PLANNING FOR WICKED PROBLEMS

Efforts to teach students pursuing graduate degrees in urban and regional planning are often frustrated by the "case books" that have been prepared for use by law professors teaching similar courses. Dawn Jourdan and Eric J. Strauss have attempted to take their concerns to heart in the design of this *Planning for Wicked Problems: A Planner's Guide to Land Use Law*.

- Each chapter begins with a planning problem that is complex and has no "correct" answer. Students should answer this hypothetically before reading the subsequent sections of each of the chapters.
- The second section of each chapter provides a primer for each topic. This primer is meant to summarize the basic principles of the law and to identify the types of question relevant to planners when such issues arise.
- The third section of each chapter includes a series of edited court opinions. The cases selected have been identified by the American Institute of Certified Planners as those fundamental to planning education.
- Each chapter concludes with an answer to the proposed wicked planning problem.

Planning for Wicked Problems has been written to demonstrate to future planners how the law may be a useful tool in helping them invent solutions to wicked planning problems. The book features additional online resources for study and review.

Dawn Jourdan is an Associate Professor and Director of the Division of Regional and City Planning at the University of Oklahoma, USA.

Eric J. Strauss is a Professor of Urban and Regional Planning and Director of Graduate Programs in the School of Planning, Design & Construction at Michigan State University, USA.

www.routledge.com/9781138012950

"This book meets a longstanding need of urban planning instructors—a text written by planners for planners on the important topic of land use law. It covers critical topics like eminent domain, regulatory takings, equal protection, and free speech in a clear and accessible way by using succinct scenarios and recommended case briefs. The book also provides much needed primer for our students on the procedural side of law and planning; it will prove very useful for core courses on planning law in planning schools across the country."

—Ellen Bassett, School of Architecture, University of Virginia

"Professors Jourdan and Strauss, both skilled planners and lawyers, have created a marvelous set of materials designed to de-mystify the law for planning professionals. This is a programmed approach that will work—wickedly interesting and relevant problems and questions, summaries of cases with bite-sized excerpts, understandable primers on legal principles, and real-world responses that build on what has been introduced. Who would have thought that something so wicked could be so good?"

—Michael Allan Wolf, Richard E. Nelson, Chair in
Local Government Law, University of Florida Levin College of Law

PLANNING FOR WICKED PROBLEMS

A Planner's Guide to Land Use Law

Dawn Jourdan and Eric J. Strauss

Routledge
Taylor & Francis Group

NEW YORK AND LONDON

First published 2016
by Routledge
711 Third Avenue, New York, NY 10017

and by Routledge
2 Park Square, Milton Park, Abingdon, Oxon OX14 4RN

Routledge is an imprint of the Taylor & Francis Group, an informa business

© 2016 Taylor & Francis

The right of Dawn Jourdan and Eric J. Strauss to be identified as authors of this work has been asserted by them in accordance with sections 77 and 78 of the Copyright, Designs and Patents Act 1988.

Library of Congress Cataloging in Publication Data
Jourdan, Dawn, author.
Planning for wicked problems : a planner's guide to land use law /
Dawn Jourdan and Eric J. Strauss. – First edition.
pages   cm
1. Land use–Law and legislation–United States.
I. Strauss, Eric J., (professor), author.   II. Title.
KF5698.J68   2015
346.7304'5–dc23   2015019718

ISBN: 978-1-138-01294-3 (hbk)
ISBN: 978-1-138-01295-0 (pbk)
ISBN: 978-1-315-79559-1 (ebk)

Typeset in Sabon
by Out of House Publishing

FOR ISAIH

CONTENTS

AUTHORS AND CONTRIBUTORS

Authors

Dawn Jourdan is an Associate Professor and Director of the Division of Regional and City Planning at the University of Oklahoma. Previously, she held a joint appointment between the College of Design, Construction, and Planning and the Levin College of Law at the University of Florida. She began her academic career as an Assistant Professor of Planning at Texas A & M University in College Station, Texas. Before returning to academia, Dawn worked for the State and Local Government Division of Holland & Knight LLP's Chicago offices. Dawn earned a Ph.D. in urban and regional planning from Florida State University in 2004, a joint degree in law and urban planning from the University of Kansas in 2000, and a B.S. in Urban Affairs and Theatre Arts from Bradley University in 1996.

Eric J. Strauss is a Professor of Urban and Regional Planning and Director of Graduate Programs in the School of Planning, Design & Construction at Michigan State University. He is a former Director of the Urban and Regional Planning Program. He has more than 40 years of experience in planning practice in both the public and private sector. Dr. Strauss has been a planner for federal and state governments, a City and County Planning Director, a City Attorney and a consultant to more than 50 organizations, both public and private, on a wide variety of planning related issues. He has prepared many comprehensive plans and land use regulations at all levels of detail for many communities.

Contributors

Kristen Dikeman is a student at the University of Oklahoma. She is pursuing a joint Master's in Regional and City Planning and Law. A graduate of OU's Native American Studies program, Ms. Dikeman aspires to serve as counsel for tribal governments.

Elizabeth Garvin is a partner with the law firm of Spencer, Fane, Britt & Browne in Denver, Colorado. Elizabeth has prepared zoning regulations and comprehensive plans for cities and counties across the country. Elizabeth is a frequent speaker at regional and national planning conferences. Prior to rejoining Spencer Fane, Elizabeth was a senior associate with Clarion Associates working in the regulatory group.

ACKNOWLEDGEMENTS

Thank you to those of you who seeded the idea for and contributed to this manuscript, including all of the students who have passed through our classrooms over the years. We appreciate the encouragement from senior editor Nicole Solano and editorial assistant Judith Newlin who have provided support throughout this process. We would like to thank Amy Trick and Allison Anderson for their editorial assistance. We would like to thank our families for their encouragement and understanding along the way.

1

INTRODUCTION

"It Depends." This is Dr. Strauss' favorite answer to any land use law question posed to him by an inquiring student. This response can be enormously frustrating. However, to Dr. Strauss' credit, "It depends" is often the best answer to most questions posed by students enrolled in such courses. As lawyers and planning practitioners will tell you, the law does not offer much definitive guidance on the complex issues planners face on a daily basis. Rather, the law, case law in particular, provides a lens that planners and lawyers may utilize in order to identify potential legal issues and some insight regarding their potential resolution in or out of the courtroom. We believe that the measure of success for a non-law student enrolled in a land use law class is whether that student can spot the presence of legal issues and speak intelligently to legal staff and decision-makers when these issues arise. Students completing a land use law course must understand that they are not lawyers, but be confident in their abilities to talk to them, as they will likely encounter a whole host of them in both public and private planning practice.

This book has been written with planning professionals in mind. This book is not a traditional casebook. Dr. Strauss and I have experimented with numerous casebooks in our classrooms over the years. We have seen our students struggle with the length and complexity of casebooks that are intended for use by law students who are often educated using the Socratic methods, a process by which the law student discovers legal principles as a result of an intensive questioning process by the instructor. This learning methodology is off-putting to planning students and has even been replaced in most law classrooms. Cases are included in this text. However, they should be considered supportive materials, providing students the opportunity to observe legal and planning principles in action. Dr. Strauss and I have aspired to include the most notable cases in land use law. This decision is based on the importance of these cases to both planning history and planning practice. The cases included also reflect the scope of the case law deemed important to the profession by the American Planning Association for the American Institute of Certified Planners examination, the certification examination for professional planners.

After introductory chapters summarizing the planning process and the origins of U.S. law, each chapter begins with a hypothetical problem. It is our hope that faculties utilizing this text will use the hypothetical as an engine to start the discussion about the topics contained in each chapter of this book. These hypotheticals have been designed to represent the complexity of typical land use law problems. Dr. Strauss and I have attempted to design "wicked problems," problems that are difficult to solve. At first glance, this approach might appear merciless. However, we believe that the tactic is useful in helping students to understand that there is no correct answer to planning problems. The "rightness" of issues is subjective and very often in the eye of the beholder. We hope these hypotheticals will engage students in dialogue about what the law requires in a situation, as well as what politics and ethics dictate.

Following the hypothetical, each chapter includes a topics section that seeks to provide a brief introduction to legal principles and relevant planning concepts. These sections have been drafted in the form of a legal treatise written with planners in mind. The information contained within is not exhaustive but will provide students with a working knowledge of the topics involved. Students should be able to answer the hypotheticals posed at the beginning of each chapter with the information contained within the topics section and with the supporting case law. Each chapter concludes with a sample answer to the posed hypothetical, as well as discussion questions that instructors may utilize to encourage critical thinking in each area of the law.

Dr. Strauss and I, along with our collaborators, hope that students and instructors utilizing this text will be able to overcome some of the traditional challenges planners face when they first encounter courses in law. We hope that students completing a land use law course will take with them the confidence that law is merely one aspect, albeit critical, of the decisions they will have to advise on or make as a part of their careers. We believe that good planning will occur when planners understand that the law is not a metaphorical box in which they have to do planning. Instead, land use law should be viewed as a basis for invention in planning practice.

Bibliography

Rittel, H. W. J. and Webber, M. M. (1973). Dilemmas in a General Theory of Planning. *Policy Sciences*, 4, 159–169.

2

THE PLANNING PROCESS

The manner in which plans have been historically crafted is separate from the legal process. This chapter seeks to introduce readers to a brief history of city planning in the United States beginning with the Industrial Revolution. The chapter will discuss how comprehensive planning and zoning processes have changed over the last 100 years. In addition, this chapter will introduce readers to terminology and fundamental concepts related to the planning process.

The planning and zoning process is relatively new in the United States. At the turn of the last century, wealthy industrialists sought the opportunity to trade with the world. One of the primary barriers to the achievement of this goal was the state of American cities. Developed to accommodate the industrial age, cities were crowded, polluted, and lacking in amenities. This small group traveled Europe to learn how to build world-class cities. They brought home with them the system of zoning, already entrenched in German city planning.

Herbert Hoover, then Secretary of Commerce, embraced this system. Understanding that planning and zoning efforts would need to be localized to be effective, Herbert Hoover drafted the Standard Planning Enabling Act (SPEA) and the Standard Zoning Enabling Act (SZEA). These acts, passed by the U.S. Congress in 1928 and 1927 respectively, divested the powers to plan and zone to the states. Copies of the original acts are available on the American Planning Association's website at: www. planning.org/growingsmart/enablingacts.htm. Within a decade, more than 20 states had enacted one or both of these acts. The states took the powers divested to them by the U.S. Congress and empowered local governments, such as those in cities and counties, to plan and zone their communities. These activities spread like wildfire.

Generally, most states adopted SPEAs and SZEAs without much modification. What is most interesting is that the majority of states adopted one or the other. This choice is meaningful to planners who now understand the symbiotic nature of comprehensive plans and zoning documents.

Components of Codes

Comprehensive plans are visioning documents. They seek to assess the state of a community at the time of the plan, based on history and resources, and project a future based on community values and demographics. Typically, the planning process begins with data analysis and gathering. This information is typically shared with the public

Figure 1 Credit: David D. Boeck

and utilized as the basis for the visioning process out of which the comprehensive plan is derived.

Comprehensive plans are typically comprised of goals, policies, and objectives that seek to cultivate abstract ideas into activities that can be implemented. For example, a city may set a goal of ensuring all residents can have easy access to fresh food. An appropriate policy would be to analyze the current location of all food stores in the city, identifying any food deserts. The affiliated objective would be to use tax incentives to recruit food sellers into these underrepresented areas. This activity is done widely for goals related to: housing, transportation, economic development, historic preservation, environmental resources, and hazards and emergency management, among others. Once adopted, the comprehensive plan serves as the guide for local development decisions.

Comprehensive plans typically contain a current and future land use map. These maps establish the appropriate land uses for property within a municipality both now and in the future. If a property owner seeks to develop his property differently from the zoning, he or she must seek permission from the legislative process for a rezoning. A rezoning application is first filed with city planning staff. Upon review of the rezoning application, planning staff issue a recommendation to the planning commission. The local planning commission is an appointed body of local residents who are empowered to review such request. Upon review at a public meeting, the planning commission passes its recommendation to the City Council. The City Council, a local elected body, holds a public meeting that allows the property owner and community members to comment on the proposed rezoning. At the end of the meeting, the City Council will issue a decision to accept or deny the rezoning. A property owner who is disappointed by this decision may seek legal appeal. A court will typically review a city council's denial to rezone to determine if it was arbitrary and capricious.

On their own, comprehensive plans are weak tools for controlling the land development process. These plans gain "teeth" when paired with zoning ordinances. Zoning ordinances regulate land use and intensity. These regulations give property owners notice of what can be built on their land and where, as well as the details of that development from height to setbacks to design features. New development must comply with the terms of these regulations or developers must use the planning process to make changes. A landowner who seeks to build in a manner not permitted by zoning regulations must seek a variance from the regulations. This process begins with an application to the planning department. The application is transmitted to the Zoning Board of Adjustment. The board acts in a quasi-judicial capacity, holding a court-like hearing where the property owner, planner, and neighbors may weigh in on the proposed modification sought. If an application or objector is unhappy with the determination made by the board, they may appeal to the city council and then to the courts.

Consistency with Comprehensive Planning

In some jurisdictions, states require local governments to prepare and adopt comprehensive plans and zoning regulations. In Florida, for example, the state has long required the preparation of both documents. By law, these documents must be referenced and build upon each other. If the comprehensive plan establishes an objective to rectify food deserts, the zoning ordinance must be devoid of barriers to this objective. A deviation from the consistency requirement, in Florida at least, can have huge consequences. In *Pinecrest Lakes v. Shidel*, 795 So. 2d 191 (2001), a multi-family housing developer was required to tear down occupied housing units after a state court ruled that the permitted development did not comply with the local government's comprehensive plan.

New Inventions in Land Development

Since the advent of the SZEA, local governments have struggled with the rigidity of their zoning requirements. They have sought to insert flexibility into this process, as further chronicled in Chapter 7. In the late 1990s, Andres Duany presented local governments with a new option for regulating local development. Known as the smart code or the form-based code, this tool seeks to regulate land development in the absence of land use. Rather than zoning individual properties, the form-based code is built on the creation of transects. These transects are similar to urban design districts, as further described in Chapter 14. They are built on the premise that any land use can be placed next to any other if appropriately designed.

Form-based codes have received wide attention and acceptance in communities across the United States, even in places where political will has not favored zoning regulations. While often embraced because they appear to be anti-zoning, the majority of communities that have embraced these new codes have kept their land use designation systems. These new codes, referred to as hybrid form-based codes, seek to regulate land use and aesthetics. It is possible that form-based codes and their hybrids may generate better designed developments. However, it is still too early to tell what their legacy may be. For now, zoning remains the primary tool utilized by cities to govern land use.

Discussion Prompts

- What is planning?
- Can planning happen without a comprehensive plan or a unified zoning code? Discuss Houston, Texas.
- What are the primary reasons motivating the recent growth of the use of form-based codes by communities across the United States?

Bibliography

Duerksen, Christopher, Dale, C. Gregory, and Elliot, Donald L. (2009). *The Citizen's Guide to Planning* (4th edn.). Chicago: American Planning Association.

Garvin, Elizabeth and Jourdan, Dawn (2008).Through the Looking Glass: Analyzing the Potential Legal Challenges to Form-Based Codes. *Journal of Land Use and Environmental Law*, 23:2, 395–421.

Hall, Peter (1996). *Cities of Tomorrow* (updated edn.). Malden, MA: Blackwell Publishers.

Hoch, Charles J., Dalton, Linda C., and So, Frank S. (2000). *The Practice of Local Government Planning* (3rd edn.). Washington, DC: International City/County Management Association.

Kelly, Eric Damian and Becker, Barbra (2000). *Community Planning: An Introduction to the Comprehensive Plan*. Washington, DC: Island Press.

3

ORIGINS OF U.S. LAW

The United States is a relatively new country. The laws of this nation evolved from a number of legal traditions and continue to demonstrate the influences of French, English, and Spanish legal systems. The most dominant, of course, is English common law. English common law is based on a tradition of the evolution of law through precedent. Law is not typically codified in statute. Rather, law evolves as a result of legal decisions that build upon each other. The United States is not governed by English common law. However, federal, state, and local statutes, in many instances, have evolved from the principles originating from common law traditions. The content and applications of these statutes, which are made by legislative bodies and enforced by executive agencies, are kept in check by the judiciary. As such, U.S. law continues to evolve and grow in the same way that English common law continues to expand.

Rather than letting U.S. law simply evolve, the founding fathers adopted a constitution to establish principles they identified as crucial to the future of the nation. In the constitution, these men sought to ensure that the new country would never become a monarchy. Instead, they created a system of government comprised of three independent branches: the legislative, the executive, and the judiciary. Each was vested with a specific and distinct function. The purpose of the three tiers of governance was to ensure that each branch of government could work to keep the others in check, precluding any one branch from obtaining too much power.

The legislative branch at the national level includes the Congress and the House of Representatives. These bodies are both comprised of elected representatives who make the law. For example, let us assume that the nation is uniformly concerned about an increase in natural disaster events such as hurricanes, earthquakes, tornadoes, floods, wildfires, and drought. There is some reliable evidence that the number and severity of these events will increase in the next 50 years as a by-product of climate dynamics. Congress, responsible for approving the country's budget, is concerned that the current approach, which compensates affected property owners for losses associated with these events, will bankrupt the nation. A representative in the U.S. House of Representatives proposes a piece of legislation that would limit compensation to property owners to a "one time only" policy. The owners of properties damaged by tornadoes, for instance, would only be compensated once. They would be encouraged to use the funds to rebuild in a manner more resistant to storm damage or, in the alternative, to use the money to rebuild in an area less likely to be affected by natural disasters. This proposed bill would be debated by members of the House. If approved, the bill would be sent to the U.S. Senate to be reviewed, debated, and either

Figure 2 Credit: David D. Boeck

approved or denied. If approved by both the House and the Senate, the bill would be sent to the President of the United States for either veto or ratification.

The executive branch is charged with approving or vetoing the laws adopted by the legislative bodies and then implementing these new proscriptions. Those serving in executive capacities, such as the U.S. President and members of his or her cabinet, are often called upon to create policies that fill the gaps in legislation. Building upon the scenario above, the President would review the proposed limitation on remuneration for those whose property is affected by natural disasters. Assuming that the President thinks this legislation is in the best interest of the nation, he or she approves the new law, and works with cabinet members to implement it. A law of this nature might involve multiple executive agencies from the Federal Emergency Management Agency (FEMA) to the U.S. Department of Housing and Urban Development. Representatives of these agencies will work with the President and the cabinet members to craft implementing rules. These rules are the "how to." They are intended to work out the details of new laws and to fill in any gaps left open in adopted legislation. While these rules are supposed to embrace the spirit of legislation, they are often the subject of legal controversy when disagreement arises about the intent of a particular law. Understanding the knowledge and expertise of federal agencies, courts are quick to defer to interpretations rendered by those associated with the executive branch of the U.S. government.

The judiciary is the third branch of the federal government. The federal judiciary is comprised of three tiers of courts. Individuals who seek to file grievances about the contents or application of a law file suit in a trial court. At the federal level, these courts are known as federal district courts. Aggrieved parties are referred to as plaintiffs. They file suit in the district court associated with the state in which they live. A map of the districts is available at: www.uscourts.gov/uscourts/images/CircuitMap.pdf.

U.S. district courts are the first step for parties that allege a grievance as a result of the adoption or application of a federal law. They file a lawsuit in the appropriate federal court, establishing their right to be in court and the grounds for their complaint. The defendant to the lawsuit is the party who is sued by the plaintiff. Upon receiving the plaintiff's lawsuit, the defendant is given a specific period to respond. The defendant will seek to establish that the plaintiff is not entitled to bring suit or, in the alternative, that his or her suit lacks merit. The defendant will likely ask the district court to dismiss the plaintiff's lawsuit. The district court will review requests for dismissal prior to holding a trial. If the court agrees that the lawsuit lacks merit, it may dismiss the plaintiff's lawsuit. However, if the suit alleges issues that require further factual inquiry, the court will set a date for trial. It may take more than a year, sometimes three to five, for a case to find its way to trial. The litigation process is not dormant for this period of time. Rather, both parties are collecting evidence, deposing witnesses, and preparing for a trial. Sometimes, cases find an end before reaching the trial date, either because they settle or because the controversy no longer exists.

A judge presides over the trial. In some cases, a jury may be assigned to hear the matter. In either instance, the plaintiff's attorney offers his case first. He presents evidence substantiating the ways in which his client is aggrieved by the application of a law to his or her property. In cases related to property, a plaintiff will have to prove that she is the owner of the property and further that she has been harmed by the adoption of an unconstitutional law or the application of a regulation. Upon the presentation of evidence by the plaintiff's attorney, counsel for the defendant may ask the judge to rule that the plaintiff's attorney has not met his evidentiary burden. If the judge agrees, she may choose to dismiss the case. In this instance, the trial is over. The plaintiff's only recourse is to appeal the judge's decision. In the instance that the judge finds that the plaintiff has met his evidentiary burden, the burden of proof will shift to the defendant's attorney. Upon the conclusion of the presentation of arguments by the plaintiff's and defendant's attorneys, the judge will deliberate. Once she is ready, her decision will be reduced to a written statement in the form of a judgment. The judgment will represent the district court's final decision.

To continue our previous hypothetical, let us assume that a hurricane rips through the middle of a coastal state, doing billions of dollars of damage. The federal government declares the event a disaster, enabling Congress to provide more than $1.5 billion of federal aid. All property owners apply to FEMA for a share of this distribution. Fred and Maggie Jones own a home that was ravaged by the hurricane. Their home was valued at $1 million prior to the storm. They have not yet filed a claim for compensation but fear that they will be denied because they have been previously compensated for damages to their property. They file suit in the district court alleging that the law violates the Fifth Amendment to the U.S. Constitution and thereby infringes their personal property rights. In response, FEMA asks the court to dismiss the claim because it is unripe.

Ripeness is an important threshold issue for all litigation. This term refers to the readiness of a claim for consideration by a court. Typically, especially in cases involving property rights, a claim will not be ready for legal review until a final decision has been rendered by a governmental entity. In the case of our hypothetical, the Jones have not yet applied to FEMA for compensation for the losses that they suffered as a result of the hurricane. Chances are that their claim will be found unripe until they file for compensation and are denied. In certain circumstances, however, a claim may be brought before achieving this degree of ripeness if the plaintiff can demonstrate that exhausting these processes and or administrative remedies would be futile because the outcome is already predetermined. In this case, a court would likely dismiss this case, as it applies to the Jones' damaged property, particularly if the new legislation contains a procedure that allows affected property owners to appeal denials for compensation.

Either party may seek to appeal the final decision of the district court judge. Typically, appeals are brought by the losing party. Appeals of district court judgments are filed with the U.S. Court of Appeals. Such appeals are heard by a panel of appellate court judges. These U.S. Court of Appeals judges are appointed by the President and approved by Congress. These judges represent the same geographic boundaries as the U.S. district courts.

Rarely is a litigant entitled to an appeal as of right. Rather, the appealing party, otherwise known as the appellant, must submit a short appellate brief stating grounds for appeal. In the case of our hypothetical, the Jones' attorney may allege that the district court judge made an error in dismissing the case for lack of futility. The appellee, in this case the government's attorney, will write a responsive brief. This attorney will likely defend the decision of the judge based on the facts of the case and the supporting law. Based on these short briefs, the appellate court will decide if there is merit in commissioning full briefs. Upon completion of the briefing schedule, a panel of judges will hear oral arguments on the case. Attorneys for both parties will each be given 15 minutes to present their cases to the judges. At this hearing, the judges may ask questions at will. The purpose of these arguments is to offer clarifying answers to the court's questions. The court will issue its decision in the form of a ruling, much like the cases in this book. These opinions are binding on courts within that jurisdiction.

Appeal may be made of an appellate court decision to the U.S. Supreme Court. The U.S. Supreme Court, comprised of nine justices appointed by the President and confirmed by the Senate, hears roughly 15–20 cases per year. These cases typically center around challenges to the interpretation of the U.S. Constitution or federal statutes or rules. Typically, the Supreme Court agrees to hear these cases because there is a split of opinions in the U.S. Court of Appeals. Zoning cases are sometimes heard by the high court as a result of their constitutional underpinnings. Supreme Court cases are the controlling law in the United States. This is the last stop for unsatisfied litigants unless they choose to pursue a legislative modification.

The federal system of courts is separate from the state judicial system. Each state government is organized similarly to the federal government with three independent branches of government. These separate systems of state and federal governance were important to the founding fathers, who felt that federal governance would be similar to living in a monarchy. The constitution specifically spells out the rights entitled to U.S. citizens by the federal government. Further, the constitution assigns all powers not vested in the federal government to the states. States, then, have the power to adopt their own constitutions (so long as they do not conflict with the federal constitution) and to govern cities.

10

It is not easy to decipher whether a challenge to a zoning decision should be filed in a state or federal court. Typically, zoning cases will only begin in the federal system if they involve the interpretation of a federal statute, a federal agency, or present a case of first impression as it relates to the interpretation of the U.S. Constitution. These matters may also reach federal court if they involve conflicts between citizens of two states, which is often the case in challenges involving natural resources such as water. In most instances, zoning cases will work themselves through the state court system.

4

NUISANCE LAW

Zoning-like issues predated the appearance of modern zoning codes. When asked to review a private dispute between neighbors, courts relied on the principles of nuisance law in resolving disputes. The principles of nuisance law were, to a large degree, codified with the passage of the Standard Enabling Legislation. These principles still guide courts in areas of the law that are either emerging or unsettled.

Nuisance Wicked Problem

You are an Assistant Attorney General in a strong right-to-farm state. As part of your responsibilities you work with the State Department of Agriculture to enforce regulations involving Confined Animal Feeding Operations (CAFO). Your cousin, a local municipal attorney, has requested a quick meeting after you have spoken at a continuing legal education event on this subject. It seems a local farmer who raises chickens has filed a site plan to erect a building to increase the size of his flock from 100 chickens to 1,000 chickens. All the neighbors built their homes knowing full well that there was a "small" farm next door and several bought their home because of the agricultural character of the area.

Your cousin would like advice on the following issues:

1. Will the neighbors be able to sue the farmer for creating a "private" nuisance?
2. Can you help out your cousin by filing a lawsuit alleging that the expanded operation is a "public" nuisance?
3. Must litigation wait until the farmer has started operations with 1,000 chickens?
4. Would the litigation be any different if the farmer wanted to increase his flock to 200 chickens? Or 5,000 chickens?
5. How does the doctrine of "coming to the nuisance" affect these cases?
6. Has the enactment of a zoning ordinance reduced the need for these types of lawsuit?
7. What is the character of the neighborhood?
8. Do the CAFO regulations adequately protect public health, safety, and welfare?
9. Do right-to-farm laws always trump nuisance lawsuits?

Figure 3 Credit: David D. Boeck

10. Should the local township enact a government regulation defining "agriculture" as less than 1,000 chickens to solve this problem?
11. Could a judge order the farmer to compensate the neighbors for loss of property value while still continuing to have 1,000 chickens?
12. Could a judge order the neighbors to all contribute to a fund to buy out the chicken farmer and force the operation to relocate?

Cases

The following cases will be useful to you as you attempt to analyze this chapter's wicked problem:

Boomer v. Atlantic Cement Co., 257 N.E.2d 870 (N.Y. 1970)
Rodrigue v. Copeland, 475 So. 2d 1071 (La. 1985)
Spur Industries v. Del Webb, 494 P.2d 700 (Ariz. 1972)

Boomer v. Atlantic Cement Co.

257 N.E.2d 870 (N.Y. 1970)

Facts

Individual property owners near Atlantic Cement Company's cement plant near Albany, New York filed for injunctive relief and damages for the dirt, smoke, and vibrations created by the cement plant. The trial and lower appellate court both found a nuisance existed, but denied injunctive relief.

Issue

When may injunctive relief be avoided even though a nuisance is established?

Held

If there exists a large disparity between the consequences of injunction and of the act causing the nuisance, permanent injunction should be avoided. The lower courts had found that Atlantic Cement did create a nuisance, which had damaged neighboring properties. Precedent in New York dictated that when a nuisance created a substantial continuing damage, injunctive relief was the remedy. Given the economic importance of the plant's continuing operation, and reasoning any injunction or requirement that Atlantic Cement cease the nuisance would effectively shut down the plant, New York's highest appellate court decided the optimal alternative was to compensate the harmed property owners for past and future economic damages.

Discussion

The court in *Boomer* admittedly struggled with whether it should directly address the issue posed by the litigants or if the litigation should be used to address larger environmental concerns regarding air pollution. The dissent argued the majority's decision was unconstitutional in that the plaintiffs are forced to suffer a continuous nuisance.

Case Excerpt

The rule in New York has been that such a nuisance will be enjoined although marked disparity be shown in economic consequence between the effect of the injunction and the effect of the nuisance.

The problem of disparity in economic consequence was sharply in focus in *Whalen v. Union Bag & Paper Co.* (208 N.Y. 1). A pulp mill entailing an investment of more than a million dollars polluted a stream in which plaintiff, who owned a farm, was "a lower riparian owner". The economic loss to plaintiff from this pollution was small. This court, reversing the Appellate Division, reinstated the injunction granted by the Special Term against the argument of the mill owner that in view of "the slight advantage to plaintiff and the great loss that will be inflicted on defendant" an injunction should not be granted (p. 2). "Such a balancing of injuries cannot be justified by the circumstances of this case", Judge WERNER noted (p. 4). He continued: "Although the damage to

14

the plaintiff may be slight as compared with the defendant's expense of abating the condition that is not a good reason for refusing an injunction" (p. 5).

Thus the unconditional injunction granted at Special Term was reinstated. The rule laid down in that case, then, is that whenever the damage resulting from a nuisance is found not "unsubstantial", viz., $100 a year, injunction would follow. This states a rule that had been followed in this court with marked consistency (*McCarty v. Natural Carbonic Gas Co.*, 189 N.Y. 40; *Strobel v. Kerr Salt Co.*, 164 N.Y. 303; *Campbell v. Seaman*, 63 N.Y. 568).

There are cases where injunction has been denied. *McCann v. Chasm Power Co.* (211 N.Y. 301) is one of them. There, however, the damage shown by plaintiffs was not only unsubstantial, it was non-existent. Plaintiffs owned a rocky bank of the stream in which defendant had raised the level of the water. This had no economic or other adverse consequence to plaintiffs, and thus injunctive relief was denied. Similar is the basis for denial of injunction in *Forstmann v. Joray Holding Co.* (244 N.Y. 22) where no benefit to plaintiffs could be seen from the injunction sought (p. 32). Thus if, within *Whalen v. Union Bag & Paper Co.* (*supra*) which authoritatively states the rule in New York, the damage to plaintiffs in these present cases from defendant's cement plant is "not unsubstantial", an injunction should follow.

Rodrigue v. Copeland

475 So. 2d 1071 (La. 1985)

Facts
Neighboring property owners sought injunctive relief to prohibit Copeland from erecting his commercial-sized Christmas display in their residential neighborhood. The annual display, which included both lights and music, attracted large crowds nightly during the holiday season to the limited access subdivision, thereby creating increased traffic and restricting neighbors' accessibility to their properties. Noise, public urination, and property damage also resulted from the visitors.

Issue
Did the trial court err in failing to find that neighbors suffered real damage from Copeland's annual Christmas display?

Held
Yes. To determine whether a use constitutes a real damage or a mere inconvenience to neighbors, the courts consider the reasonableness of the conduct in the context of the area's character, the extent of the intrusion, and the activity's impact on the health and safety of neighbors. Copeland's display, albeit seasonal, constituted a private nuisance because of its unreasonable character in its residential setting, causing real damage to neighbors. The court ordered Copeland to reduce the physical size of his display to prevent the attraction of

large crowds to the neighborhood and to reduce the sound so as to not be audible within neighbors' homes.

Discussion
In *Rodrigue*, the Supreme Court of Louisiana held that while property owners have extensive rights, which can inconvenience neighbors to a degree, an owner could be prohibited from utilizing the property in a manner that causes real damage and interferes with the right of others to enjoy their own properties.

Case Excerpt
Plaintiffs contend that defendant's exhibition constitutes a commercial use of his premises in violation of the Jefferson Parish zoning ordinance. The neighborhood is zoned solely for residential use. Plaintiffs support their allegation with defendant's testimony that the cost of the display, $30,000–$50,000, has been borne by his business, A. Copeland Enterprises, Inc., since 1980. Defendant owns 100% of the stock in A. Copeland Enterprises, Inc. This corporation is the parent company of Popeye's Famous Fried Chicken, Inc.

Richard Tatalluto, the assistant comptroller of A. Copeland Enterprises, testified that the costs of the display are handled as a business expense of the company. He also stated that although he does not prepare the tax returns, he was aware that the company deducted its business expenses for tax purposes. Further support for plaintiffs' allegation is found in Burton Klein's testimony that he had observed, on television, a Popeye's sign which was located in the front yard of defendant's home.

Defendant maintains that his display is not an advertisement, but rather that it is intended simply as his personal expression of the spirit and meaning of Christmas. He contends that he immediately removed a small Popeye's Famous Fried Chicken sign from his front yard on one occasion several years prior to the suit. According to Copeland the sign had been placed upon the premises without his consent by his advertising department and it remained on his premises for just one day.

The Comprehensive Zoning Ordinance for Jefferson Parish generally restricts the use of property zoned "R-1 residential" to non-commercial uses. If defendant's display was primarily intended to promote his commercial enterprises, it would be prohibited.

Our analysis of the facts and law lead us to affirm the lower courts' finding that the display did not constitute a commercial use of defendant's property. Therefore, defendant's display is not barred by the zoning ordinance.

Although the expenses of the display have been borne by defendant's business, the lower courts reasonably could have concluded that the display was intended primarily for defendant's personal satisfaction. The display is temporary in nature. With the exception of one day, several years prior to this suit, it has not included any reference to his business interests. The evidence does not indicate that the display has been used in any media advertisements of defendant's business. Based on these facts, the lower courts could conclude that the display did not constitute a commercial use of his premises.

OBLIGATIONS OF NEIGHBORHOOD (C.C. arts. 667–669)

Owners of immovable property are restrained in the use of their property by certain obligations. These obligations include the responsibilities imposed by articles 667–669 of the Civil Code:

"Although a proprietor may do with his estate whatever he pleases, still he cannot make any work on it, which may deprive his neighbor of the liberty of enjoying his own, or which may be the cause of any damage to him." C.C. 667.

"Although one be not at liberty to make any work by which his neighbor's buildings may be damaged, yet every one has the liberty of doing on his own ground whatsoever he pleases, although it should occasion some inconvenience to his neighbor.

Thus he who is not subject to any servitude originating from a particular agreement in that respect, may raise his house as high as he pleases, although by such elevation he should darken the lights of his neighbors's [neighbor's] house, because this act occasions only an inconvenience, but not a real damage." C.C. 668.

"If the works or materials for any manufactory or other operation, cause an inconvenience to those in the same or in the neighboring houses, by diffusing smoke or nauseous smell, and there be no servitude established by which they are regulated, their sufferance must be determined by the rules of the police, or the customs of the place." C.C. 669.

These obligations of vicinage are legal servitudes imposed on the owner of property. These provisions embody a balancing of rights and obligations associated with the ownership of immovables. As a general rule, the landowner is free to exercise his rights of ownership in any manner he sees fit. He may even use his property in ways which "… occasion some inconvenience to his neighbor." However, his extensive rights do not allow him to do "real damage" to his neighbor.

At issue in this case is whether Copeland's light and sound display has caused a mere inconvenience or real damage to his neighbors and their right to enjoy their own premises.

In determining whether an activity or work occasions real damage or mere inconvenience, a court is required to determine the reasonableness of the conduct in light of the circumstances. This analysis requires consideration of factors such as the character of the neighborhood, the degree of the intrusion and the effect of the activity on the health and safety of the neighbors.

In the past, this court has borrowed from the common law of nuisance in describing the type of conduct which violates the pronouncements embodied in C.C. 667–669. In *Robichaux v. Huppenbauer*, 258 La. 139, 150, 245 So.2d 385, 389 (1971), we considered whether a horse stable located in the City of New Orleans could be abated under C.C. 669. We stated the following test:

"Thus noxious smells, rats, flies and noise may constitute an actionable nuisance although produced and carried on by a lawful business, where they result in *material injury to neighboring property or interfere with its comfortable use and enjoyment by persons of ordinary sensibilities. McGee v. Yazoo & M.V.R. Co.*, 206 La. 121, 19 So.2d 21 (1944)." (Emphasis added).

This test has also been applied by the courts of appeal: *McCastle v. Rollins Environmental Services of Louisiana, Inc.*, 415 So.2d 515, 519 (La.App. 1st

Cir.1982) ("... whether the alleged nuisance produces serious or material discomfort to persons of ordinary sensibilities in a normal state of health."). *Allen v. Paulk,* 188 So.2d 708, 709 (La.App. 2d Cir.1966) ("... whether the alleged nuisance produces such a condition as, in the judgment of reasonable men, naturally produces actual physical discomfort to normal persons of ordinary sensibilities, tastes, and habits.").

Although the common law of nuisance has no binding, precedential value in the courts of this state, that body of law does correspond to some extent with the obligations of neighborhood established by C.C. 667–669. Therefore, the analysis employed by the courts of our sister states has been useful as persuasive authority regarding the application of our law.

In *Hero Lands Co. v. Texaco Inc.,* 310 So.2d 93, 98 (La.1975), we recognized that the prohibitions contained in C.C. 667–669 were not limited to the physical invasion of neighboring premises. According to the court:

"... The damage may well be intrinsic in nature, a combination of facts and conditions which, taken together, do not involve a physical invasion but which, under the circumstances, are nevertheless by their nature the very refinement of injury and damage." (Citations omitted).

Since plaintiffs seek injunctive relief, they must prove irreparable injury in addition to the necessary showing of real damage under C.C. 667–669. C.C.P. 3601; *Salter v. B.W.S. Corp., Inc.,* 290 So.2d 821 (La.1974); *Hilliard v. Shuff,* 260 La. 384, 256 So.2d 127 (1972). Applying the foregoing principles to this case, we conclude that defendant's display has occasioned real damage, not mere inconvenience, upon plaintiffs. Likewise, we conclude that plaintiffs will be irreparably harmed unless injunctive relief is granted.

Defendant's exhibition constitutes an unreasonable intrusion into the lives of his neighbors when considered in light of the character of the neighborhood, the degree of the intrusion and its effect on the use and enjoyment of their properties by his neighbors.

The record demonstrates that the affected area is a single family residential neighborhood. Access to the neighborhood is restricted to residential streets and Transcontinental Drive, a divided paved thoroughfare which ends at Folse Drive, just to the east of defendant's residence. There is no access to and from defendant's premises from the north since the Lake Pontchartrain levee is located immediately to the rear of the lots fronting on Folse Drive.

The damage suffered by plaintiffs during the operation of defendant's display is extensive, both in terms of its duration and its size. Defendant's display becomes operative in early December and remains in operation until January 5. During this period, plaintiffs are forced to contend with a flow of bumper to bumper traffic through their limited access neighborhood. In addition, they must endure the noise and property abuse associated with the crowd of visitors who congregate near the display.

The display begins operation at dusk each evening and continues until 11:00 p.m. on weekdays and 12:00 midnight on weekends. The display is occasionally operational beyond midnight. While in operation, it features an extravagant display of lights which are located across the front of defendant's residence, on the roof and in the enclosed yard to the west of the residence. Some of the lights comprising the display are shaped into figures such as a star, a reindeer, a snowman, three angels and a depiction of Santa and his reindeer. Lights are also located in the trees and shrubs. In addition to the lights, the display features a tapestry proclaiming "Glory to God in the Highest" and a creche.

Noise emanates from the display and from the visitors. The display is accompanied by traditional Christmas music which is amplified through loudspeakers located on the second floor of defendant's residence. The music is audible inside the home of Mary Borrell. The plaintiffs also complain of noise emanating from car engines, car horns, the slamming of car doors and police whistles.

The record clearly indicates that traffic in the neighborhood is congested due to the slow progress of vehicles carrying spectators by the display. The traffic has seriously impaired the ability of plaintiffs to gain access to and from their premises. Furthermore, on street parking for plaintiffs or their guests becomes virtually nonexistent. As a result of the traffic congestion and lack of parking, plaintiffs and children of defendant's neighbors cannot have their own Christmas celebrations and gatherings.

Defendant contends that the sheriff's traffic plan has minimized any damage to the plaintiffs. Although the plan has facilitated a smoother (quicker) flow of traffic, the remaining problems still exist. The plaintiffs still experience extended delay in reaching and leaving their premises. The noise associated with the display and the crowds remains. Furthermore, the duration of the display has been unaffected by the plan.

The increased traffic attracted to the display has some impact on the health and safety of the residents. The response time for emergency services is increased due to the traffic congestion. However, the record indicates that this danger was minimized under the sheriff's plan through the creation of an emergency lane on Transcontinental and the presence of two motor scooters to be used in medical emergencies. If the physical health and safety of the plaintiffs had been the only factor to consider, we would not have deemed it necessary to restrain defendant's display. However, in consideration of all the factors, the district court committed clear error in failing to find that plaintiffs suffered damage under C.C. 667–669 and irreparable injury. Likewise, the court of appeal erred in affirming the district court.

Plaintiffs' injury stems from the nature and size of the display which render it incompatible with a restricted access, residential neighborhood. Defendant is enjoined from erecting and operating a Christmas exhibition which is calculated to and does attract an unusually large number of visitors to the neighborhood.

In complying with our order, defendant is specifically enjoined from placing oversized lighted figures, such as the reindeer and snowman, in his yards or upon the roof of his residence. The proper place for these "commercial size" decorations is not within a quiet, residential neighborhood. Defendant is also specifically ordered to reduce the volume of any sound accompanying the display so that it is not audible from within the closest homes of his neighbors.

In limiting his display, the burden is placed on defendant to reduce substantially the size and extravagance of his display to a level at which it will not attract the large crowds that have been drawn to the neighborhood in the past.

Of course, defendant is free to maintain his display unrestricted, at a location which is appropriate. The injunction granted herein is limited to activity at defendant's premises on Folse Drive.

Spur Industries, Inc. v. Del E. Webb Development Co.

494 P.2d 700 (Ariz. 1972)

Facts

Beginning in the 1950s, developers started establishing suburban cities geared towards retirees in the areas surrounding Phoenix, which until then, had been primarily used for agriculture. Spur Industries owned 25 feedlots that contained an estimated 20,000 to 30,000 cattle. In 1959, Del Webb purchased 20,000 acres of farmland in the vicinity of Spur Industries for $15 million to begin developing the urban area of Sun City. By 1967, 1,300 of Webb's lots were unfit for sale as a result of the odor and flies produced by Spur's operations in the vicinity.

Issue

Can a business operation that was legal at its inception become a nuisance because of new residential areas in the proximity and, thereby, be enjoined from operation?

Held

Yes. Spur Industries became both a public and private nuisance when its operations were engulfed by Webb's development. However, in such instances, it is fair and reasonable for developers who seize the opportunities presented by developing large tracts of rural land to compensate those who are forced out as a result. Webb was ordered by the court to compensate Spur for the cost of relocation or ceasing operations.

Discussion

Spur is distinguished from other so-called "coming to the nuisance" cases because at the operation's inception, it was in a remote area with no indication that a new urban area would rapidly develop around it.

Case Excerpt

The difference between a private nuisance and a public nuisance is generally one of degree. A private nuisance is one affecting a single individual or a definite small number of persons in the enjoyment of private rights not common to the public, while a public nuisance is one affecting the rights enjoyed by citizens as a part of the public. To constitute a public nuisance, the nuisance must affect a considerable number of people or an entire community or neighborhood. City of Phoenix v. Johnson, 51 Ariz. 115, 75 P.2d 30 (1938).

Where the injury is slight, the remedy for minor inconveniences lies in an action for damages rather than in one for an injunction. Kubby v. Hammond, 68 Ariz. 17, 198 P.2d 134 (1948). Moreover, some courts have held, in the "balancing of conveniences" cases, that damages may be the sole remedy. See Boomer v. Atlantic Cement Co., 26 N.Y.2d 219, 309 N.Y.S.2d 312, 257 N.E.2d 870, 40 A.L.R.3d 590 (1970), and annotation comments, 40 A.L.R.3d 601.

Thus, it would appear from the admittedly incomplete record as developed in the trial court, that, at most, residents of Youngtown would be entitled to damages rather than injunctive relief.

We have no difficulty, however, in agreeing with the conclusion of the trial court that Del Webb's City were concerned.

§ 36–601, subsec. A reads as follows:

"§ 36–601. Public nuisances dangerous to public health

"A. The following conditions are specifically declared public nuisances dangerous to the public health:

"1. Any condition or place in populous areas which constitutes a breeding place for flies, rodents, mosquitoes and other insects which are capable of carrying and transmitting disease-causing organisms to any person or persons."

By this statute, before an otherwise lawful (and necessary) business may be declared a public nuisance, there must be a "populous" area in which people are injured:

"* * * [I]t hardly admits a doubt that, in determining the question as to whether a lawful occupation is so conducted as to constitute a nuisance as a matter of fact, the locality and surroundings are of the first importance. (citations omitted) A business which is not per se a public nuisance may become such by being carried on at a place where the health, comfort, or convenience of a populous neighborhood is affected. * * * What might amount to a serious nuisance in one locality by reason of the density of the population, or character of the neighborhood affected, may in another place and under different surroundings be deemed proper and unobjectionable. * * *." MacDonald v. Perry, 32 Ariz. 39, 49–50, 255 P. 494, 497 (1927).

It is clear that as to the citizens of Sun City, the operation of Spur's feedlot was both a public and a private nuisance. They could have successfully maintained an action to abate the nuisance. Del Webb having shown a special injury in the loss of sales, had a standing to bring suit to enjoin the nuisance. Engle v. Clark, 53 Ariz. 472, 90 P.2d 994 (1939); City of Phoenix v. Johnson, supra. The judgment of the trial court permanently enjoining the operation of the feedlot is affirmed.

MUST DEL WEBB INDEMNIFY SPUR?

A suit to enjoin a nuisance sounds in equity and the courts have long recognized a special responsibility to the public when acting as a court of equity:

§ 104. Where public interest is involved.

"Courts of equity may, and frequently do, go much further both to give and withhold relief in furtherance of the public interest than they are accustomed to go when only private interests are involved. Accordingly, the granting or withholding of relief may properly be dependent upon considerations of public interest. * *." 27 Am.Jur.2d, Equity, page 626.

In addition to protecting the public interest, however, courts of equity are concerned with protecting the operator of a lawfully, albeit noxious, business from the result of a knowing and willful encroachment by others near his business.

In the so-called "coming to the nuisance" cases, the courts have held that the residential landowner may not have relief if he knowingly came into a neighborhood reserved for industrial or agricultural endeavors and has been damaged thereby:

"Plaintiffs chose to live in an area uncontrolled by zoning laws or restrictive covenants and remote from urban development. In such an area plaintiffs cannot complain that legitimate agricultural pursuits are being carried on in the vicinity, nor can plaintiffs, having chosen to build in an agricultural area, complain that the agricultural pursuits carried on in the area depreciate the value of their homes. The area being *primarily agricultural,* any opinion reflecting the value of such property must take this factor into account. The standards affecting the value of residence property in an urban setting, subject to zoning controls and controlled planning techniques cannot be the standards by which agricultural properties are judged.

"People employed in a city who build their homes in suburban areas of the county beyond the limits of a city and zoning regulations do so for a reason. Some do so to avoid the high taxation rate imposed by cities, or to avoid special assessments for street, sewer and water projects. They usually build on improved or hard surface highways, which have been built either at state or county expense and thereby avoid special assessments for these improvements. It may be that they desire to get away from the congestion of traffic, smoke, noise, foul air and the many other annoyances of city life. But with all these advantages in going beyond the area which is zoned and restricted to protect them in their homes, they must be prepared to take the disadvantages." Dill v. Excel Packing Company, 183 Kan. 513, 525, 526, 331 P.2d 539, 548, 549 (1958). See also East St. Johns Shingle Co. v. City of Portland, 195 Or. 505, 246 P.2d 554, 560–562 (1952).

And:

"* * * a party cannot justly call upon the law to make that place suitable for his residence which was not so when he selected it. * * *." Gilbert v. Showerman, 23 Mich. 448, 455, 2 Brown 158 (1871).

Were Webb the only party injured, we would feel justified in holding that the doctrine of "coming to the nuisance" would have been a bar to the relief asked by Webb, and, on the other hand, had Spur located the feedlot near the outskirts of a city and had the city grown toward the feedlot, Spur would have to suffer the cost of abating the nuisance as to those people locating within the growth pattern of the expanding city:

"The case affords, perhaps, an example where a business established at a place remote from population is gradually surrounded and becomes part of a populous center, so that a business which formerly was not an interference with the rights of others has become so by the encroachment of the population * * *." City of Ft.

We agree, however, with the Massachusetts court that:

"The law of nuisance affords no rigid rule to be applied in all instances. It is elastic. It undertakes to require only that which is fair and reasonable under all the circumstances. In a commonwealth like this, which depends for its material prosperity so largely on the continued growth and enlargement of manufacturing of diverse varieties, 'extreme rights' cannot be enforced. * * *." Stevens v. Rockport Granite Co., 216 Mass. 486, 488, 104 N.E. 371, 373 (1914).

There was no indication in the instant case at the time Spur and its predecessors located in western Maricopa County that a new city would spring up, full-blown, alongside the feeding operation and that the developer of that city would ask the court to order Spur to move because of the new city. Spur is required to move not because of any wrongdoing on the part of Spur, but because of a proper and legitimate regard of the courts for the rights and interests of the public.

Del Webb, on the other hand, is entitled to the relief prayed for (a permanent injunction), not because Webb is blameless, but because of the damage to the people who have been encouraged to purchase homes in Sun City. It does not equitably or legally follow, however, that Webb, being entitled to the injunction, is then free of any liability to Spur, if Webb has in fact been the cause of the damage Spur has sustained. It does not seem harsh to require a developer, who has taken advantage of the lesser land values in a rural area as well as the availability of large tracts of land on which to build and develop a new town or city in the area, to indemnify those who are forced to leave as a result.

Having brought people to the nuisance to the foreseeable detriment of Spur, Webb must indemnify Spur, or a reasonable amount of the cost of moving or shutting down. It should be noted that this relief to Spur is limited to a case wherein a developer has, with foreseeability, brought into a previously agricultural or industrial area the population which makes necessary the granting of an injunction against a lawful business and for which the business has no adequate relief.

It is therefore the decision of this court that the matter be remanded to the trial court for a hearing upon the damages sustained by the defendant Spur as a reasonable and direct result of the granting of the permanent injunction. Since the result of the appeal may appear novel and both sides have obtained a measure of relief, it is ordered that each side will bear its own costs.

Primer on Easements as an Issue for Planners

Introduction

Nuisance law has been used primarily as a way to settle disputes between neighboring property owners. Courts have controlled the development of land by deciding which uses belong in which areas based on compatibility and/or an injury demonstrated by the affected party. There is a long history of these issues being decided through actions interpreting the common law.

These actions are separate from state statutes that often define the same activities as a nuisance and provide for fines or criminal penalties. Common law nuisances, on the other hand, are reactive in that they arise when intentional damage is proved. There is no "planning" involved in trying to predict the land use future of an area that relies solely on common law nuisance cases to resolve disputes. Therefore, zoning has been used as a substitute to provide advance knowledge of the growth of an area. However, the enactment of a zoning ordinance does not mean the end of nuisance lawsuits.

Nuisance law retains vitality for a number of reasons. It is the primary method of resolving land use compatibility issues where there is no zoning in place. In addition, if a permitted activity is conducted in a way that causes harm to a neighbor, the relief is through a nuisance lawsuit. In addition, courts have used nuisance law principles to help frame discussions about the Takings clause of the Fifth Amendment to the United States Constitution.

Common law nuisances are classified in two different categories. They are either public or private or they are nuisances per se or nuisances per accidens (based on specific facts). The most common occurrence is a private nuisance per accidens because it involves factual disputes between adjacent property owners. A public nuisance is an unreasonable interference with the right of the public that involves public health, welfare, and safety. It may or may not involve a property right and the state government is responsible for bringing lawsuits alleging a public nuisance.

A private nuisance is an unreasonable interference with a property owner's use of land. The common law permits every property owner to enjoy the benefits of ownership free from the activities of others that affect the use of their land. Of course, every landowner has a responsibility not to use land in a way that damages their neighbor. Usually, a private nuisance lawsuit involves intentional activity and must cause damage on a continuing basis.

A nuisance lawsuit is different from trespass in that there is no actual occupation of a neighbor's property. But there is an invasion of property rights in these lawsuits. A private nuisance lawsuit interferes with an owner's right to the use and enjoyment of that property.

In reality, there is often little difference between public and private nuisances. A single activity can be both and can result in multiple lawsuits by various individuals.

A nuisance per se is an action that is always a nuisance under any circumstance in any place. It is a question of law and not one of fact. An activity that has governmental permission to operate cannot be determined to be a public nuisance. On the other hand, such an activity, even though licensed by the state, can be a nuisance per accidens. A nuisance in fact is a nuisance in terms of its location or how it is conducted.

Most nuisance situations are nuisances per accidens because circumstances differ as to location. A funeral home located in a residential neighborhood may or may not be a nuisance, depending upon its operation or its effect on neighboring property values. It is a balancing test to determine the impacts of this particular land use. The most valuable land use will get protection.

Of course, the land use that is determined to be the most "valuable" changes over time, varies by different location, and is dependent upon a judge's ruling. There is no way that nuisance law can fix the future of a neighborhood. That is the function of comprehensive planning and zoning.

Public Nuisances and Remedies

A public nuisance is any activity that interferes with the rights of the public. In this case these rights would include everything that constitutes the public interest, e.g. health, welfare, safety, and morals. Offending activities could include such things as blocking access to public streets or emissions from publicly owned facilities. While land uses such as bars, adult entertainment venues and group homes have been alleged to be public nuisances, typically courts have not found these activities to be violations of public rights.

Public nuisances affect the rights of the public while private nuisances affect individual property owners. Clearly an activity can be both a private nuisance and a public nuisance. An activity such as excessive noise that bothers many individuals, may have both public and private aspects. This situation has often been referred to as a "mixed" nuisance.

It is important to remember that public nuisances may not involve the violation of property rights. In the case of an allegation of a land use that violates community aesthetics, there is no specific individual property right that is harmed. Many public nuisances are controlled through environmental pollution control laws, e.g. air and water quality standards. Landowners would ordinarily pursue violators through this statutory mechanism rather than depend upon common law doctrines.

The state prosecutes public nuisances. Therefore, the state can declare activities to be nuisances, either at common law or by statute. However, if a state wishes to stop a public nuisance through the common law, a judge will have to decide whether that activity is a public nuisance.

An activity with a state license or state permission to operate is usually immune from a public nuisance lawsuit. A court may have to find this intention in the statute. Immunity from private nuisance litigation is also conferred by state legislation, particularly in right-to-farm laws. This is discussed in the section "Response to Wicked Problem." Some courts may not believe that these laws provide an unconditional exemption from private nuisance lawsuits that satisfy constitutional provisions, including due process.

Public nuisances that are stopped by the state usually do not owe compensation to the property owner for damages or losses occurred after the public nuisance is stopped. A public nuisance may also give rise to a criminal complaint initiated by the state. Public nuisances may also be enjoined but these actions are separate from activities designed to enforce criminal statutes. In addition, an individual can almost always sue the operator of a public nuisance alleging special damages. That is, the harm to this individual is so great that it goes beyond a normal private nuisance complaint. Usually, a lawsuit that alleges a private nuisance asks for damages to compensate for the loss. A lawsuit involving "special" damages for the effect of public nuisances could also involve an injunction. That would stop the continued operation of the nuisance. As will be discussed, this alternative is not often available in private nuisance cases.

Private Nuisances and Remedies

A private nuisance is an unreasonable interference with the use and enjoyment of land. That is, one should not use one's property in a way that harms the property of one's neighbor. In other words, an individual has the right to use their land in a manner that is free from interference from their neighbor.

The factors that determine a private nuisance are balanced by a court. Issues include how often there is a problem, how long has there been a problem, how long has the property (including the surrounding land) been in its current use and the character of the neighborhood. Courts will look at the value of the activity, including economics, as well as the ability of the defendants to avoid the harm. The private nuisance lawsuit depends upon the facts in an individual case. This means that an activity that is a nuisance in one place may or may not be a nuisance in another place. Therefore, it is almost impossible to predict whether a court will or will not find a nuisance on a particular set of facts.

It is this outcome that leads to the belief that nuisance law is actually "judicial zoning." A court decides if this activity, assumed to be reasonable, is unreasonable in this particular area. Given the history of nuisance law, it is residential uses that receive the highest level of protection. That is, non-residential uses have a history of being eliminated if the area is residential in nature. If the neighborhood is non-residential, there is much more leeway given to the continuation of existing uses.

Courts, in their role as "judicial zoning" experts, also consider the future development of an area. If the property owner engages in the first non-agricultural (or even agricultural) use in a neighborhood, that fact alone does not guarantee that the area must be developed in that way. Courts may decide otherwise. This is despite a "coming to the nuisance" defense that suggests the first landowner in the area controls the type of future development. Where this doctrine is recognized, it becomes only one factor in a balancing test used by a judge to decide the outcome of a lawsuit.

Private nuisances usually, but not always, involve some actual physical harm such as cement dust or smells from a feedlot. However, psychological interference with the use of property can also be deemed a private nuisance. Disturbances of this type that do not involve physical harm have included the location of a funeral home in a residential neighborhood or a residential facility for ex-prisoners. A determination that these activities are nuisances is not very common. Furthermore, nuisances with aesthetic considerations, such as "ugly" houses or signs, are usually not found to be nuisances. This is because courts are reluctant to deal with subjective issues such as the state of mind of individuals or to give attention to the definition of the term "beauty." The key to determining whether an activity is a private nuisance is to determine whether there was intent to cause a neighbor an injury through the use of property. Aesthetic violations can have a difficult time meeting this standard.

Damages for private nuisance violations are the most common form of remedy. A plaintiff can recover, depending on the harm, money for both past and present injuries. The court will determine the fair market value of the property both with and without the nuisance. If the action was done deliberately, punitive damages are available.

An injunction is also possible but is harder to secure. It involves the court balancing the hardship to the plaintiff of continuing to live with the nuisance as opposed to the hardship to the defendant of stopping the activity.

It is often difficult to prove the connection between an injury to an individual and a nuisance. Such information necessary to prove this linkage is often not readily available. Furthermore, it may take many years for damages to appear after the original injury occurs. If the problem is widespread throughout a neighborhood, a public nuisance action might be more appropriate, even if it is more difficult to prove. For these reasons, environmental pollution control laws may provide a better solution to a problem that in the past was solved by a nuisance lawsuit.

Response to Wicked Problem

1. A private nuisance is an unreasonable interference with someone's use of their property. Usually, a court will prevent a landowner from damaging a neighbor's property. In this case, the answer first depends upon whether a building that contains 1,000 chickens is an "unreasonable" use of the property. The available acreage is important. The wicked problem contains no information on the size of the parcel, e.g. 1 acre or 100 acres. In *Rodrigue v. Copeland,* the standard to be met to determine unreasonableness was "real" damage to property and not mere inconvenience. The court would have to determine if this building with the extra chickens was "irreparable" harm, considering the character of the neighborhood. A ten-fold increase in the number of chickens would seem to present some additional negative impacts, e.g. noise, smell, and waste, that a judge would consider.
2. A public nuisance injures the entire neighborhood and need not affect individual property rights. The question is whether any rights of the public are negatively impacted by the expansion of the local chicken farmer. The neighbors might argue that the use generates additional traffic (for supplies) or additional water and air pollution as consequences. The problem with these arguments is that these impacts are already covered by state statutes or local ordinances. Courts are often reluctant to look at the common law for relief if a neighborhood property owner can sue a polluter or responsible government to stop pollution under a statute. In this instance, the existence of a recognized CAFO would make it difficult to bring a public nuisance lawsuit.
3. In order to prove interference with property rights, a neighboring landowner must show "substantial" harm to property values. This means that the neighbors will need to demonstrate the effects of a nuisance after it has begun. Courts have ruled that this must be a continuing and not isolated occurrence in order to show real damages. Therefore, it is very unlikely that a court will issue an injunction against the site plan approval, building permit issuance or actual land use until it has been underway for some time.
4. It would be almost impossible to show "substantial" harm with an increase of 100 chickens. An increase to 5,000 chickens would make it easier to meet this standard, assuming the neighbors would be able to prove damage to their property.

5. "Coming to the nuisance" is a shorthand phrase for a defense designed to stop lawsuits by neighbors who moved into a neighborhood with pre-existing land uses. In other words, the land use that was there first has the priority for protection. This doctrine would prevent an individual from coming to an area with depressed property values and then getting excess profit if the "offensive" land use was removed. Of course, this "defense" to a nuisance lawsuit is dependent on the facts of this case. In the wicked problem, the chickens appear to have been there first.

6. The relationship between a zoning ordinance and a nuisance lawsuit is complex. Most courts will rule that a zoning ordinance cannot completely protect an activity from being classified as a nuisance. In other words, even with the appropriate zoning, conditions could exist where a neighboring property owner could prove the existence of a nuisance. Other courts may defer to the judgment of the local government. Each state will have a different approach to the use of nuisance law as "judicial zoning" and different ways in which judges actively take a role in determining the land use of a neighborhood.

7. As an agricultural area, the neighborhood in the wicked problem can be viewed in land use terms as a "transitional" area. It may remain primarily as a location for farms or it may be redeveloped into a more intense land use (e.g. single family dwelling units). Being a resident in an area does not, of course, give a property owner the right to determine the future land use of the area. In the wicked problem, the character of the neighborhood is ultimately not important since even if the lawsuits are successful, the chicken farm will remain with a certain number of animals.

8. CAFO is a term to describe an agricultural operation regulated by the federal government. Large numbers of confined animals can cause excessive pollution, especially to surrounding waters. The United States Environmental Protection Agency has classified the size of CAFOs by the number of animals at that particular location. The number of chickens in the wicked problem is considered to be a "small" CAFO and would not be automatically subject to federal regulation.

9. Because farmers have often lost private nuisance lawsuits, particularly on land that is being developed for housing, states have enacted "right-to-farm" laws. These laws protect a "farmer" who engages in "agriculture" by taking away the right to bring a nuisance lawsuit against these individuals. The definition of these terms and the amount of protection provided if someone is covered by these laws varies from state to state. These laws provide protection for agricultural operations against claims of a public or private nuisance, assuming that the activity has been in existence for the designated period of time. The expansion of pre-existing farm uses is usually allowed. These "right-to-farm" laws usually, but not always, prevent neighbors from bringing successful lawsuits.

10. Most "right-to-farm" laws do not allow a local government to define terms to either include or exclude certain land uses or farming techniques or methods. In the wicked problem, even if the township was able to define "agriculture" in this way, it might not be a solution to the problem. A private nuisance lawsuit might be filed under these circumstances as well.

11. The *Boomer v. Atlantic Cement* Co. case stands for the proposition that a landowner may compensate the neighboring property owners for damages

while still allowing the nuisance to continue. In that case, a cement factory emitted dust that caused damage to nearby residences. Instead of ordering an injunction to stop the nuisance, the court awarded permanent damages for the loss of property values. The loss to the community of the jobs and the capital investment of the company was important to the court. In the wicked problem, a court would need to balance the cost to the farmer and the township of stopping the farm as opposed to the benefit given to the neighbors of living in a nuisance-free environment.

12. The *Spur Industries v. Del Webb* case dealt with a situation where a nuisance was forced to cease but was compensated by the surrounding landowners. A feedlot operator was sued by a developer who built an exurban residential development near Phoenix. The residents of the subdivision, many of whom were retirees, complained about the odor. The court ordered the developer to pay the feedlot operator for the costs of removal and relocation. Of course, the feedlot operator retained the ownership of the land that could be put to another land use. In the wicked problem, damages to the farmer might be an appropriate remedy, particularly if they involve compensation for the loss of a larger farming operation.

Discussion Prompts

- What are the primary differences between public and private nuisances?
- In what ways has Euclidean zoning served to reduce claims based on nuisance?
- The greening of neighborhoods, including the installation of solar panel and wind turbines, as well as the encouragement of urban agriculture, has served as an impetus for the resurgence of nuisance suits. How might these operations inspire such litigation?
- Many land use types cause nuisance effects. How much interference should a property owner have to bear as a result of a neighbor's legal use of his or her property?

Bibliography

Bishop, Patrick and Jenkins, Victoria (2011). Planning and Nuisance: Revisiting the Balance of Public and Private Interests in Land Use Development. *Journal of Environmental Law*, 23(2), 288–310.

Ford, John D. (1993). Planning a Nuisance. *Cambridge Law Journal*, 52(1), 15–17.

5

PRIVATE LAND USE CONTROLS

Private landowners have engaged in quasi-zoning efforts to protect the use and values of their properties and those around them. These covenants and easements add another layer in discussions about the future development of affected properties. Readers should be aware of these tools and the rights that accompany them.

Private Land Use Controls Wicked Problem

You are a municipal planner for a city that has historically relied on private covenants instead of zoning to control land use. The Planning Commission has asked you to review some major land use issues that have occurred in the city that have been caused by various covenants. How have further covenants attempted to solve these problems? Would a solution contained in the zoning ordinance be a better way to solve these issues?

1. Each family can have no more than two adult animals of any species on their property, unless the City agrees through use of a Special Use Permit.
2. Vegetable gardens are not permitted unless the harvested crops are sold at an established Farmers Market.
3. Swimming pools and solar collectors may be permitted with the permission of each of the surrounding property owners. Such permission may be revoked by the Owners Association.
4. The Owners Association may grant permission for the following activities:

    a. Visits by relatives for more than 90 days
    b. More than one night's parking for recreational vehicle

5. Home occupations performed by residents of the property, other than child day care, are prohibited. Child day care is not permitted unless the child is biologically related to the property owner or has a similar racial background.
6. Outbuildings that are no more than 10 percent of square footage of the principal structure are only allowed with plans reviewed by the Architectural Review Board.
7. Once the developer of the property owns no platted lots in the subdivision, a majority of the property owners may amend or delete one of these covenants in each calendar year following this event.

Figure 4 Credit: David D. Boeck

Cases

The following cases will be useful to you as you attempt to analyze this chapter's wicked problem:

Shelley v. Kraemer, 334 U.S. 1 (1948)
Runyon v. Paley, 416 S.E.2d 177 (N.C. 1992)

Shelley v. Kraemer

334 U.S. 1 (1948)

Facts

In 1911, property owners in a neighborhood in Saint Louis created a restrictive covenant that would prevent African Americans from owning property in the neighborhood for a period of 50 years from the date of the covenant. In 1945, the Shelleys, an African American couple, entered into contract on a home in the neighborhood without any knowledge of the covenant. Neighbors brought suit, asking the court to restrain the Shelleys from taking title to the home. The trial court denied neighbors' prayer for relief, which was reversed by the Supreme Court of Missouri, holding that enforcement of the covenant did not violate any rights guaranteed by the Fourteenth Amendment.

Issue

Can the State of Missouri enforce the restrictive covenant excluding Shelley from property ownership solely on the basis of race?

Held

No. As private agreements between individuals, restrictive covenants cannot be held to be violations of the equal protection of laws guaranteed by the Fourteenth Amendment. However, once the Supreme Court of Missouri, as a state actor, proceeded to enforce the covenant at the behest of Kraemer, the covenant became unconstitutional.

Discussion

In *Shelley*, the Court mentioned that it is clear given the context surrounding the adoption of the Fourteenth Amendment, that the framers of the Constitution clearly intended to extend its protections to the enjoyment of property rights, which were considered a necessary prerequisite to the realization of other basic rights guaranteed by the Amendment.

Case Excerpt

Against this background of judicial construction, extending over a period of some three-quarters of a century, we are called upon to consider whether enforcement by state courts of the restrictive agreements in these cases may be deemed to be the acts of those States; and, if so, whether that action has denied these petitioners the equal protection of the laws which the Amendment was intended to insure.

We have no doubt that there has been state action in these cases in the full and complete sense of the phrase. The undisputed facts disclose that petitioners were willing purchasers of properties upon which they desired to establish homes. The owners of the properties were willing sellers; and contracts of sale were accordingly consummated. It is clear that but for the active intervention of the state courts, supported by the full panoply of state power, petitioners would have been free to occupy the properties in question without restraint.

These are not cases, as has been suggested, in which the States have merely abstained from action, leaving private individuals free to impose such discriminations as they see fit. Rather, these are cases in which the States have made available to such individuals the full coercive power of government to deny to petitioners, on the grounds of race or color, the enjoyment of property rights in premises which petitioners are willing and financially able to acquire and which the grantors are willing to sell. The difference between judicial enforcement and nonenforcement of the restrictive covenants is the difference to petitioners between being denied rights of property available to other members of the community and being accorded full enjoyment of those rights on an equal footing.

The enforcement of the restrictive agreements by the state courts in these cases was directed pursuant to the common-law policy of the States as formulated by those courts in earlier decisions. In the Missouri case, enforcement of the covenant was directed in the first instance by the highest court of the State after the trial court had determined the agreement to be invalid for want of the requisite number of signatures. In the Michigan case, the order of enforcement by the trial court was affirmed by the highest state court. The judicial action in each case bears the clear and unmistakable imprimatur of the State. We have noted that previous decisions of this Court have established the proposition that judicial action is not immunized from the operation of the Fourteenth Amendment simply because it is taken pursuant to the state's common-law policy. Nor is the Amendment ineffective simply because the particular pattern of discrimination, which the State has enforced, was defined initially by the terms of a private agreement. State action, as that phrase is understood for the purposes of the Fourteenth Amendment, refers to exertions of state power in all forms. And when the effect of that action is to deny rights subject to the protection of the Fourteenth Amendment, it is the obligation of this Court to enforce the constitutional commands.

We hold that in granting judicial enforcement of the restrictive agreements in these cases, the States have denied petitioners the equal protection of the laws and that, therefore, the action of the state courts cannot stand. We have noted that freedom from discrimination by the States in the enjoyment of property rights was among the basic objectives sought to be effectuated by the framers of the Fourteenth Amendment. That such discrimination has occurred in these cases is clear. Because of the race or color of these petitioners they have been denied rights of ownership or occupancy enjoyed as a matter of course by other citizens of different race or color. The Fourteenth Amendment declares "that all persons, whether colored or white, shall stand equal before the laws of the States, and, in regard to the colored race, for whose protection the amendment was primarily designed, that no discrimination shall be made against them by law because of their color." *Strauder* v. *West Virginia, supra* at 307. Only recently this Court had occasion to declare that a state law which denied equal enjoyment of property rights to a designated class of citizens of specified race and ancestry, was not a legitimate exercise of the state's police power but violated the guaranty of the equal protection of the laws. *Oyama* v. *California*, 332 U.S. 633 (1948). Nor may the discriminations imposed by the state courts in these cases be justified as proper exertions of state police power. Cf. *Buchanan v. Warley, supra.*

Respondents urge, however, that since the state courts stand ready to enforce restrictive covenants excluding white persons from the ownership or occupancy of property covered by such agreements, enforcement of covenants excluding colored persons may not be deemed a denial of equal protection of the laws to the colored persons who are thereby affected. This contention does not bear scrutiny. The parties have directed our attention to no case in which a court, state or federal, has been called upon to enforce a covenant excluding members of the white majority from ownership or occupancy of real property on grounds of race or color. But there are more fundamental considerations. The rights created by the first section of the Fourteenth Amendment are, by its terms, guaranteed to the individual. The rights established are personal rights. It is, therefore, no answer to these petitioners to say that the courts may also be induced to deny white persons rights of ownership and occupancy on grounds of race or color. Equal protection of the laws is not achieved through indiscriminate imposition of inequalities.

Nor do we find merit in the suggestion that property owners who are parties to these agreements are denied equal protection of the laws if denied access to the courts to enforce the terms of restrictive covenants and to assert property rights which the state courts have held to be created by such agreements. The Constitution confers upon no individual the right to demand action by the State which results in the denial of equal protection of the laws to other individuals. And it would appear beyond question that the power of the State to create and enforce property interests must be exercised within the boundaries defined by the Fourteenth Amendment. Cf. *Marsh v. Alabama*, 326 U.S. 501 (1946).

The problem of defining the scope of the restrictions which the Federal Constitution imposes upon exertions of power by the States has given rise to many of the most persistent and fundamental issues which this Court has been called upon to consider. That problem was foremost in the minds of the framers of the Constitution, and, since that early day, has arisen in a multitude of forms. The task of determining whether the action of a State offends constitutional provisions is one which may not be undertaken lightly. Where, however, it is clear that the action of the State violates the terms of the fundamental charter, it is the obligation of this Court so to declare.

The historical context in which the Fourteenth Amendment became a part of the Constitution should not be forgotten. Whatever else the framers sought to achieve, it is clear that the matter of primary concern was the establishment of equality in the enjoyment of basic civil and political rights and the preservation of those rights from discriminatory action on the part of the States based on considerations of race or color. Seventy-five years ago this Court announced that the provisions of the Amendment are to be construed with this fundamental purpose in mind. Upon full consideration, we have concluded that in these cases the States have acted to deny petitioners the equal protection of the laws guaranteed by the Fourteenth Amendment. Having so decided, we find it unnecessary to consider whether petitioners have also been deprived of property without due process of law or denied privileges and immunities of citizens of the United States.

Runyon v. Paley

416 S.E.2d 177 (N.C. 1992)

Facts

In 1937, Gaskins acquired four acres of land in the Village of Ocracoke. In 1954, Gaskins conveyed one and one-half acres to Runyon, who reconveyed it to Gaskins on January 6, 1960. Two days later, Gaskins conveyed a lake-front lot and a 15-foot-wide strip of land to Runyon. The following day, Gaskins conveyed the remainder of the parcel to Brugh, with a covenant restricting the land to no more than two residences. Brugh's lot was then acquired by Paley, who subsequently entered into a contract to construct condominium units on the lot.

Issue
Was Paley's property subject to the restrictive covenant forbidding the construction of condominiums?

Held
Yes. Restrictive covenants are considered to be real covenants, meaning it remains with the land after transferred ownership, if (1) the covenant touches and concerns the land; (2) there is privity of estate between the enforcing and non-enforcing parties; (3) and the original covenanting parties intended for the covenant to "run with the land." In the present case, Williams, Gaskin's daughter who inherited her estate, established Gaskins had intended the restrictive covenants to be enforceable by the property owner. However, the Runyons, as co-plaintiffs, did not have substantial evidence to meet their burden of proof and were thus barred from enforcing against Paley.

Discussion
As long as restrictions do not disregard public policy, property owners are able to sell their property with any restrictions, in the form of covenants, as they deem fit.

Case Excerpt
In order to enforce a restrictive covenant on the theory of equitable servitude, it must be shown (1) that the covenant touches and concerns the land, and (2) that the original covenanting parties intended the covenant to bind the person against whom enforcement is sought and to benefit the person seeking to enforce the covenant. 5 *Powell on Real Property* 673[1], at 60–44.

Whether a covenant is of such a *character* that it touches and concerns land is determined according to the same principles applicable to real covenants running at law. Unlike with real covenants, however, it is not always necessary to show that both the burden and the benefit touch and concern land. To enforce a restrictive covenant as an equitable servitude, it is only necessary to show that the covenant is of such a nature as to bind the party sued and to be enforceable by the party suing. The covenant itself establishes these rights and obligations between the original covenanting parties as well as any named parties intended to be benefitted thereby. Thus, the touch and concern element need only be established where the covenant is sought to be enforced either by or against successors in interest to the original or named parties to the covenant. Where, for example, a covenantee or a named beneficiary seeks to enforce the restriction against the covenantor's successor in interest, the party seeking enforcement need not show that the benefit touches and concerns his land but need show only that the burden touches and concerns the land of the party against whom he seeks to enforce the restriction. *See Bauby,* 107 Conn. 109, 139 A. 508. Similarly, a successor in interest to the covenantee or to a named beneficiary who seeks to enforce the restriction against the original covenantor must show only that the benefit of the restriction touches and concerns the successor's land. Where, however, the covenant is sought to be enforced by *and* against parties neither of whom were the covenanting parties or named beneficiaries, the party seeking to enforce the restriction must show that the covenant touches and concerns the land of both...

A party who seeks to enforce a covenant as an equitable servitude against one who was not an original party to the covenant must show that the original covenanting parties intended that the covenant bind the party against whom enforcement is sought. To meet this requirement, the party seeking to enforce the covenant must show that the covenanting parties intended that the burden run to successors in interest of the covenantor's land.

If the party seeking enforcement was not an original party to the covenant, he must show that the covenanting parties intended that he be able to enforce the restriction. Maurice T. Brunner, Annotation, *Comment. Note – Who May Enforce Restrictive Covenant or Agreement as to Use of Real Property,* 51 A.L.R.3d 556, 573 (1973). It is presumed in North Carolina that covenants may be enforced only between the original covenanting parties. *Stegall,* 278 N.C. at 101, 178 S.E.2d at 828. However, this presumption may be overcome by evidence that (1) the covenanting parties intended that the covenant personally benefit the party seeking enforcement, or (2) the covenanting parties intended that the covenant benefit property in which the party seeking enforcement holds a present interest. *B.C.E. Dev. v. Smith,* 215 Cal.App.3d 1142, 1147, 264 Cal.Rptr. 55, 59 (1989). The latter may be shown by evidence of a common scheme of development, *e.g., Higdon v. Jaffa,* 231 N.C. 242, 56 S.E.2d 661 (1949); of succession of interest to benefitted property retained by the covenantee, *e.g., Sheets v. Dillon,* 221 N.C. 426, 20 S.E.2d 344 (1942); or of an express statement of intent to benefit property owned by the party seeking enforcement, *e.g., Lamica v. Gerdes,* 270 N.C. 85, 153 S.E. 2d 814 (1967)...

It is well settled in our state that a restrictive covenant is not enforceable, either at law or in equity, against a subsequent purchaser of property burdened by the covenant unless notice of the covenant is contained in an instrument in his chain of title. N.C.G.S. § 47-18 provides:

No conveyance of land shall be valid to pass any property interest as against purchasers for a valuable consideration but from the time of registration thereof in the county where the land lies... N.C.G.S. § 47-18(a) (1984). Unlike in many states, actual knowledge, no matter how full and formal, is not sufficient to bind a purchaser in our state with notice of the existence of a restrictive covenant. *Turner v. Glenn*, 220 N.C. 620, 625, 18 S.E.2d 197, 201 (1942).

A purchaser is chargeable with notice of the existence of the restriction only if a proper search of the public records would have revealed it... If the restrictive covenant is contained in a separate instrument or rests in parol and not in a deed in the chain of title and is not referred to in such deed a purchaser, under our registration law, has no constructive notice of it...

While it would be advisable to include an express provision with respect to the rights of enforcement in the conveyance that creates them, we do not agree that such notice, as defendants demand, is required. An examination of our case law reveals that we have required the certainty of an express statement in the chain of title only with respect to the *existence* of a restrictive covenant. *See Reed*, 246 N.C. 221, 98 S.E.2d 360; *Turner*, 220 N.C. 620, 18 S.E.2d 197. "'If the restrictive covenant is contained in a separate instrument or rests in parol and [is] not [referred to] in a deed in the chain of title,'" a subsequent purchaser will take the property free of restrictions. *Reed*, 246 N.C. at 230, 98 S.E.2d at 367 (quoting *Turner*, 220 N.C. at 625, 18 S.E.2d at 201). Where, however, the restriction is contained in the chain of title, we have not hesitated to enforce the restriction against a subsequent purchaser when the court may reasonably infer that the covenant was created for the benefit of the party seeking enforcement...

This is not to say that a restrictive covenant, the existence of which is clearly set forth in the chain of title, may be enforced by any person who is able to show by any means possible that the covenanting parties intended that he be permitted to enforce the covenant. For a restrictive covenant to be enforceable against a subsequent purchaser, there must be *some* evidence in the public records from which it reasonably may be inferred that the covenant was intended to benefit, either personally or as a landowner, the party seeking enforcement.

Primer on Covenants as an Issue for Planners

What is a Covenant?

Covenants are a common method used by individuals to control the land use on their property and that of their neighbors. A covenant is a contract between a buyer and seller of land that is "mutually advantageous." Each person signing the agreement reaps some benefit from the restrictions placed on the property. Typically, the seller will achieve a higher price from the property for the restrictions and the buyer is purchasing the value of the belief that changing these restrictions is difficult and time-consuming. As noted in *Runyon v. Paley*, 416 S.E.2d 177 (N.C. 1992), a case involving the restriction of land to the building of no more than two residences, an owner of land has the right to sell the land subject to any restrictions that he or she may impose, as long as they are not contrary to public policy.

Covenants are mostly concerned today with looks and behavior, particularly as it affects property values. There are two parties to a covenant, who both sign the document. A covenantor originally creates the restriction and a covenantee originally agrees to some restriction on the total use of the property. Covenants can be positive (e.g. requiring review of all buildings in a subdivision by an architectural review committee) or negative (e.g. prohibiting the construction of fences between neighbors). While some covenants may be personal (all residents must be at least 55 years of age), this chapter will discuss those covenants that affect real property.

What are the Advantages and Disadvantages of a Covenant?

Modern covenants clearly have advantages for both the property owner and the local government. They allow each subdivision, for example, to offer those amenities that its residents want and can afford. This relieves, to some extent, the burden of local government (and its taxpayers) from providing such services. Of course, access to public facilities in areas without such covenants (typically older and/or poorer neighborhoods) may be a problem. Covenants often have no set expiration date; they will outlast the original signers. As discussed later, this permanent nature makes them attractive.

Disadvantages of covenants are also quite common. First of all, because they are not technically related to zoning, they tend to be overlooked and forgotten. This is particularly true if the neighborhood association becomes inactive as the subdivision grows older. The covenants often place a lien on the property, so homeowners are required to pay for any activities that are consistent with the covenant (e.g. homeowner association dues). Covenants can be an invasion of privacy requiring a homeowner to do or not to do things that they consider to be out of bounds for the public's concern. Finally, the question of what is a reasonable and what is an unreasonable use of the property may be a matter that is best resolved by a court. The question of reasonableness may or may not be an easy matter to decide. For example, if a covenant limits a property to residential use, does this prohibit the owners from turning the property into a bed-and-breakfast while they still live there?

These restrictions are not government regulations. They are enforced by private individuals, either alone or in groups (e.g. homeowner associations). Governments often review covenants prior to their starting date. This is often done as part of a subdivision plat review. Covenants are of interest to planners for two reasons. First, governments cannot be made responsible for covenants without their express consent. Planners need to make sure they are not obligated in any way when covenants are signed unless they wish to be a "third party beneficiary." More importantly, when covenants provide for the maintenance and construction of improvements normally associated with government (e.g. streets, parks, open spaces), planners need to make sure that the covenants provide public facilities that are built to existing standards. If not, these improvements may be inadequate and the government may be faced with the politically popular but fiscally expensive task of accepting substandard improvements and rebuilding them to current specifications.

Where are Covenants Used?

In some places, covenants are used as substitutes for public land use controls. In Houston, Texas, for example, the city has not adopted a zoning ordinance. Instead, it relies on covenants, deed restrictions, and subdivision plats to control land use, particularly for residential areas. A Texas statute gives the city the right to enforce existing covenants, even though they were not a party to the original document. This is an important point to remember. Covenants are typically used in residential settings. They are most commonly found where individuals want to build homes and are used to reassure initial and subsequent property owners that the presence of covenants retains property values. Of course, when the property is subject to a zoning ordinance, there is a possibility that it might conflict with a restrictive covenant. Assuming that the restrictive covenant is valid, courts will usually enforce the "stricter" or more restrictive of the two documents.

Covenants are written and placed in deeds to pieces of property. They are indicated by reference or actually placed in the document that goes from each buyer and seller. Every sale of the property after the first one must refer in some way to these covenants in order to make sure the "chain of title" of the property always maintains the legality of these restrictions. There are a number of legal requirements that are historically associated with covenants. They were developed through court decisions in England that interpreted the common law. While some or all of these principles may be superseded or amended by a particular state statute, it is useful to remember at least two of these common-law principles.

What are the Requirements of a Covenant?

As noted in *Runyon v. Paley,* a covenant runs with the land of the "dominant" and "servient" estate only if (1) the subject of the covenant "touches and concerns" the land, (2) there is privity of estate between the party enforcing the covenant and the party against whom the covenant is being enforced, and (3) the original parties to the covenant intended this result. First, before discussing these ideas, it is important to remember that in order for covenants to be effective, they need to be valid between subsequent buyers and sellers. One of the aspects of this ability to enforce these rules long after the original signers of the first deed have sold their property is a legal doctrine known as "running with the land" or "touching and concerning the land." Essentially this means that the subject matter of the covenants must involve the use of land or the buildings placed on each parcel. Examples might include the payment of annual assessments for a homeowner association to benefit the subdivision or requirements for certain design elements of a building, e.g. roofing material or siding.

Can Covenants be Used to Accomplish Objectives against Public Policy?

Covenants were the principal method through which land developers enforced racial and religious segregation. In order to protect the property values in their subdivision, "undesirable" people such as Jews, Catholics, and/or African Americans were excluded from ownership and/or residency in that neighborhood. This particular use of covenants was effectively ended in 1948 with the case of *Shelley v. Kraemer*, 334 U.S. 1. The United States Supreme Court ruled that racially restrictive covenants do not automatically violate the Equal Protection clause of the United States Constitution. However, enforcement of these requirements are against public policy and do violate the U. S. Constitution. Therefore, the Supreme Court opinion did not technically change any restrictive covenants that are currently on deeds but ruled they could not be enforced. Other laws, particularly fair housing statutes and group home siting statutes, have affected the enforcement of covenants. For example, in many states a covenant that requires only single-family residences cannot be used to stop the construction of a group home for individuals with recognized disabilities. The potential impact on these individuals is enough to make sure these covenants are not enforced. This leads to some interesting questions that planners need to consider. For example, many subdivisions offer amenities (e.g. walking trails, tennis courts, swimming pools) for use only by residents of the subdivision. These facilities may be unavailable to residents with disabilities. Is it a violation of federal and/or state law to build subdivisions with these amenities? Should disabled persons owning houses in the subdivision have to pay for amenities that they are unable to use at any time? Similar questions can be asked regarding issues of religious freedom (can a residence be used as a public site for worship?) or free speech (can all signs be prohibited?).

How are Covenants Enforced?

Enforcement of covenants has become a major issue to planners. Covenants are designed so that enforcement is "automatic," in the sense that individuals and/or neighborhood associations are given the right to implement these provisions. If the property owner is found by a court to have violated the covenants, the property owner pays all the costs, including those of litigation. To overturn covenants, the person challenging them must prove they are "unreasonable." This may be difficult to do if the property owner purchased the property with knowledge of the restriction. If the provision is discriminatory, arbitrary, or irrational, it may be easier to deny enforcement of those provisions of the covenant that do not meet legal standards. However, as a general rule, courts have been reluctant to overturn these contracts between private individuals.

A well-written covenant makes provisions for change once conditions are different than at the time the covenant was signed. Traditionally, covenants could not be changed unless every single individual with an interest in the property affected by these covenants agreed to the change. Today, covenants can be changed by less than 100 percent agreement. Covenants may also have a "sunset" provision in which they automatically expire after a certain period of time. Planners can expect that as neighborhood land use changes (e.g. smaller homes being converted to offices), more problems will occur. Approval of such changes will or will not occur outside the government's system of planning and zoning.

When a government acquires a property by purchase and that property is subject to a covenant, the government is treated by the courts just like any other property owner. It must obey all the restrictions that affect the neighbors. However, government often acquires a property by eminent domain. Does the compensation given to the property owner include the value of the covenant? In most states the answer is yes.

What Compensation is Available when Covenants are Violated?

There are remedies available to property owners or homeowner associations who wish to enforce covenants. Typically, an injunction will be issued by a judge to prevent conduct. In other cases a specific performance decree is necessary to force an individual to live up to the terms of the covenant.

It is possible, although less common, for property owners and/or homeowner associations to receive damages from the violation of the covenant's provisions. Property is unique and the language in the documents is individually tailored to meet specific needs. Therefore, courts may have a difficult time determining value and the loss of that value that is attributable to the lack of enforcement of the covenant. It is also possible, but not very likely, to receive damages from a local government that revises a zoning code to make it inconsistent with an established covenant.

The planning and zoning system does, however, set the framework in which covenants operate even though the two methods of land use control are separate. The covenants represent "mutual coercion, mutually agreed upon" between a willing buyer and seller. While planners need to be aware of such issues, resolution of problems with covenants is best left to attorneys with expertise in real property litigation.

What is an Easement?

Another type of contract is an easement. It is a restriction on property signed by the property owner in return for a benefit to that property. An easement gives permission to the non-property owner to enter the property to provide a service to the owner. This limitation of property rights is a "shared arrangement" that provides more stability than a simple public license. Public services, such as water, sewerage, telephone, and so forth are the most common subject of easements.

There are three types of easements that are of interest to planners. An easement in gross is an easement placed in the public records, usually at the time of the initial subdivision or development of the property. This is a very common type of restriction often used by utility companies to provide services over and/or under the surface of the property. Compensation is usually not given to the landowner; access to the service is seen as the benefit provided in return for the easement. However, some easements, such as high-voltage electric lines, do involve a payment to the landowner.

A second type of easement is an easement appurtenant. These usually benefit a neighbor. In other words, one property owner has the right to go over an adjacent owner's land. The neighbor has the "dominant" tenement while the landowner has the "servient" tenement. Usually this easement is intentionally created at the time properties are developed. Planners may be affected by these easements if they plan a public improvement that changes access to a road. Often times a new "easement by necessity" will be recognized to provide road access, particularly if two parcels once had a single original owner. These easements are almost never overturned as a result of litigation.

Finally, prescriptive easements may impact a local development proposal. This type of easement is created through adverse use, using your neighbor's land without permission, for example. It has to be used in an "open, notorious, and hostile" manner and relies on the landowner's unwillingness to contest the use of land by another. Eventually, a court will grant the adjacent landowner a permanent easement based on these activities. Often times, landowners are unaware of their property boundaries and this could affect requests for development or additions to structures.

Another type of easement that planners may become familiar with is a conservation easement. This is an agreement that is personal to the property owner; it does not, in the language of covenants, "run with the land." This is an agreement between a property owner and a government agency and a government agency and/or non-governmental organization to keep the land in its current use, usually undeveloped, for the life of the property owner. The ownership then passes to the government or group that holds the easement in order to preserve the open space. The conservation easement often permanently restricts what can be done with the land. The easement takes away the development potential of the property by restricting the current land use. Because of the reduced property value, there are usually diminished property and/or estate taxes for property covered by conservation easements. This is an important tool when drawing up implementation of environmental land use plans.

Response to Wicked Problem

1. Many cities regulate the number of animals that are permitted in a structure for the purposes of public health and safety. This is done through the zoning ordinance in order to provide consistency throughout the jurisdiction. Often times more than the minimum number may be accommodated if the city grants a permit for a "kennel." Controlling this subject through the use of a covenant raises a number of concerns. Does the number of animals on a parcel "touch and concern" the land? Why would neighbors or the homeowner association be concerned with this issue? Is this a reaction to a perceived problem of "animal hoarding"? Does the property owner have the right to have as many animals as he or she wants? Should a covenant distinguish between animals (e.g. a horse and a goldfish)?

2. Many zoning ordinances regulate accessory uses, e.g. those uses that complement the principal use of the property. The idea is to protect the land use integrity of the neighborhood by controlling both the dominant and subsidiary ways in which the property realizes the intent of the zoning ordinance. This provision seems to go against that idea by indirectly forbidding the consumption of these vegetables in the residence. In fact, this covenant may violate the zoning ordinance by permitting a commercial function in a residential neighborhood. Why should covenants control this problem? Who has an interest in solving this problem? Is it a problem?

3. Some accessory uses of the property raise issues of concern to the city, particularly if installations come after the neighborhood has been constructed. Of course, the zoning ordinance protects pre-existing uses that were legally begun before a zoning ordinance was enacted or amended. Solar panels depend upon the neighboring property not interfering with direct access to the sun (*Prah v. Maretti* 318 N.W. 2d 404 (Wisc. 1981)). Swimming pools raise questions of aesthetics, noise, and safety. Should this be the responsibility of the property owner alone? What if there is a state statute or local regulation that decides the issue? This provision would seem to give the Owners Association the right to take down an existing solar panel or fill in an existing swimming pool. Is this a good policy?

4. There are many temporary uses that can occur on a property. The zoning ordinance will define a temporary use of the property. Is parking a vehicle on your

property a "use" of land? Many neighbors can become concerned about "temporary" uses that last longer than they believe to be appropriate. These two provisions are drawn to raise these questions in light of the interests of the property owner, neighbor, and city. Who defines a "relative"? Why not allow a recreational vehicle parked in the driveway? Shouldn't the city's interest be limited to oversize vehicles parked in the street? The current provision does not distinguish between a vehicle owned by the property owner and one owned by a visitor. Should this distinction be made?

5. Many communities have sought to accommodate the interests of individuals to operate a home-based business. Usually, these issues are covered in a zoning ordinance. Some individuals believe that the interests of the neighbors are not adequately covered in this way. This provision is intentionally strict and parts of it would not be enforced because of the ruling in *Shelley v. Kraemer*. Apparently, babysitting of a non-relative on the property would violate this covenant. Is this appropriate? What is the role of this type of instrument in allowing property owners to live in harmony? Since zoning ordinances provide for public hearing and comment, should these issues be discussed in the open before a decision is reached?

6. Many covenants seek to maintain the original architectural look of a neighborhood. Additional buildings are regulated in a way that does not upset the "look" of a neighborhood. Many times this is accomplished through an architectural review committee of an owners association. These individuals may or may not be residents of the subdivision. What are the property rights of the individual to build outbuildings or additions to the main residence? What is the interest of the neighbors in this regard? Does the city care about the appearance of its residential areas? Many communities regulate aesthetics through design review plans and ordinances. Should the neighbors have responsibility for this issue or should the city?

7. Covenants in theory are permanent, assuming they are consistent with any applicable laws, regulations, and court opinions. Circumstances can change. Sometimes the property owners want to change these provisions. How easy should this be? There is often a distinction between covenants adopted by a developer (to encourage sale of the lots and construction of new homes) and those adopted by property owners (to prevent changes that diminish existing property values). This provision allows a majority of the property owners to pick one covenant per year to amend or delete. Is this reasonable? Should the city care at all about these provisions? Is this a matter that can be regulated by the zoning ordinance?

Discussion Prompts

- Houston is often characterized as an unplanned city. However, development on a substantial number of properties in the City is limited by restrictive covenants. In what ways do these covenants operate like land use controls?
- Those who seek to preserve historic structures or to conserve undisturbed landscapes often utilize easements and covenants to accomplish their intended purposes. How do these tools aid in preservation?

Bibliography

Alexander, Gregory S. (1999). The Publicness of Private Land Use Controls. *Edinburgh Law Review*, 3:2, 176–190.

Ellickson, R. C. (1973). Alternatives to Zoning: Covenants, Nuisance Rules, and Fines as Land Use Controls. *The University of Chicago Law Review*, 40:4, 681–781.

Tarlock, Dan (1989). Private Land Use Controls: What is in the Public Interest. *Land Use Law and Zoning Digest*, 41:9, 3–7.

6

ZONING LAW

The zoning ordinance is the bread and butter of modern planning practice. It is the rule book that sends notice to property owners of how public and private property in a community can be developed and used. This chapter seeks to introduce readers to the use categories most common to zoning and the applicable requirements. Readers will also be introduced to the tools that allow for modification of these requirements, as well as the property rights implications of zoning schemes.

Zoning Law Wicked Problem

As part of its current zoning ordinance, a county has placed a parcel of land of over 100 acres in an exclusive zone with the purpose of building a campus-like industrial park emphasizing "high-tech" industry. The property in question has not been developed as an industrial park as of yet. There is, however, a cheese factory located in the district. No group homes are currently located within the county boundaries.

One day a new developer comes to the planning office. In other counties, the company holds a license from the state to build group homes for convicted embezzlers. The group home is actually a series of interconnected mobile homes, none of which meet the current county standard for residential dwellings. The company proposes to put these recovering embezzlers in a group home next to the cheese factory. In addition, the company proposes to open an income tax preparation service that caters to the factory workers with the former embezzlers as employees. This is a commercial use.

Shortly after the developer spoke to the planner, the Board of County Commissioners amended the zoning ordinance with the following provisions:

A) The property is now zoned exclusively agricultural instead of industrial.
B) Group homes may be granted by a special use permit with appropriate conditions.
C) All group homes are to be considered industrial uses for the purposes of the zoning ordinance.
D) All group homes must be at least 500 square feet in size and located on a lot of 10,000 square feet.
E) Any rezoning out of the agricultural district must be made on the condition that land be donated to the county for a cell tower for 911 service.

Figure 5 Credit: David D. Boeck

You have been asked to prepare a staff report on the following issues:

1. The cheese factory wishes to open a retail store in the plant to sell surplus production. Is this an expansion of an existing nonconforming use? Is it an accessory use?
2. Is the cheese factory an agricultural use?
3. What appropriate conditions will be required for the group home to be located in this district?
4. What type of variance is required for the location of the income tax service?
5. Is the mobile home a single-family home?
6. The mobile homes are only 300 square feet in size. Can the developer challenge this regulation?
7. The lot size is only 2,000 square feet. Can the developer challenge the new regulation on size of lot for group homes?
8. On what grounds can the developer challenge the rezoning?
9. What if the cheese factory had applied for a building permit for the new store before the rezoning went into effect?
10. Is it legal to require donation of land for public use?

Cases

The following case will be useful to you as you attempt to analyze this chapter's wicked problem:

Village of Euclid v. Ambler Realty, 272 U.S. 365 (1926)

Village of Euclid, Ohio v. Ambler Realty Co.

272 U.S. 365 (1926)

Facts

In 1922, the Village of Euclid, a suburb of Cleveland, enacted an ordinance establishing a comprehensive zoning plan to regulate and restrict the placement of different land uses, as well as the specific building requirements for each type of use. The ordinance also created a system for enforcement and appeals. Ambler Realty Company owned nearly seventy acres in Euclid, parts of which were zoned after passage of the ordinance for both multi-family residences and industrial use. Being situated in the vicinity of two railroad tracks and near industry, the market value of Ambler's property was severely undermined by its residential classification. Ambler claimed that the ordinance was unconstitutional, depriving it of property without due process and denying it equal protection of the law.

Issue

Was Euclid's zoning ordinance constitutional?

Held

Yes. The validity of a government's exercise of police power, while dependent on the particular circumstances, is constitutional when it bears a rational relationship to promoting the health, safety, and general welfare of a community. In the interest of promoting safety, preserving open space, and reducing noise and air pollution, Euclid's zoning ordinance is a valid exercise of its police powers.

Discussion

By the early twentieth century, the courts recognized that increased urbanization necessitated restrictions on the use of private land. In legitimizing zoning as a constitutional exercise of police powers, *Euclid* ushered in a new era of municipal regulation.

Case Excerpt

The matter of zoning has received much attention at the hands of commissions and experts, and the results of their investigations have been set forth in comprehensive reports. These reports, which bear every evidence of painstaking consideration, concur in the view that the segregation of residential, business, and industrial buildings will make it easier to provide fire apparatus suitable for the character and intensity of the development in each section; that it will increase the safety and security of home life; greatly tend to prevent street accidents, especially to children, by reducing the traffic and resulting confusion in residential sections; decrease noise and other conditions which produce or intensify nervous disorders; preserve a more favorable environment in which to rear children, etc. With particular reference to apartment houses, it is pointed out that the development of detached house sections is greatly retarded by the coming of apartment houses, which has sometimes resulted in destroying the entire section for private house purposes; that in such sections very often the apartment house is a mere parasite, constructed in order to take advantage of the open spaces and attractive surroundings created by the residential character of the district. Moreover, the coming of one apartment house is followed by others, interfering by their height and bulk with the free circulation of air and monopolizing the rays of the sun which otherwise would fall upon the smaller homes, and bringing, as their necessary accompaniments, the disturbing noises incident to increased traffic and business, and the occupation, by means of moving and parked automobiles, of larger portions of the streets, thus detracting from their safety and depriving children of the privilege of quiet and open spaces for play, enjoyed by those in more favored localities, – until, finally, the residential character of the neighborhood and its desirability as a place of detached residences are utterly destroyed. Under these circumstances, apartment houses, which in a different environment would be not only entirely unobjectionable but highly desirable, come very near to being nuisances.

If these reasons, thus summarized, do not demonstrate the wisdom or sound policy in all respects of those restrictions which we have indicated as pertinent to the inquiry, at least, the reasons are sufficiently cogent to preclude us from saying, as it must be said before the ordinance can be declared unconstitutional, that such provisions are clearly arbitrary and unreasonable, having no substantial relation to the public health, safety, morals, or general welfare. *Cusack Co. v. City of Chicago, supra,* pp. 530–531; *Jacobson v. Massachusetts,* 197 U.S. 11, 30–31.

It is true that when, if ever, the provisions set forth in the ordinance in tedious and minute detail, come to be concretely applied to particular premises, including those of the appellee, or to particular conditions, or to be considered in connection with specific complaints, some of them, or even many of them, may be found to be clearly arbitrary and unreasonable. But where the equitable remedy of injunction is sought, as it is here, not upon the ground of a present infringement or denial of a specific right, or of a particular injury in process of actual execution, but upon the broad ground that the mere existence and threatened enforcement of the ordinance, by materially and adversely affecting values and curtailing the opportunities of the market, constitute a present and irreparable injury, the court will not scrutinize its provisions, sentence by sentence, to ascertain by a process of piecemeal dissection whether there may be, here and there, provisions of a minor character, or relating to matters of administration, or not shown to contribute to the injury complained of, which, if attacked separately, might not withstand the test of constitutionality. In respect of such provisions, of which specific complaint is not made, it cannot be said that the land owner has suffered or is threatened with an injury which entitles him to challenge their constitutionality. *Turpin v. Lemon,* 187 U.S. 51, 60. In *Railroad Commission Cases,* 116 U.S. 307, 335–337, this Court dealt with an analogous situation. There an act of the Mississippi legislature, regulating freight and passenger rates on intrastate railroads and creating a supervisory commission, was attacked as unconstitutional. The suit was brought to enjoin the commission from enforcing against the plaintiff railroad company any of its provisions. In an opinion delivered by Chief Justice Waite, this Court held that the chief purpose of the statute was to fix a maximum of charges and to regulate in some matters of a police nature the use of railroads in the state. After sustaining the constitutionality of the statute "in its general scope" this Court said: "Whether in some of its details the statute may be defective or invalid we do not deem it necessary to inquire, for this suit is brought to prevent the commissioners from giving it any effect whatever as against this company." Quoting with approval from the opinion of the Supreme Court of Mississippi it was further said: "Many questions may arise under it not necessary to be disposed of now, and we leave them for consideration when presented." And finally: "When the commission has acted and proceedings are had to enforce what it has done, questions may arise as to the validity of some of the various provisions which will be worthy of consideration, but we are unable to say that, as a whole, the statute is invalid."

The relief sought here is of the same character, namely, an injunction against the enforcement of any of the restrictions, limitations or conditions of the ordinance. And the gravamen of the complaint is that a portion of the land of the appellee cannot be sold for certain enumerated uses because of the general and broad restraints of the ordinance. What would be the effect of a restraint imposed by one or more of the innumerable provisions of the ordinance, considered apart, upon the value or marketability of the lands is neither disclosed by the bill nor by the evidence, and we are afforded no basis, apart from mere speculation, upon which to rest a conclusion that it or they would have any appreciable effect upon those matters. Under these circumstances, therefore, it is enough for us to determine, as we do, that the ordinance in its general scope and dominant features, so far as its provisions are here involved, is a valid exercise of authority, leaving other provisions to be dealt with as cases arise directly involving them.

And this is in accordance with the traditional policy of this Court. In the realm of constitutional law, especially, this Court has perceived the embarrassment which is likely to result from an attempt to formulate rules or decide questions beyond the necessities of the immediate issue. It has preferred to follow the method of a gradual approach to the general by a systematically guarded application and extension of constitutional principles to particular cases as they arise, rather than by out of hand attempts to establish general rules to which future cases must be fitted. This process applies with peculiar force to the solution of questions arising under the due process clause of the Constitution as applied to the exercise of the flexible powers of police, with which we are here concerned.

Use Categories

Permitted Uses

Each zone contains a list of permitted uses. There are two approaches to this issue. One is to have a long and detailed list of acceptable uses, perhaps based on model language from some organization. In this way the purpose of the zoning district is clear. Administrative discretion is limited. The other approach is to be vague, e.g. "retail." Language would be added that allows similar uses that would increase the flexibility of the zoning administrator to allow innovative land uses. The potential for litigation exists within each classification scheme. For example, a service station sells gasoline, is a grocery store, a liquor store, and often times serves food (e.g. a restaurant). If it has an ATM it is a financial institution under some zoning ordinance definitions. Classifying this use in a particular district may be challenging. One trend that is no longer popular is to provide a list of prohibited uses.

Cumulative vs. Exclusive Uses

The idea of use zoning was approved by the United States Supreme Court in the *Village of Euclid v. Ambler Realty* case. The idea is that every particular land use has an appropriate place in the community and it is the government's responsibility to allocate these uses in a reasonable manner consistent with the property rights of the individual landowner. The *Euclid* case created a system of cumulative and exclusive zones that might be visualized as a pyramid. The detached single-family home is at the top of the zone and it is "exclusive" in that only single-family homes are allowed in that district. This is the type of land use that deserves the most protection. The next level of the pyramid is non-single family residential uses, followed by commercial uses and industrial uses. All uses other than single-family homes are "cumulative" in that they include all the previously mentioned uses. In other words, under this system any permitted land use is possible in an industrial zone. Extensive use of cumulative zoning may lead to the creation of nuisances, as incompatible land uses may be located next to each other. Cumulative zoning has been decreasing as a trend in zoning regulations.

Accessory Uses and Home Occupations

In general, zoning laws contain provisions that property owners can use their land for principal uses and any uses that are accessory to that use. An accessory use is contained on the same lot and may be considered subordinate and customarily associated with the principal use. For example, parking is often associated with a business. It is a separate land use but it is normally part of a commercial enterprise. An accessory use is usually smaller than a principal use, in the sense that a garage is smaller than a residence. Property owners have certain expectations about the use of their property and their neighborhood when they purchase a house. Some accessory uses may not meet these expectations; many times these uses are ancillary to home occupations. Historically, single-family homes have been used by their occupants for a variety of businesses, usually involving personal services: e.g. beauty salons, tax preparation services, day care, etc. The question is whether these home occupations are customarily associated with the expectations of that community or neighborhood. Some communities have adopted special provisions regulating home occupations covering permitted and prohibited activities, hours of operation, presence of non-resident employees, time of delivery, location of the home occupation, etc. The goal of such regulations is to balance the rights of the property owner with the character of the neighborhood.

Single-Family Homes

As mentioned, the goal of most zoning ordinances is to provide the maximum protection to the single-family home. The "good city" was seen as a suburban refuge from the problems of the city. This concept was initiated when the typical "family" had the male parent go to work, the female parent stayed home and the three or four children all walked to school. This social arrangement is no longer so common. In addition, this preference may promote urban sprawl, unnecessarily destroy valuable environments, and promote economic and even racial segregation. On the other hand, it is extremely popular with homeowners and provides economic and social stability to neighborhoods that have been developed with this type of housing. If future generations no longer desire the protection of this type of housing, the rationale behind zoning will have to be readjusted.

Group Homes

A group home is a supervised residential facility for individuals with special needs. These include persons with physical and mental disabilities, the elderly, persons recovering from substance abuse issues and post-prison locations for ex-prisoners. Placing these facilities in residential zones has often been controversial. The group has often been characterized as the functional equivalent of a family and thus deserving of location in a single-family neighborhood. Arguments against this use in a neighborhood include resident turnover, extra traffic and the potential for criminal activity. The federal government, through the Fair Housing Act and the Americans with Disabilities Act provide some protection for individuals with certain disabilities who wish to live in group homes. Many states prohibit local governments from completely excluding certain types of group homes from a jurisdiction. They do so by providing a zone of last resort, usually a residential land use district. Under this state rule, group homes would be permitted in this district unless the local government permitted them by right in another type of zoning district.

Agricultural Uses

When zoning was first introduced into the United States, the country was considerably less urban. Zoning was not meant to include agriculture or agricultural uses and it was common for city residents to have gardens or even perhaps raise a few animals. Questions such as loss of productive farmland or diminution of open space were not important. This has now changed and farmland preservation is an important topic. Agricultural zoning is quite common and will permit any activities that are associated with agriculture. These could include feedlots, farm markets, and even processing plants. Most agricultural zones are "non-exclusive" in that they allow the construction of single-family homes on large lots; "exclusive" zones do not permit this activity or require a special permit for permission. The idea was to allow multi-generations of a family to continue to live on a farm. The rise of these types of zones has led to a trend to ban some farming and types of animals from urban residential zones. Communities will define these terms to allow domesticated pets in these areas and not the same type of animals that were permitted 100 years ago when zoning was introduced.

Industrial and Commercial Uses

There are many ways by which a local government can provide for these uses. As land uses have become more complex, simple commercial and industrial zones have moved into separate categories for shopping centers, offices, industrial parks, and so forth. Zoning practice now favors exclusive industrial and commercial zones as opposed to the cumulative nature originally implemented. If there is a market for this land as zoned, both the property owners and the community benefit. If there is an imbalance of either too little or too much of this land in these districts, litigation alleging constitutional problems such as takings may occur. Also, an alternative way has been developed to zone these lands, particularly industrial uses. Performance zoning involves the creation of standards to measure the impacts of these activities using indicators of such items as smoke, dust, noise, and light.

Buffer Zones

Land on the edge of a district may be impacted by or impact land in an adjacent district. Since single-family homes land receives the most protection in a zoning ordinance, great care is often taken to shield these districts from incompatible uses, usually thought to be heavy commercial or industrial uses. Therefore, many communities place multi-family districts between these two other uses in order to protect single-family residences. Buffering considerations are also present within individual districts. Screening, fencing, landscaping, and distance from the property line are all added measures of protection for the affected use.

Public Uses

Governmental uses of land have proven to be quite controversial in zoning ordinances. Furthermore, governments do things directly, through licenses or use agents to accomplish their responsibilities. Although the Standard Zoning Enabling Act (SZEA) did not exempt such activity from an ordinance, courts have inferred it through a variety of means. The federal government is immune from regulation by state and local governments due to the supremacy clause of the United States Constitution. In addition, courts have recognized the common law doctrine of sovereign immunity. In this case that means the "superior" level of government cannot be regulated unless it agrees to such treatment. Local zoning is thus preempted in many cases. Each state has a different set of rules as to which activity exercised by which organization (either public or private) is not subject to local zoning.

NIMBYs and LULUs

Other categories of land use are referred to as NIMBYs (Not in My Back Yard) or LULUs (Locally Unwanted Land Use). Some land uses must be located on a site that benefits a community but has negative impacts on adjoining landowners. There are many such examples of these circumstances and often involve public land uses such as prisons, landfills, and sewage treatment plants. Most communities are able to resist NIMBYs and LULUs unless the activity is either a public use or the state has adopted a regional general welfare standard. In that case, the local government must show that the region will be better served by locating it elsewhere. Of course, if all the communities in a region refuse to locate such an activity, a local government must locate this facility as a service to the region. This analysis has also been extended to private land uses such as cemeteries, large-scale retail operations and junkyards.

Nonconforming Uses

A nonconforming use is a land use that was permitted when it was created but is now prohibited due to the initial enactment of the regulations or a change in the existing zoning ordinance. The goal of zoning is to create uniform land use within each district. Nonconforming uses do not conform to regulations and so most regulations have a policy of eliminating these uses. Once a land use is legally created, it is allowed to continue indefinitely. This is due to a belief that stopping a pre-existing use would cause constitutional problems for the government, particularly in the area of takings and due process. The assumption was that if expansion and reconstruction were limited, these uses would eventually disappear, thus restoring uniformity to a zoning district. These natural processes of the market often take a long time. To speed things along, courts have allowed local governments to adopt regulations that will eliminate them after a certain time. First, some regulations require that nonconforming uses be amortized over a certain period. When this period is over, they are terminated. The allowable time period is dependent upon the investment of the property owner and the impact on the neighborhood. Second, zoning regulations often forbid the expansion of a nonconforming use but allow normal maintenance to keep the property in good repair. Third, if the property owner voluntarily abandons a nonconforming use for a specific time, zoning ordinances will not allow that property owner or another one to re-establish that particular use. Finally, if the nonconforming use is destroyed or damaged beyond a certain percentage of its fair market value (e.g. 50 percent), it cannot be rebuilt.

Controls on Land Use

Height Limits

Limits on the height of buildings have been approved by the courts even before the *Village of Euclid v. Ambler Realty* case. These limits are usually expressed in terms of feet. When litigation arises, it is an "as applied" case rather than a "facial" attack. Limitations based on safety or density concerns are almost always acceptable. When the regulations for building height rely on aesthetic concerns, their validity may be a little more uncertain. In addition, particular building characteristics may cause a concern. An example of this might be a church steeple that exceeds the height limit. These cases are often solved by the issuance of an area variance, discussed later in this chapter.

Lot Size

Minimum lot size may be regulated by both the zoning ordinance and subdivision regulations. Different minimums apply for different purposes, e.g. on-site waste disposal and private wells. They are especially popular when used as a tool to decrease density of single-family homes in a suburban setting. Courts have generally upheld these requirements on police power grounds, e.g. health, welfare, and safety. This is despite the rationale used by some governments to use minimum lot size as a basis to increase economic segregation and improve the tax revenues of the jurisdiction. Courts have upheld the right of communities to control their own destiny by preserving the existing character of the locality through large lot zoning. This is true in agricultural areas where lot size minimums can be very large.

Setbacks

The United States Supreme Court, in a case decided just after the *Village of Euclid v. Ambler Realty* case upheld the validity of setback lines for a variety of purposes. A setback regulates the distance a structure can be built from the property lines. It is a setback from the street and also determined as "yards," e.g. front, side, and rear. Setback requirements can be found in both the zoning regulations and the zoning ordinance. Setback lines originally served two purposes. First, they were used to meet general police power objectives, public safety, health, and light and air. They have also been used to provide more space for future street expansions. Problems with setback requirements may arise under the Takings Clause of the U.S. Constitution if the regulations take away all of the value of the undeveloped property. See Chapter 10 to further explore the dimensions of the Takings Clause.

Building Size

Building size has been used as a land use control technique in a variety of contexts. It was first used to require a minimum size for residential structures based on concerns for health (e.g. overcrowding and aesthetics). An implicit purpose of these regulations was to keep out individuals who could not afford the larger homes in a community. While these ordinances were originally approved by the courts, in recent years they have been invalidated as exclusionary zoning. A more recent example of this technique is the use of maximum building size. In the residential context, it has been used to prevent the redevelopment of residential areas with newer homes significantly larger than the structures from the original development. In the nonresidential context, they have been used to prevent the construction of large-scale retail facilities such as "big box" stores. They have been upheld on the basis of aesthetics and preservation of the character of the community.

FAR

FAR stands for floor area ratio and provides for a comparison of the square footage in a building with the square footage of an individual parcel. It is a way of promoting open space if the local government allows the construction of a taller building on the lot. A ratio of 1:1 means the entire building lot can be covered by a single-story building. A 5:1 ratio means a 5-story building can cover 20 percent of the lot. In commercial areas of large cities the ratio may be much higher, e.g. 15:1.

Zoning regulations often give increases in FAR if the developer provides amenities such as open space or public art. This is a separate calculation from the building height requirement and provides another tool for the local government to control aesthetics.

Zoning Process

Rezonings

Requirements for Legislative v. Quasi-Judicial Rezonings

Virtually every state treats a rezoning as a legislative matter. This includes complete community amendment to the zoning ordinance as well as those actions that affect a particular parcel. Government action is given the presumption of validity. Since this is a legislative matter, courts will not inquire about the motives of the decision-makers. A number of states have challenged this view about rezoning, particularly when it involves small parcels. This rationale is based on the belief that since actions affect individual property rights, governments must act like a court or conduct itself in a quasi-judicial manner. Governments no longer have the same deference with quasi-judicial decisions. Each state can characterize various actions (e.g. rezonings and plat reviews) in various ways. Procedural due process concerns are only apparent in quasi-judicial actions. These include the right to be heard, the right to a fair hearing, and the right to a record of the proceedings.

Grounds for Rezoning

The traditional standard that courts use to evaluate a rezoning is whether the action is "in accord with the comprehensive plan." Decision-makers look at the character of the neighborhood, the pattern of development, the wishes of the landowner, and the impacts on the adjacent property owners in order to reach a decision. Property values are a consideration but often not an important one. Some courts look at changes in the area before approving rezoning. The courts will look for a rational basis to permit the change (or approve a refusal to amend the zoning ordinance) on the basis of the public interest. Judges will balance the interests of the parties but the action of the government gets deference.

Spot Zoning

A spot zone refers to the creation of a parcel or parcels with a designation that is incompatible with the zoning designation of neighboring property. A spot zone may or may not be illegal under any set of circumstances. The use that is the "spot" is often times more intense than the surrounding parcels. Spot zoning is most often found to be a problem if a court does not find this activity to be "in accord with a comprehensive plan." In addition, courts will look at the surrounding neighborhood and try to determine if the activity is in the public interest. In states where spot zoning is "quasi-judicial," there is little deference to governmental actions.

Conditional Zoning

It is fairly common for governments to rezone property and attach conditions to this permission. Where rezonings are legislative, courts defer to the granting of conditions. This is also true of quasi-judicial actions with conditions. Some courts distinguish between contract zoning (a bi-lateral agreement between a landowner who agrees to provide certain improvements in return for the government's promise to rezone) and conditional zoning (a unilateral promise by the landowner to the government without requiring anything in return). Contract zoning is illegal while conditional zoning is acceptable. The reality is that often times the same activity can be characterized as either contract zoning or conditional zoning. Most courts now use a balancing test to determine whether this action is in the public interest.

Area Variances

Definition

An area variance is an administrative action authorized by a local government through the Board of Appeals or other group that allows the construction or placement of a structure in a way that is not authorized by the zoning ordinance. The underlying land use that is permitted by the zoning ordinance remains in place. It is often called a "dimensional" ordinance.

Applicable Legal Standards

Courts have often used a less stringent standard to review an area variance, called "practical difficulties." There are various considerations used by courts to balance the impact of granting such permission between the landowner, neighboring property owners, and the community. These include financial hardship, whether the building can be constructed without the area variance, the harm to the neighborhood and the community, and the public interest to be served if the variance is allowed. Courts will look at the presence of some economic hardship involved to the property owner if the property cannot be used in the way permitted by the zoning ordinance.

Use Variances

Definition

A use variance is an administrative action authorized by a local government through the Board of Appeals or other group that allows the use of land in a way that is not authorized by the zoning ordinance. A use variance creates a nonconforming use. It is the equivalent of a rezoning that may not require public notice or public hearing. There is no review by the Planning Commission nor approval by the governing body. Some states have specifically forbidden the issuance of use variances.

Applicable Legal Standards

Courts have traditionally used a strict standard in judging use variances, known as "unnecessary hardship." There are a variety of standards that the court uses to determine whether to issue a use variance. These include: a determination that the parcel, as currently zoned, cannot yield a reasonable return on investment; a finding that the problem incurred is due to unique circumstances and not one that is generally prevalent in the area; a belief that the granting of the use variance will not alter the character of the neighborhood; and a judgment that issuing the variance would be in the public interest. Self-created hardship on the part of the landowner will not be considered by the court. Conditions may be imposed by the local administrative body in the issuance of the use variance. Courts have subjected the issuance of use variances to close review and have not deferred generally to the judgment of the government on this issue.

Special Use Permits

Definition

A special permit is designed to allow certain permitted land uses that have extraordinary impacts to be located within a district after a special review process. This provision has been available to local governments since the beginning of zoning. There are two types of mechanism that essentially accomplish the same goal: a "Special Exception" issued by the Board of Adjustment and a "Conditional Use Permit" reviewed by the Planning Commission and approved by the governing body. Some examples of these unusual uses include gun clubs, day-care centers, and junkyards. Issuance of these special permits is often scrutinized for their impacts on property owners' constitutional rights, particularly in the area of equal protection and due process.

Legal Standards

Special use permits require that the authorizing regulation contain clear standards for the issuing organization to follow. Two kinds of standards exist: specific standards and general standards. The general standards are similar to the ones used for issuing variances. They include requirements that issuance occurs in the public interest, does not harm the character of the neighborhood, and does not cause incompatible land uses with surrounding property. Courts may view these general standards as being too vague or an improper delegation of power, depending upon which group is responsible for issuing a permit. If it is a legislative organization (e.g. the governing body), courts will generally defer to its judgment. If it is an administrative body (e.g. the Board of Appeals), the courts often adopt a less deferential review in order to assure that the administrative group has not substituted its own judgment for that of the legislative body.

Conditions

The ordinance may list conditions or allow the local government to impose conditions. Typical conditions might include hours of operation and length of time in which the particular land use may be operated (e.g. number of years). Conditions could also include aesthetic features, screening, and lighting. Conditions must relate to the use that is being proposed. Courts will use a balancing test between the benefit of the conditions to the community and the adjacent landowners versus the cost to the applicant. All conditions must be reasonable and presumably advance the public interest.

Vested Rights, Estoppel, and Development Agreements

When a zoning ordinance is changed, a common question is whether the new regulations apply to uncompleted projects. Traditionally, courts will apply the law in effect at the time of their decision, i.e. the new regulations. Developers often hurry to complete projects in order to finish their development and thus become a legal nonconforming use. This conflict of new vs. old has caused litigation. Courts have sought to protect the due process and equal protection rights of the property owner versus the rights of the government to determine land use policy. Two doctrines have developed to help guide the courts in this balancing exercise. The first is known as "vested rights." A property owner may acquire a vested right if it engages in substantial expenditure in good faith reliance pursuant to a valid building permit. If the property owner acquires a vested right, the new regulation has no effect. The doctrine of "estoppel" is related. A government cannot apply a new law to a property owner who makes substantial expenditure in good faith reliance on an act of government so that applying the new law would be unfair. Both doctrines are similar in nature and have the same outcome of allowing the property owner to proceed under the prior regulations. One way to avoid litigation over these concerns is to use development agreements. A development agreement is a document that sets the rights of a government and property owner on a certain date and limits the power of a government to enact new regulations that would cover the existing project. Development agreements can contain conditions and often provide for the imposition of exactions, both on-site and off-site. Usually, they are authorized by state statute. It is not a contract in the traditional sense, but has been interpreted to be similar in scope to the issuance of a special use permit.

Response to Wicked Problem

1. The cheese factory is now a legal nonconforming industrial use located in an agricultural district. As such, there are restrictions on its expansion. If there is only internal remodeling allowed, the cheese factory might claim that there is no additional activity, particularly if they are selling products already made on site. The local ordinance contains no provisions for commercial uses in this district. Other jurisdictions may have a narrower interpretation of "industrial" that does not include commercial activity. The factory might also try to claim that a retail store is an accessory activity in that retail and surplus stores are often times located at industrial plants. Of course, these uses are accessory only to permitted uses, not nonconforming uses. So the standards of subordinate and incidental use would not apply to the problem.

2. Under most definitions, processing food products can be considered as "agriculture." If agriculture is a permitted use in the district, the cheese factory could continue without being labeled a nonconforming use. The wicked problem does not contain the answer to this problem. Also, most agriculture districts provide this definition to allow the manufacturing of products grown on-site. Again, there

is no information as to whether there is a dairy farm located on the 100 acres in question.

3. The United States Supreme Court has ruled that there must be a rational basis for imposing a special permit requirement for group homes. In that instance, other similar institutions did not need a special use permit. The local government did not show that this special permission was necessary for this type of land use. The conditions imposed on the group home would have to be the same for all similar residential land uses. These might include lot size, amount of off-street parking, lighting, screening, location of structures away from the property line, and so forth. Groups may also be defined as a "family" that consists of a number of unrelated persons. This concept is discussed in Chapter 8 on Due Process and Equal Protection.

4. The income tax service is a commercial land use that is currently not permitted in the district either in the old zoning of an industrial park or the new zoning of an exclusive agricultural district. A use variance would be required for this activity, which would be the equivalent of a rezoning. The standard that a court would most probably use to grant this variance is "unnecessary hardship." The developer might suggest that since the land use will employ convicted embezzlers, the government should grant the request because the land use would benefit disabled persons. However, this type of individual currently is not protected by the Federal Fair Housing Act or the American with Disabilities Act. Therefore, it is unlikely a use variance would be issued on these grounds. A review of the causes for granting a use variance including no reasonable return on investment, unique circumstances, character of the neighborhood, and public interest would suggest that the property owner would have a difficult time in getting a use variance.

5. A mobile or manufactured home is different than a traditional "site built" structure. It is smaller, less expensive, and requires a lot less land to accommodate its footprint. It is usually not "mobile." Manufactured homes built after 1975 are subject to federal safety standards. What makes them objectionable to communities is the fear of lower property values as well as the stereotypical attributes of its residents (e.g. lower income and transiency). Many communities have required that these units be located only in mobile home parks or have tried to exclude them entirely from a community. In addition, some jurisdictions have placed aesthetic limitations on single-family homes in order to make them less obtrusive in a developed neighborhood. Without specific restrictions, a mobile home can be considered a single-family dwelling. The wicked problem has suggested the parcel is now zoned exclusively agricultural which would suggest that no single-family residences, including mobile homes, are allowed on this land.

6. The courts would inquire as to the purpose of the requirement for the minimum building size. The court would probably take notice of the fact that a group might consist of eight people in residence (six clients and two members of staff). The court will also probably realize that some, but not all, groups are unpopular in the neighborhood, depending on the characteristics of the group. The court would try to determine if these particular regulations were adopted to keep out this particular group. In this case, 500 square feet may be too small a structure for 8 people to occupy safely. The fact that the mobile home is only 300 square feet

is even harder to defend on the grounds of public welfare. Therefore it is unlikely that the developer would win this argument.

7. A minimum building size regulation is often imposed in order to protect environmentally sensitive land, control drainage, provide for a buffer zone between adjacent land uses, and improve the aesthetics of an area. A requirement that a group home contain a lot size of 10,000 square feet might be too large since there is no evidence presented that a quarter-acre lot (a typical suburban single-family residence) is necessary to accommodate a group. On the other hand, the government would point out that in a mixed use area there should be plenty of space between industrial, commercial, and residential uses. In this instance, the deference given to governmental regulations may not be enough to allow a court to approve this number.

8. The wicked problem contains no information concerning the comprehensive plan for the area. The assumption is that the original zoning for a campus-like industrial park was a part of the future land use map. The problem contains no information on whether the future land use map was changed to show the use as agricultural. Therefore, the plan and the zoning ordinance may be inconsistent, which is a separate problem to the rezoning. A court will look for a rational basis to approve a rezoning because it gives deference to a local government. The character of the neighborhood is industrial, the pattern of development has been a single factory, the wishes of the landowner are to develop this mixed use and the impacts on the adjacent property owners are unclear. The assumption is that rezoning to agriculture will severely decrease property values. There is a chance that this rezoning will not be approved by the court.

9. Applying for a building permit prior to the effective date of the new regulation in and of itself does not give the owner of the cheese factory "vested rights" or prevent the county from rezoning through the "equitable estoppel" doctrine. The building permit must have been issued and there must have been substantial expenditure incurred in good faith after the permit was issued. The facts in the wicked problem do not allow such a conclusion to be reached. The cheese factory owner may have a slightly stronger argument in preventing the county from enforcing the new ordinance. If the owner had spent considerable amounts of money in remodeling the interior of a building for an accessory use (e.g. a store) of a legally permitted use, the court might feel it unfair to apply the new law. Of course, mere application for a building permit would not necessarily confer these rights.

10. A requirement that land be donated for public use represents a difficult question for a court to resolve. Public uses are generally approved by courts and deference is shown to a government when it undertakes governmental functions. On the one hand, courts will approve conditions that are reasonable. On the other hand, this donation for public use might be seen as a taking of property without compensation. This is not a situation where the applicant is proposing to construct a cell tower and the county government demands space on the structure to improve its 911 service. The new regulation requires the applicant to provide land to the county to build a tower. As a matter of fact, the county could build the tower and lease out space to private companies, since it might not need all the room for public services. In that instance the developer would be required

to give land to the county for free so that the county might engage in a revenue generating activity. This outcome would probably not be approved by a court.

Discussion Prompts

- Zoning has been widely criticized as a tool responsible for the demise of urban form. Explain. Do you agree?
- Zoning ordinances may perpetuate social and economic segregation. Explain. Can the tools also be utilized to overcome such problems?
- In its early form, zoning did not permit for a great deal of flexibility, even in cases where common sense dictated the same. How were variances and special use permits utilized to increase flexibility? What are the problems associated with the use of these tools as a corrective device?

7

INSERTING FLEXIBILITY INTO THE ZONING PROCESS

Zoning schemes have been widely criticized. One of the most commonly expressed concerns about zoning is its inflexibility. Some might argue that in their detail, land use regulations often lack common sense and a process that allows for property owners to maximize the value and use of their properties in a way that is viable, but contrary to the regulatory approach. This chapter introduces readers to a whole host of inventions in zoning that seek to insert more flexibility into planning practice.

Flexible Zoning Wicked Problem

Greystone, Colorado, is a small mountain town and ski resort located in the central part of the state, off the beaten track and hours away from the string of ski resorts that line the main interstate highway through the Rocky Mountains. Greystone was well-known across the state and in the ski community for its collection of challenging expert runs and laid-back, "come on and join us" atmosphere. For years, Greystone was locally owned by a group of families and flourished as a small ski area that catered mostly to a regional clientele, with junior racing competitions on Saturdays and family pot-luck dinners in the lodge on Sunday afternoons. The town of Greystone had a year-round population of about 4,500 people. Historic buildings lined a two-mile-long stretch of downtown along Emmons Street that was typically about 75-percent leased with local businesses. The town had a small hospital with respected specialists in orthopedics and trauma injury, and a satellite campus of a state university. Downtown Greystone was (and is) completely surrounded by single-family residential neighborhoods. The town's full-time residents included health professionals, university professors and staff, an assortment of state agency employees who worked in the state offices in a nearby city, local business owners, professionals engaged in telework for large companies across the country, and a small number of ski resort employees. There was also a small population of part-time, second home owners. The resort was advertised by three tall but unmaintained billboards along the road into the town and there were seven sequential directional signs through town advertising the route to the resort.

That all changed when the SkiBig ownership group from California purchased the Greystone ski area to add to its collection of elite XTRA eXTreme terRAin resorts. SkiBig invested millions of dollars in the resort to add lifts, runs, and world-class snowboarding facilities on the mountain along with a new base lodge and three new resort hotels along Emmons Street. SkiBig also invested heavily in advertising its

Figure 6 Credit: David D. Boeck

newest resort, including constructing four new downtown, off-site rooftop billboards. SkiBig pushed the town to amend the already minimal sign regulations to permit extra on-site signage for each of the new resort hotels. On the front of each structure they advertised not only the name of the hotel but the names of all of the restaurants, clubs, and shops in each of the hotels.

Greystone XTRA did well and over the next 20 years the area became a marquee ski resort for both top athletes and a well-moneyed party crowd who enjoyed both the terrain and the après-ski activities. New restaurants, shops, bars, hotels, and amenities were constructed, many more second homes were built, and during this time the town approved numerous applications for new signage, allowing big and colorful on- and off-site signage to bloom across the community. Many local businesses joined in, adding neon and blinking signage to their storefronts and windows all along Emmons Street.

During this time, a small group of community members became concerned about the overall amount of signage across the town in general and specifically along Emmons Street, complaining that the number and square footage of sign space overshadowed the historic nature of downtown, contributed to traffic accidents, made pedestrian travel unsafe, and made the whole place look cheap. They also identified a number of signs that had been abandoned across the community and urged the town to take action to clean up or remove those signs.

BigSki, apparently unaware of the local anti-sign movement, has recently applied to the town to replace the ski resorts' original three billboards, the four newer billboards, and all of the directional signs through town with fully or partially animated electronic signage. The resort owners wanted the ability to advertise on- and off-mountain activities and amenities to tourists. Local residents were appalled by the request and shared their anger and concerns about property values, traffic accidents, and overall community aesthetics with elected officials at the public hearing on the sign applications. The town immediately passed a moratorium on the issuance of sign permits and set about drafting and adopting updated sign regulations.

What regulatory options does the town have in its legal arsenal to address these issues?

Cases

The following cases will be useful to you as you attempt to analyze this chapter's wicked problem:

Dallen v. City of Kansas City, 822 S.W.2d. 429 (1991)
Ecogen, LLC v. Town of Italy, 438 F.Supp.2d 149 (W.S.N.Y. 2006)
Crooked Creek Conservation and Gun Club, Inc. v. Hamilton County North Board of Zoning Appeals, 677 N.E. 2d 544 (1997)
Rodgers v. Village of Tarrytown, 302 N.Y. 115 (1951)
Collard v. Incorporated Village of Flower Hill, 421 N.E.2d 818 (NY. 1981)
Cheney v. Village 2 New Hope, Inc., 241 A.2d 81 (Pa. 1968)

Dallen v. City of Kansas City

822 S.W.2d. 429 (1991)

Facts
Dallen owned a gas station within Kansas City's Main Street Corridor Special Review District, a zoning overlay district designed to preserve the area's unique character through additional building and site regulations. Dallen sought to remodel the property in a manner that was consistent with the area's underlying zoning, but in conflict with the Special Review District's more stringent standards and regulations under Ordinance 59380. When Dallen filed suit for relief, the trial court held that the ordinance's requirement of ten-foot setbacks from the street was so burdensome that it was confiscatory, and therefore, unconstitutional.

Issue
Did the trial court err in finding Ordinance 59380, requiring more stringent regulations in the Main Street Corridor Special Review District, unconstitutional?

Held
No. The City's zoning ordinance provided that special district requirements could not modify the underlying district's regulations, yet as applied to Dallen, several provisions of Ordinance 59380 conflicted with the property's underlying zoning requirements. Furthermore, the ordinance's requirement of ten-foot setbacks rendered the property useless as a gas station, which was so burdensome to Dallen as to be confiscatory.

Discussion
Zoning ordinances are presumed to be constitutional; however, the reasonableness of any ordinance can be overcome when it is proved that the ordinance is unreasonable either on its face or when applied to a particular property. The property owner challenging the reasonableness of an ordinance bears the burden of proof.

Ecogen, LLC v. Town of Italy

438 F.Supp.2d 149 (W.S.N.Y. 2006)

Facts

Ecogen, a wind-energy developer, sought to build a wind substation in the town of Italy to complement finished wind turbines in the neighboring town of Prattsburgh and future turbine projects in Italy. In 2004, the town of Italy passed a moratorium on the construction of wind turbine towers and supporting facilities until the town had created a plan to regulate such facilities in cohesion with the town's comprehensive zoning regulations. The moratorium was only intended to last six months but was renewed continuously for two years, preventing Ecogen from completing the projects in Prattsburgh that depended on the completion of the substation in Italy. The moratorium included a hardship exception, for which Ecogen never applied.

Issue

Did the town of Italy's moratoria on wind energy facilities violate Ecogen's substantive due process rights?

Held

No. Municipal ordinances are presumed to be constitutional if the ordinance bears a substantial relationship to a permissible government objective. Ecogen failed to prove that Italy had no conceivable basis for the moratorium. The court ordered Italy to either enact a comprehensive zoning plan or to decide on Ecogen's hardship application.

Discussion

Moratoria are designed to give municipalities time to study an arising issue and are popular responses to emerging or problematic land uses. There are no definitive rules regarding their duration and at what point they begin to trample on constitutional rights, but moratoria that last more than one year are considered suspect.

Crooked Creek Conservation and Gun Club, Inc. v. Hamilton County North Board of Zoning Appeals

677 N.E. 2d 544 (1997)

Facts

Crooked Creek operated a trap and skeet-shooting club for over 45 years in Marion County until increased urbanization of the surrounding area compelled the gun club to find a more rural location in Hamilton County. The property of choice was zoned for agricultural, large-lot residential, and flood plain uses by Hamilton County, with gun clubs permitted upon special exception. The

County's Board of Zoning Appeals denied the club's application for an exception, which was later affirmed by the trial court.

Issue

Did the County's Board of Zoning Appeals err in denying Crooked Creek's application for a special exception permit?

Held

No. The zoning ordinance in question afforded the county significant discretion in reviewing the club's exception application. For approval, Crooked Creek needed to prove to the board that their desired use would be consistent with neighboring land uses while not harming the community or affecting neighboring property values. Opponents presented evidence that the club would harm the community and Crooked Creek failed to prove that their use would meet the aforementioned criteria. As experts in zoning, the board had the discretion to weigh the evidence presented and decide as it did.

Discussion

Special exception permits, also known as variances, provide property owners with the ability to amend their property's zoning district. However, as *Crooked Creek* demonstrates, potential and current property owners can face significant burdens during the application process.

Rodgers v. Village of Tarrytown

302 N.Y. 115 (1951)

Facts

The village of Tarrytown adopted an ordinance that would amend the municipality's general zoning ordinance from seven to eight district zones. The ordinance created a new district, "Residence B-B," which allowed buildings for multiple occupancy with a maximum of 15 families on a minimum of 10 acres. In 1948, Tarrytown passed a successive ordinance allowing a residential property meeting the requirements of the ordinance to be rezoned as "B-B." Rodgers, a neighboring property owner, filed suit against Tarrytown.

Issue

Can Tarrytown amend their zoning ordinance to create a new district, the boundaries of which are not delineated on the zoning map, but change as eligible individual property owners apply for rezoning?

Held

Yes. While stability is crucial to zoning, communities are allowed to amend their ordinances as they deem fit to meet changing needs; as such, property owners are not guaranteed that their properties will be zoned a particular way in perpetuity. Tarrytown concluded that the community needed additional housing and it was well within its authority to create a new zoning district to accommodate the construction of garden apartments because it did so in accordance with the comprehensive plan.

Discussion
Tarrytown helped solidify the validity of "floating zones" within land use regulations. Contrary to Rodger's allegations, floating zones are fundamentally different than "spot zoning," because they are designed to address the entire community's welfare as part of a comprehensive plan, whereas spot zoning benefits individual property owners.

Collard v. Incorporated Village of Flower Hill

421 N.E.2d 818 (NY. 1981)

Facts
Collard owned property in the village of Flower Hill that had been previously rezoned from a General Municipal and Public Purposes District to a Business District. The approved rezoning application, with an accompanying declaration of covenants, came with a stipulation that no new structure could be built or enlarged on the property without the consent of Flower Hill's Board of Trustees. When Collard's application to extend the property's existing structure was denied without any explanation, Collard moved to have the denial deemed capricious and to compel a construction permit.

Issue
Can a municipality be compelled to permit rezoning or provide justification for failing to do so?

Held
No. Flower Hill could not be required to consent, or explain a lack of consent, absent a provision in the declaration of covenants that such consent could not be unreasonably withheld.

Discussion
The Court offered several reasons for not requiring Flower Hill's consent or an explanation of non-consent. Although many critics refer to conditional rezoning as "spot zoning," benefiting individuals rather than conforming to a community's zoning plan, the test for spot zoning is whether the rezoning is not part of a community's comprehensive plan. And although the legislature did not expressly grant municipalities authority to conditionally rezone, neither did the legislature forbid the practice. The Court further handled the declaration of covenants as a contract and was hesitant to implement additional provisions, such as requiring only reasonable non-consent, upon one side where uncertainty may exist.

Cheney v. Village 2 New Hope, Inc.

241 A.2d 81 (Pa. 1968)

Facts
In 1965, New Hope, Pennsylvania's Borough Council enacted Ordinance 160, which created a new zoning district known as a Planned Unit Development (PUD). Consequently, Ordinance 161 amended the zoning of a large tract of land from low-density residential, destined to become single-family homes, to PUD. The Borough's Planning Commission issued building permits to Village 2 New Hope, a developer whose plans for the recently rezoned PUD had been approved. The Board of Adjustment denied neighboring property owners' appeals; the Court of Common Pleas held the ordinances invalid for failure to comply with the Borough's comprehensive zoning plan.

Issue
Did the Board of Adjustments abuse their discretion or commit an error of law by upholding the Borough Council's PUD ordinances?

Held
No. Under state enabling legislation, a municipal planning body has a broad range of powers to regulate land uses to promote the general health and welfare of the community. The neighboring property owners were mistaken in asserting the comprehensive zoning plan was binding; so long as a legislative body passes new zoning ordinances with the community as a whole in mind, comprehensive plans can be amended. Furthermore, the borough's ordinances did not constitute spot zoning.

Discussion
Density zoning, in the form of PUD districts, provides municipalities a flexible alternative to more stringent, traditional zoning districts. PUD districts permit a greater range of permissible uses, allowing self-sufficient communities to be built within a single zoning district.

Primer on Flexible Zoning as an Issue for Planners

The Need for Flexibility

Zoning regulations have been widely criticized for their relative lack of flexibility in terms of variety of uses, patterns of development, and ability to address design issues. In the early years of zoning, inflexibility was the goal – regulations were intended to lock in local development preferences and allow the community to reject projects that did not conform to those preferences. Once adopted, however, zoning regulations are typically in place in a community for a minimum of ten years, and in most communities for much longer. Development uses and types frequently change over

Table 1 Flexible Zoning Tools

	Uses	Density	Dimensions	Development Standards	Review Process
	P – Primary Application		S – Secondary Application		
Floating Zones	P	P	S		P
Planned Unit Development	S	P	P	S	P
Conditional Zoning	P			S	P
Incentive Zoning					
Performance Zoning	P	P	P	P	P
Interim Zoning and Moratoria	P				P
Overlay Zoning	P	P	P	P	P
Form-Based Code	P	P			P

that timeframe. Suburban communities who desired increased density to limit sprawl in the 1980s and urban communities who encouraged mixed-use infill development in the 2000s learned this problem the hard way. Older zoning regulations, when not updated, form a very effective barrier to change, even when new patterns and uses are specified by the comprehensive plan.

At a smaller scale, most traditional zoning regulations also assumed that individual lots in a district were all identical and developable under a blanket set of regulations. This was almost always not the case; in any given district individual lots would have issues with topography, developable area, or adjacent uses that the standard regulations were not designed to accommodate.

And finally, many traditional zoning codes drafted before the early 1980s did not address the design of either sites or structures. Developers were permitted to design however they pleased, but the results did not always please the surrounding property owners.

In an effort to combat the relative inability of traditional zoning regulations to address these issues, communities have tested and incorporated a variety of more flexible tools into their zoning regulations. While each of the flexible zoning tools described in this section has a specific name and underlying concept, the common goal has been to balance the need to have a cohesive zoning approach with the specifics of designing a project to meet the requirements of the lot and the demands of the real estate market. Creative efforts have been made in communities across the country to establish regulatory flexibility in or across one or more areas of the four basic aspects of zoning regulation: use allocation, dimensional standards, density requirements, and design standards. Each flexible approach has been paired with a review process to memorialize the regulatory changes that were approved to incorporate the changes into the overall regulatory approach and allow the continued use and enforceability of the full zoning ordinance in the future. The overview of each of these tools, provided in Table 1, identifies where each tool promotes additional flexibility in a typical zoning regulation.

This chapter provides a general description of each of these tools. Practitioners may find that these general descriptions do not exactly match the way the tool is used locally. This should be expected; land use regulations are, for the most part, an on-going state and local experiment and they rarely work uniformly across multiple jurisdictions.

Floating Zones

Floating zones were one of the earliest approaches used to add flexibility to traditional zoning. A floating zone is a zone district that is established in the text of the zoning regulations but not applied to any particular location, i.e., not "mapped," until requested by a property owner. Floating zones are typically designed to encourage or limit a specific use or density, such as big box development or higher density development, in an area where that use or density would not otherwise be permitted by the existing zoning. The original floating zone was created to encourage increased residential density immediately following World War II in a community that had an abundance of large-lot development. The floating zone was used to permit medium density residential development that was designed to blend with the larger, single-family surrounding lots. One of the primary goals of floating zones was to create a zoning structure linked to the master plan while avoiding a spot zoning challenge. See *Rodgers v. Village of Tarrytown*, 302 N.Y. 115 (1951). Once the floating zone is approved it becomes a base or underlying zone district.

A floating zone typically includes a number of specific development standards, such as minimum density, parcel size limit, or required mix of uses, which standards are linked to the specific development desired. A floating zone is not placed on the zoning map until requested for a variety of reasons, including: (a) anticipation that only some development proposals will conform to the requirements of the floating zone; (b) potential impact of the proposed development type on property values, either increasing or decreasing the site or surrounding properties; and (c) uncertainty about the ability of the underlying site to meet the conditions of the zone in advance of site-specific information provided by property owners.

Planned Unit Developments

The planned unit development (PUD, also called "planned development" or PD) was created at about the same time as floating zones in an effort to provide more big-picture flexibility in development patterns. PUD is a development designed according to a site-specific master plan that does not necessarily conform to the individual standards or districts of the adopted zoning regulations. See *Cheney v. Village 2 at New Hope, Inc.*, 241 A.2d 81 (Pa. 1968). The PUD approach allows a developer with a property of a certain size, typically five acres or larger, to creatively redesign or opt out of the standard zone districts and subdivision standards and establish a district unique to that property. This approach is permitted to allow the applicant to design the project to meet the standard objectives of PUD: (1) achieve flexibility; (2) provide a more desirable living environment than would be possible through the strict application of zoning ordinance requirements; (3) encourage developers to use a more creative approach in their development of land; (4) encourage a more efficient and more desirable use of open land; and (5) encourage variety in the physical development pattern of the city.

The benefits to the applicant can be increased flexibility in site design, use allocation, and density (for some projects). Local government typically employs the PUD process to impose design standards and the benefit to the community can be a better designed project. Because PUD is typically negotiated, improved outcomes for either the applicant or the community are not always certain. Regulations usually take one of two types of approach. The first category is PUD regulations that work like a master-variance process. In these regulations, the property is usually assigned a "base" district from the regular zoning districts, and the applicant is permitted specific modifications of the regulations. For example, an applicant may be allowed to reduce standard setbacks by up to 70 percent, reduce standard lot size by 20 percent, or increase overall density by 15 percent. The result of this PUD approach tends to be a more clustered and sometimes more dense layout than would otherwise be allowed, but overall the development pattern has similarities to development that would be allowed under the standard zoning district.

The second category of PUD regulation is the standard-based approach. Here, applicants submit a site plan that is measured against a series of standards established in the regulations. The standards can range from general – "the plan is consistent with good land planning and site engineering design principles, particularly with respect to safety" – to specific – "the design of the PUD is as consistent as practical with the preservation of natural features of the site such as flood plains, wooded areas, steep slopes, natural drainage ways, or other areas of sensitive or valuable environmental character." In contrast to master-variance PUD regulations, standard-based regulations tend to result in a more negotiated and less uniform development pattern.

The PUD approval process is very similar to subdivision approval. In most communities, a developer submits a preliminary plan for approval by the governing body and then submits a final plan for approval either by the governing body or the planning commission. While there can be individual variations to this process, it is typically a multi-approval process that moves from general site design to specific design.

Approval criteria are established as part of the PUD ordinance and each application must meet the criteria. For master-variance PUD regulations, this includes a determination that all of the specifically measurable standards have been met. For a standard-based PUD, this means that the site design has been agreed upon by both the applicant and the reviewing staff. If a PUD application meets these criteria, it can be approved. Once in place, a PUD becomes its own mini zoning code and is usually subject to long-term administration based on the conditions and requirements of its approval.

Conditional Zoning

Conditional zoning evolved in response to the uncertainties and shortcoming of "as of right" zoning. It is really two concepts, used differently by different jurisdictions, with a shared title and a shared approach of establishing individual conditions regarding the use of a specific property. Most traditional zone districts included a laundry-list of uses that gave property owners a wide variety of options for use of the property "as of right" – that is without further local approval and typically without regard to impacts on neighboring properties. The zone district also included fixed bulk and dimensional standards that did not provide property owners with any real flexibility with respect to the application of development standards to their lot. This caused two problems: (1) adjacent property owners did not like the uncertainty of not knowing whether their neighbor would develop a grocery store or a car dealership; and (2) all developers were expected to build within the same imaginary box; if the applicant wanted to do anything unique with the lot, the only way to change the regulations was to either seek a variance or change the text of the code.

Depending on the jurisdiction, two types of conditional zoning were established to address these issues. Voluntary-restriction conditional zoning allows an applicant to voluntarily limit the use of a property and thereby obtain a rezoning with minimal protest. This approach is described in *Collard v. Village of Flower Hill*, 421 N.E.2d 818 (1981). Voluntary-design conditional zoning both proposes specific uses and imposes dimensional and design standards that differ from those required by the zoning regulations but that are locally viewed as an improvement over the minimal requirements and are also aimed at obtaining a favorable rezoning outcome. In both cases, the final conditions can be approved as part of a development agreement between the developer and local government and/or recorded as property covenants. Conditional zoning is not illegal contract zoning because the conditions are reviewed and agreed to, and can also be rejected, as part of the regular review and approval process. In other words, conditional zoning does not commit the elected body to a future action.

Conditional zoning can be accomplished at multiple levels and scales. At the smallest scale conditions such as minimum lot size or structure location are placed on individual uses. For example, an applicant seeking approval for doggy day care on a property may voluntarily restrict two acres of the lot to only that use. See *Crooked Creek Conservation and Gun Club v. Hamilton County North Board of Zoning Appeals*, 677 N.E.2d 544 (1997). At a larger site or structure scale, construction of a building above a certain height can be conditional on approval of a design that limits the amount of shadow thrown on adjacent public plazas. And at the district scale, rezoning with higher density can be conditional on the applicant providing attainable housing or other community amenity. Once the conditions are in place, communities typically take one of two approaches to ensure that the conditions are met: (1) postponing the final adoption of the rezoning until the conditions have been met or a development agreement has been entered into, or (2) reversing (or automatically reverting) the rezoning at some later date if the project is not in compliance with the approval.

Incentive Zoning

As the name suggests, incentive zoning – also referred to as bonus zoning – introduces flexibility into the zoning process by providing development incentives for preferred development types or patterns. This can be done through additional floor area ratio (FAR), extra building square footage, increased density, fee waivers, expedited review, measurement exceptions, reduced parking requirements, or changes to whatever development standard the community believes to be helpful or useful. For example, a community may want to encourage public plazas and so may allow additional building height where a ground-level plaza of a certain size is provided. In many communities incentive zoning is linked to the provision of affordable or attainable housing. Developers may elect to build affordable units in exchange for additional square footage on another project, or they may pay an in-lieu fee for the same exchange.

Incentive zoning is used more frequently in large urban areas where return on investment for additional density, share footage, and height, make more applicants consider the incentives calculation. Incentives can be difficult to calibrate, however, and many communities find that either the incentive has been made too "expensive" for an applicant to desire and consequently is not requested, or the incentive has been provided too "cheaply" and all applicants request the incentive. Additionally, communities inadvertently fail to close other doors that make the incentive available, allowing developers to choose the easiest route to the desired result without necessarily providing the off-setting community benefit.

Performance Zoning

Performance zoning was promoted in the early 1970s as a method to shift the regulatory process from an internal look at the use on the lot to an external look at the impacts of the development on surrounding lots and the community as a whole. The goals of performance zoning were to: (1) place less emphasis on use restrictions and instead mitigate the impacts of development through performance standards; (2) shift to a stronger emphasis on the relationship of building to open space and resource protection; and (3) quantify acceptable levels of impact at the property line to ensure compatibility of uses. If properly administered, a performance code could permit a residential use next to an industrial use without complaint by either. This was done through detailed measurement of multiple potential impacts of the proposed development with the establishment of accompanying off-setting development requirements.

Early in the development of performance zoning, a small number of zoning codes were built entirely around this approach. In general, the code included several zone districts that could be used to identify the character of an area. Within each district, individual development applications were measured against a series of standards: FAR, open space ratio, impervious surface ratio, noise measurements, vibration measurements, and so forth. Once properly measured, the development was designed to minimize impacts through siting, landscaping, open space, and the overall size of the project. Performance zoning was detailed and exceedingly difficult to administer in communities that did not have sufficient expert planning staff to perform the necessary measurements and calculations. Ultimately, this approach did not catch on as a new way to zone. However, it did provide the idea of performance standards that many communities have incorporated into the manufacturing and industrial standards of their zoning codes to help measure the impact of heavier uses on the neighborhood.

Interim Zoning and Moratoria

The flexibility of interim zoning and moratoria is not in the actual technique but in the time it takes for a community to revise existing regulations to better address a problem. Adoption of a moratorium is an act by an elected body that stops the processing of some or all development or an aspect of development for a specified period of time. A moratorium on wind farm development is described in *Ecogen, LLC v. Town of Italy*, 438 F. Supp.2d 149 (W.S.N.Y. 2006). During the period of time established in the moratorium, the local government reviews the existing zoning regulations related to the subject issue and replaces those regulations or creates new regulations designed to alleviate or eliminate the problem that was or could have been created by additional development. While researching and drafting the new regulations, the local government can also elect to put interim zoning in place that may allow some development applications to proceed where the project will not have a negative impact on the community.

This approach is best explained by example: In a community where the existing zoning ordinance was silent about the permissibility of keeping domestic chickens in residential districts, planning staff recognized that there was a growing population of backyard chickens and accompanying coops, not all of which were adequately designed to protect the poultry. The local government enacted a moratorium on new domestic chicken-keeping for six months. During that time, the planning staff prepared an ordinance specifying the site requirements and conditions for the permitted keeping of domestic chickens. The ordinance was adopted and applied to all future chicken applications. Applicants with other urban farming issues such as community gardens or beekeeping that were already addressed by the existing regulations were permitted to submit applications pursuant to the interim regulations in place during the moratorium.

Overlay Zoning

Overlay districts were created by communities to reflect that specialized zoning is sometimes required for a geographic area – such as an environmentally sensitive area, a downtown, or a transit stop – where the area to be regulated already has existing zoning in place. An overlay district is a set of development standards organized to be applicable within the specific geographic area that overlays the existing base zone districts in that geographic area. The standards in the overlay district may supplement, enhance, or supersede the requirements of the base district and, in most cases, provided that the standards are well-written, the overlay district standards will govern. See *Dallen v. City of Kansas City*, 822 S.W.2d 429 (1991). The flexibility in overlay districts tends to be to the benefit of the community more so than the developer; however, overlay districts have been used to change single-use districts to mixed-use districts in some communities.

Form-Based Codes and Traditional Neighborhood Development

Form-based codes and traditional neighborhood development (referred to collectively as "form-based codes" and intended to refer to the full range of form-based codes) are both a reaction to and a departure from the roots and current realities of traditional zoning and subdivision. Neo-traditional design theory is highly critical of modern, automobile-dependent development types which are easily recognized in our current landscape and frequently tagged as "sprawl." The source of sprawl development, simply, is traditional zoning and subdivision. And while there is room for debate about zoning and subdivision as the sole sources of suburban development patterns, there is no question that most pre-1990 traditional zoning and subdivision certainly required and reinforced these patterns.

Form-based development seeks to establish a street and lot layout that is reminiscent of traditional cities and residential districts where pedestrian activity is maximized through a mix of uses in a compact space and automobile use is minimized. In terms of regulations, this means:

- allowing a variety of uses in order to create vitality and bring many activities of daily living within walking distance of homes;
- fostering mixed residential density and housing types;
- developing contextual design standards that ensure new development responds to the typical architecture style of the city or region;
- creating compact, walkable centers and neighborhoods served by public transit;
- enhancing streetscape and civic life; and
- shaping metropolitan regions with public space, farmland, and natural areas.

Accordingly, form-based codes are not at all flexible when it comes to the design of streets, structures, and neighborhoods. Form-based theory recognizes that where the community has a good structure, uses can come and go but the buildings remain. This dynamic plays out in many downtowns and main streets across the country. Shops and restaurants are used by multiple tenants in succession but the nature and character of the area remains functional and vibrant. To ensure the easy exchange of uses, many form-based codes require only an administrative permit for use change, lowering the barrier to use change once the structure of the neighborhood is established.

Response to the Flexible Zoning Wicked Problem

Flexibility in zoning is often important in helping to produce an environment that is easy to navigate and attractive. Flexible zoning tools would allow a town to create an overlay district. In this case, one element of the overlay district may be reduced signage requirements. Care should be taken to ensure that the laws of the First Amendment are observed.

In addition, the town might contemplate passing a temporary moratorium on electronic or digital signs. The moratorium would provide the community with the opportunity to assess the demand for these signs and to investigate best practices for their display. This type of moratorium should be used sparingly and only for the time needed to study this problem.

Another tool that would be potentially useful in regulating signs in this context is through the PUD process. By their very nature, PUDs tend to have an urban design component. Allowing development by PUD in this area would allow developers to set the parameters for sign regulation.

Discussion Prompts

- Developers have long decried the inflexibility of zoning codes. Provide an example of this type of inflexibility and the traditional processes in place to help alleviate the burdens of these rules.
- Planned unit developments (PUDs) are a commonly utilized tool. Sometimes they are misused. In what instances is a PUD most appropriate?

Bibliography

Acker, F. W. (1991). Performance Zoning [notes]. *Notre Dame Law Review*, 67:2, 363–402.

Freilich, R. H. (1971–1972). Interim Development Controls: Essential Tools for Implementing Flexible Planning and Zoning. *Journal of the Urban Lawyer*, 49, 65.

Krasnowiecki, J. Z. (1980). Abolish Zoning. *Syracuse Law Review*, 31, 719.

Porter, D. R., Phillips, P. L., and Lassar, T. J. (1988). *Flexible Zoning: How it Works*. Washington, DC: Urban Land Inst.

Reno, R. R. (1963). Non-Euclidean Zoning: The Use of the Floating Zone. *Maryland Law Review*, 23, 105.

8

DUE PROCESS AND EQUAL PROTECTION

Knowledge of the key principles of the U.S. Constitution is vital to planners. Due process and equal protection offer fundamental protections to private property owners ensuring that planning occurs in an open and transparent process and that they are treated fairly in decision-making.

Due Process and Equal Protection Wicked Problem

After a recent child abduction by a registered sex offender, the city of Z seeks to take action to prevent another such incident from occurring. The city has decided that, based on the best science available, it will create an ordinance that identifies where a sex offender is allowed to live based on the level of risk associated with their previous offenses. Before taking up residence in the city, a sex offender must register with law enforcement and submit to a psychological exam administered by a police psychologist. The sex offender is notified of the results of the evaluation. He may then proceed to find a place to live based on the exam results. Level one sex offenders cannot live within 1,000 feet of any school, park, church, or daycare center. Level two sex offenders cannot live within 2,500 feet of those places. Level three sex offenders must live in group homes established by the city and monitored full-time by resident probation offices.

1. Does the evaluation scheme violate the due process rights of sex offenders who have been released from jail?
2. Is there a rational basis to justify this type of disproportionate treatment pursuant to the equal protection clause of the constitution?

Cases

The following cases will be useful to you as you attempt to analyze this chapter's wicked problem:

Village of Belle Terre v. Boraas, 416 U.S. 1 (1974)
City of Cleburne v. Cleburne Living Center, 473 U.S. 432 (1985)

Figure 7 Credit: David D. Boeck

Village of Belle Terre v. Boraas

416 U.S. 1 (1974)

Facts
In the 1970s, the village of Belle Terre was a small community with a population of less than 1,000 people. Belle Terre's land use ordinance was restricted to one-family dwellings, allowing only two people unrelated by blood, marriage, or adoption to live together. In 1971, the Dickmans leased their Belle Terre home to six college students, none of whom were related to another by blood, marriage, or adoption. When the Dickmans were served with an ordinance violation, the owners and three of the tenants brought suit, requesting the court to declare the ordinance unconstitutional.

Issue
Was Belle Terre's ordinance limiting the number of unrelated persons who could live together unconstitutional?

Held
No. Belle Terre's ordinance did not infringe upon any fundamental right guaranteed by the constitution. If it can be shown that regulations are reasonable and as such bear a rational relationship to achieving a permissible state objective, then the Court will uphold the regulation as constitutional. Legislative deference was given to Belle Terre's definition of family as comprised of two unrelated

persons and under the broad concept of public welfare, Belle Terre had the right to draft their ordinances in a manner to promote a small, quiet community.

Discussion

Multi-family housing can pose urban problems such as increased traffic, noise pollution, and create a demand for parking. Municipalities have the ability to draft ordinances limiting the number of unrelated persons living together.

Case Excerpt

The present ordinance is challenged on several grounds: that it interferes with a person's right to travel; that it interferes with the right to migrate to and settle within a State; that it bars people who are uncongenial to the present residents; that it expresses the social preferences of the residents for groups that will be congenial to them; that social homogeneity is not a legitimate interest of government; that the restriction of those whom the neighbors do not like trenches on the newcomers' rights of privacy; that it is of no rightful concern to villagers whether the residents are married or unmarried; that the ordinance is antithetical to the Nation's experience, ideology, and self-perception as an open, egalitarian, and integrated society.

We find none of these reasons in the record before us. It is not aimed at transients. Cf. *Shapiro* v. *Thompson,* 394 U. S. 618. It involves no procedural disparity inflicted on some but not on others such as was presented by *Griffin* v. *Illinois,* 351 U. S. 12. It involves no "fundamental" right guaranteed by the Constitution, such as voting, *Harper* v. *Virginia Board,* 383 U. S. 663; the right of association, *NAACP* v. *Alabama,* 357 U. S. 449; the right of access to the courts, *NAACP* v. *Button,* 371 U. S. 415; or any rights of privacy, cf. *Griswold* v. *Connecticut,* 8*8 381 U. S. 479; *Eisenstadt* v. *Baird,* 405 U. S. 438, 453–454. We deal with economic and social legislation where legislatures have historically drawn lines which we respect against the charge of violation of the Equal Protection Clause if the law be "reasonable, not arbitrary" (quoting *Royster Guano Co.* v. *Virginia,* 253 U. S. 412, 415) and bears "a rational relationship to a [permissible] state objective." *Reed* v. *Reed,* 404 U. S. 71, 76.

It is said, however, that if two unmarried people can constitute a "family," there is no reason why three or four may not. But every line drawn by a legislature leaves some out that might well have been included. That exercise of discretion, however, is a legislative not a judicial, function.

It is said that the Belle Terre ordinance reeks with an animosity to unmarried couples who live together. There is no evidence to support it; and the provision of the ordinance bringing within the definition of a "family" two unmarried people belies the charge.

The ordinance places no ban on other forms of association, for a "family" may, so far as the ordinance is concerned, entertain whomever it likes.

The regimes of boarding houses, fraternity houses, and the like present urban problems. More people occupy a given space; more cars rather continuously pass by; more cars are parked; noise travels with crowds.

A quiet place where yards are wide, people few, and motor vehicles restricted are legitimate guidelines in a land-use project addressed to family needs. This goal is a permissible one within *Berman* v. *Parker, supra*. The police power is not confined to elimination of filth, stench, and unhealthy places. It is ample to lay out zones where family values, youth values, and the blessings of quiet seclusion and clean air make the area a sanctuary for people.

City of Cleburne v. Cleburne Living Center

473 U.S. 432 (1985)

Facts

Hannah purchased a building with the intention of leasing it to Cleburne Living Center (CLC), for the operation of a home for adults with learning difficulties. Under the City of Cleburne's zoning ordinance, a special use permit was necessary for such an activity, but the permit was denied. CLC filed suit against the City, alleging that the ordinance violated the equal protection rights guaranteed to CLC and its potential residents under the Fourteenth Amendment.

Issue

Did the City of Cleburne's zoning ordinance violate protections guaranteed under the Fourteenth Amendment?

Held

Yes. The City did not require a special use permit for a variety of other uses involving multiple unrelated persons living together such as apartments, fraternity or sorority houses, dormitories, and nursing homes, yet mandated one for the operation of a home for adults with learning difficulties. Since there was no evidence that CLC would threaten the city's legitimate interests in a way that other permitted uses would not, the ordinance is invalid. The city's arguments for denying the permit, including negative attitudes of nearby property owners, its location near a school and in the 500-year floodplain, and the number of people who would live there, all failed.

Discussion

The Court acknowledges that there is no room for fear, negative attitudes, or stereotypes in zoning procedures. Cleburne's denial of a special use permit rests on an "irrational prejudice" against the intellectually disabled in the community.

Case Excerpt

The Equal Protection Clause of the Fourteenth Amendment commands that no State shall "deny to any person within its jurisdiction the equal protection of the laws," which is essentially a direction that all persons similarly situated should be treated alike. *Plyler* v. *Doe*, 457 U. S. 202, 216 (1982). Section 5 of the Amendment empowers Congress to enforce this mandate, but absent controlling congressional direction, the courts have themselves devised standards for determining the validity of state legislation or other official action that is challenged as denying equal protection. The general rule is that legislation is presumed to be valid and will be sustained if the classification drawn by the statute is rationally related to a legitimate state interest. *Schweiker* v. *Wilson*, 450 U. S. 221, 230 (1981); *United States Railroad Retirement Board* v. *Fritz*, 449 U. S. 166, 174–175 (1980); *Vance* v. *Bradley*, 440 U. S. 93, 97 (1979); *New Orleans* v. *Dukes*, 427 U. S. 297, 303 (1976). When social or economic legislation is at issue, the Equal Protection Clause allows the States wide latitude, *United States Railroad Retirement Board* v. *Fritz, supra*, at 174; *New Orleans* v. *Dukes, supra*, at 303, and the Constitution presumes that even improvident decisions will eventually be rectified by the democratic processes.

The general rule gives way, however, when a statute classifies by race, alienage, or national origin. These factors are so seldom relevant to the achievement of any legitimate state interest that laws grounded in such considerations are deemed to reflect prejudice and antipathy – a view that those in the burdened class are not as worthy or deserving as others. For these reasons and because such discrimination is unlikely to be soon rectified by legislative means, these laws are subjected to strict scrutiny and will be sustained only if they are suitably tailored to serve a compelling State interest. *McLaughlin* v. *Florida*, 379 U. S. 184, 192 (1964); *Graham* v. *Richardson*, 403 U. S. 365 (1971). Similar oversight by the courts is due when state laws impinge on personal rights protected by the Constitution. *Kramer* v. *Union Free School District No. 15*, 395 U. S. 621 (1969); *Shapiro* v. *Thompson*, 394 U. S. 618 (1969); *Skinner* v. *Oklahoma ex rel. Williamson*, 316 U. S. 535 (1942).

Legislative classifications based on gender also call for a heightened standard of review. That factor generally provides no sensible ground for differential treatment. "[W]hat differentiates sex from such non-suspect statutes as intelligence or physical disability ... is that the sex characteristic frequently bears no relation to ability to perform or contribute to society." *Frontiero* v. *Richardson*, 411 U. S. 677, 686 (1973) (plurality opinion). Rather than resting on meaningful considerations, statutes distributing benefits and burdens between the sexes in different ways very likely reflect outmoded notions of the relative capabilities of men and women. A gender classification fails unless it is substantially related to a sufficiently important governmental interest. *Mississippi University for Women* v. *Hogan*, 458 U. S. 718 (1982); *Craig* v. *Boren*, 429 U. S. 190 (1976). Because illegitimacy is beyond the individual's control and bears "no relation to the individual's ability to participate in and contribute to society," *Mathews* v. *Lucas*, 427 U. S. 495, 505 (1976), official discriminations resting on that characteristic are also subject to somewhat heightened review. Those restrictions "will survive equal protection scrutiny to the extent they are substantially related to a legitimate state interest." *Mills* v. *Habluetzel*, 456 U. S. 91, 99 (1982).

We have declined, however, to extend heightened review to differential treatment based on age:

"While the treatment of the aged in this Nation has not been wholly free of discrimination, such persons, unlike, say, those who have been discriminated against on the basis of race or national origin, have not experienced a 'history of purposeful unequal treatment' or been subjected to unique disabilities on the basis of stereo-typed characteristics not truly indicative of their abilities." *Massachusetts Board of Retirement* v. *Murgia*, 427 U. S. 307, 313 (1976).

The lesson of *Murgia* is that where individuals in the group affected by a law have distinguishing characteristics relevant to interests the State has the authority to implement, the courts have been very reluctant, as they should be in our federal system and with our respect for the separation of powers, to closely scrutinize legislative choices as to whether, how, and to what extent those interests should be pursued. In such cases, the Equal Protection Clause requires only a rational means to serve a legitimate end.

Against this background, we conclude for several reasons that the Court of Appeals erred in holding mental retardation a quasi-suspect classification calling for a more exacting standard of judicial review than is normally accorded economic and social legislation...

Such legislation thus singling out the retarded for special treatment reflects the real and undeniable differences between the retarded and others. That a civilized and decent society expects and approves such legislation indicates that governmental consideration of those differences in the vast majority of situations is not only legitimate but also desirable. It may be, as CLC contends, that legislation designed to benefit, rather than disadvantage, the retarded would generally withstand examination under a test of heightened scrutiny. See Brief for Respondents 38–41. The relevant inquiry, however, is whether heightened scrutiny is constitutionally mandated in the first instance. Even assuming that many of these laws could be shown to be substantially related to an important governmental purpose, merely requiring the legislature to justify its efforts in these terms may lead it to refrain from acting at all. Much recent legislation intended to benefit the retarded also assumes the need for measures that might be perceived to disadvantage them...Especially given the wide variation in the abilities and needs of the retarded themselves, governmental bodies must have a certain amount of flexibility and freedom from judicial oversight in shaping and limiting their remedial efforts.

Doubtless, there have been and there will continue to be instances of discrimination against the retarded that are in fact invidious, and that are properly subject to judicial correction under constitutional norms. But the appropriate method of reaching such instances is not to create a new quasi-suspect classification and subject all governmental action based on that classification to more searching evaluation. Rather, we should look to the likelihood that governmental action premised on a particular classification is valid as a general matter, not merely to the specifics of the case before us. Because mental retardation is a characteristic that the government may legitimately take into account in a wide range of decisions, and because both State and Federal Governments have recently committed themselves to assisting the retarded, we will not presume that any given legislative action, even one that disadvantages retarded individuals, is rooted in considerations that the Constitution will not tolerate.

Our refusal to recognize the retarded as a quasi-suspect class does not leave them entirely unprotected from invidious discrimination. To withstand equal protection review, legislation that distinguishes between the mentally retarded and others must be rationally related to a legitimate governmental purpose. This standard, we believe, affords government the latitude necessary both to pursue policies designed to assist the retarded in realizing their full potential, and to freely and efficiently engage in activities that burden the retarded in what is essentially an incidental manner. The State may not rely on a classification whose relationship to an asserted goal is so attenuated as to render the distinction arbitrary or irrational. See *Zobel* v. *Williams,* 457 U. S. 55, 61–63 (1982); *United States Dept. of Agriculture* v. *Moreno,* 413 U. S. 528, 535 (1973). Furthermore, some objectives – such as "a bare ... desire to harm a politically unpopular group," *id.,* at 534 – are not legitimate state interests. See also *Zobel, supra,* at 63. Beyond that, the mentally retarded, like others, have and retain their substantive constitutional rights in addition to the right to be treated equally by the law.

Primer on Due Process and Equal Protection as an Issue for Planners

The Fourteenth Amendment to the U.S. Constitution establishes the right of due process under the law. The Amendment states: "Nor shall any state deprive any person of life, liberty, or property, without due process of the law." This guarantee of due process has been interpreted to offer substantive and procedural due process protections.

Substantive Due Process

In the context of city planning and land use regulation substantive due process guarantees that the substance of the law will be applied fairly across all landowners. In terms of land use, the due process clause means "that land use controls must advance legitimate governmental interests that serve the public health, safety, morals, and general welfare." Land use regulations may not be applied in a fashion which is arbitrary and capricious no matter what procedural protections apply.

Substantive due process regulations must advance a legitimate governmental interest, and challenges do not typically survive. The legal standard by which these cases are judged is highly deferential in favor of the local government. These claims are most likely to be upheld if the challenger can demonstrate that the local government's actions have impeded a fundamental right to which he or she is entitled. In the absence of a fundamental right, all the local government has to do is show that its regulations advance a legitimate governmental interest. Some courts, however, require more of an entitlement to bring suit, including the vesting of a right and the exhaustion of administrative remedies where appropriate.

An administrative decision affecting property rights will be found to be a substantive due process violation, when it "shocks the conscience." Courts will require more proof and defer less to the government. When a challenge is to a legislative action, courts rely on the "arbitrary and irrational test." Courts defer more to the local government, requiring less proof. A litigant cannot make a substantive due process claim if another, more specific, claim is available. A plaintiff must have an entitlement to bring a substantive due process claim; thus, the claimant must show that the law entitles him to do what he wants to his land.

Procedural Due Process

The due process clause requires that localities adopt constitutionally acceptable procedures for administrative and quasi-judicial decision-making. These may include, but are not limited to: (1) notice; (2) hearing and (3) findings of fact on variance decisions.

The degree of procedural due process to which a property owner is entitled is dependent entirely upon the types of decision being made: legislative, administrative, or quasi-judicial. Legislative decisions are those decisions made by a local government that affect the community at large. An example of this might be when a city council adopts a comprehensive plan or zoning ordinance, or an amendment to either. These changes affect all property owners generally. As such, they must all be generally notified and invited to participate in a public hearing on the proposed ordinance or change thereto. With legislative decisions, notice may be given in the newspaper. Property owners are allowed to comment on the proposed change at the public hearing. They are not entitled to know, however, the reasons upon which the local governing body based its decision.

By contrast, administrative decisions are actions that may be taken by the planning department or the building code official as long as the applicant's proposal complies with the law. For example, a historic district may have a particular paint palate that requires homeowners who wish to paint their homes to seek permission to do so from a city's historic preservation planner. Typically, the applicant will bring a paint chip to the preservation planner. If it is an approved paint color, the planner will issue a permit for the homeowner to paint the home. Such decisions are made on a case by case basis by an administrator with limited discretion. Had the applicant brought a paint chip of an unapproved color before the historic preservation planner, he or she would have had to seek approval from the planner or the board designated for review.

Sometimes local governing bodies act in a similar way to courts. For example, Zoning Boards of Adjustment make decisions about the issuance of variances to allow individual property owners to deviate from bulk requirements like setbacks. When a decision stands to directly benefit one property owner to the potential detriment of neighboring property owners, notice and hearing requirements are increased. By statute, neighboring property owners within a specified distance must be notified by certified mail of impending hearings on variances. If they are not reached by certified mail, efforts must be made by the local government to post notice by placard on the affected property. The nature of the hearing held on quasi-judicial actions also varies significantly when compared to legislative actions. At such hearings, the Zoning Board of Adjustment acts as a tribunal. Parties may be represented by legal counsel. Witnesses are sworn under oath and may be cross-examined. Evidence is entered into the record. Upon conclusion, a Zoning Board of Adjustment will issue a written decision detailing the reasons for the decision and the facts upon which the decision is based.

Procedural due process is perhaps one of the most important guarantees put in place to help guard private property rights. These rights only protect those with a real entitlement to them, not a speculative property right. Failure of a local government to honor due process requirements is a legal "trump card." In instances where procedural due process rights have not been honored, courts will be quick to invalidate decisions made in the absence of proper process.

Equal Protection

Equal protection rights also emanate from the Fourtenth Amendment to the U.S. Constitution. These rights only apply to actions of the states and, therefore, local governments. The purpose of the equal protection clause is to prevent differential treatment of people or, in the alternative, to guarantee that the disparate treatment of people is justified. It is important, for the purposes of land use law, to note that the equal protection clause applies to people rather than properties. In equal protection challenges, courts will be reviewing local decisions affecting properties to see if a particular person or class of person is being treated differently than another individual or group.

While all U.S. citizens are guaranteed equal protection under the laws, some residents, because of special characteristics, are guaranteed higher levels of protection. For example, regulations that treat racial groups differently will only be allowed to stand if the regulator can demonstrate a compelling interest for the disparate treatment. The same is true in terms of identified fundamental rights like free speech, privacy, and voting, among others. These groups are afforded the highest level of protection under the Equal Protection Clause.

Zoning decisions frequently have a disparate impact on racial groups, whether intentional or accidental. Even if differential treatment is unintended, it is still problematic as demonstrated in *Village of Arlington Heights v. Metropolitan Housing Dev. Corp.*, 429 U.S. 252 (1976). This case involved the village's denial of a rezoning which would have allowed the Metropolitan Housing Development Corporation (MHDC) to construct a federally subsidized multi-family housing development. Relying on the Equal Protection Clause, MHDC challenged the village's denial of the rezoning as discriminatory in its intention and effect. The Supreme Court, finding in favor of MHDC, held that if a protected class can prove even the slightest discriminatory intent, the burden of proof shifts to the local government to justify zoning classification. In this case, the high court ruled that the village had failed to offer a compelling justification for its differential treatment.

A second tier of protections applies to quasi-suspect classes. Differential treatment based on gender is the most common quasi-suspect class. In order to justify disparate treatment based on gender, the governmental entity must prove that it has a substantial interest in crafting a regulation that favors one gender over another.

Courts are often called upon to decide if the groups contained within each classification should be expanded. In *City of Cleburne v. Cleburne Living Center*, 473 U.S. 432 (1985), the U.S. Supreme Court was asked to determine if mental retardation was a quasi-suspect class under the Equal Protection Clause. At the heart of this case was a decision by city officials denying an application for a special use permit to operate a group home to house those with developmental disabilities in an area zoned for multi-family residential use. On appeal, the U.S. Supreme Court found that the developmentally disabled were not a quasi-suspect class under the Equal Protection Clause. However, the court ruled that the denial of the permit was unconstitutional under the rational relationship test because of an absence of threats to legitimate governmental interests supporting the denial of the application based on concerns expressed by neighbors.

Differences, not otherwise specified by case law, are treated under the third tier of equal protection. A regulator must prove that disparate treatment is rationally related to a legitimate governmental interest. This is the tier of legal analysis that most commonly applies to planning challenges. The rights of sex offenders, the subject of this chapter's wicked problem, fall under this classification scheme.

City ordinances may intend to treat groups differently. In college towns, for example, cities often seek to craft regulations that will ensure that neighborhood vitality does not decline as a result of student rentals. Such regulations are typically justified because students are short-term residents who rent properties, often originally developed for families. Occupants of these rentals are typically unrelated and may not occupy single-family houses in the same way that typical families do. In response to this problem, many cities have passed unrelated persons ordinances. These ordinances typically define the term family, thereby limiting the number of unrelated persons who can live together. In *Belle Terre v. Boraas*, 416 U.S. 1 (1974), the U.S. Supreme Court upheld differential treatment based on familial status because the regulation had a rational purpose, i.e. preserving the integrity of neighborhoods comprised of single-family homes.

While courts generally talk about protected "groups" in equal protection cases, such challenges are appropriate for individuals, often referred to as "classes of one." *Willowbrook v. Olech*, 528 U.S. 562 (2000) offers a good demonstration of how third-tier analysis applies to people who feel they have received unfair treatment by local decision-makers in zoning cases. In *Willowbrook*, the city council sought to require a property owner to grant the city a 33-foot easement across their property in exchange for connection to city water services. The property owner sued the city on the grounds that they were treated differently than neighbors, who were only required to grant the city a 15-foot easement for the same connection to water services. On appeal to the U.S. Supreme Court, the high court recognized, for the first time, that equal protection claims could be brought by single plaintiffs who were treated differently than another similarly situated individual.

Response to Wicked Problem

Sex offenders are not a protected class for the purposes of the equal protection clause. As such, regulations that target this particular group will be found to be a violation of the equal protection clause only if the regulation imposed is not rationally related to a legitimate government interest. This is the lowest level of protection afforded under the equal protection clause. A reviewing court will examine such a regulation to see if there is a rational basis for the classification that serves the public interest. Here, as in *Doe v. White*, the court is likely to find that such regulations are necessary given the expanse of the types of crime that brand someone a sex offender for life. This type of differential treatment would allow cities and/or the penal system to allow those sex offenders who may have committed lesser crimes, like public nudity, to more freely move about a city upon release, while simultaneously limiting the living opportunities of felons who were convicted of serial sex offenses.

While this sort of regulation is likely to survive scrutiny on grounds of equal protection, the classification system may be more vulnerable if subjected to due process analysis. Procedural due process entitles affected parties the opportunity to receive notice to participate in a public hearing at which they are allowed to comment. This standard is less for general legislative acts that affect the city as a whole. Arguably, this city-wide ordinance falls into such a classification. While the enactment of the ordinance may not be problematic, the application of the ordinance might be vulnerable to attack. The problem with this ordinance is not with the buffer requirements; they would likely be upheld. The problem lies with the process of classification. A police psychologist is being allowed, on his or her own, to determine into which level of sex offender a released sex offender falls. This process of classification is under-developed and does not provide any recourse for released sex offenders who feel like they have been improperly labeled. To avoid such an issue, the city might revise its regulation to coincide with the crimes for which the sex offenders were convicted. However, care should be taken to contemplate an appeal's process that allows review of such designations over time.

Some issues, like this one in particular, are not typical planning issues. They are, perhaps, more appropriately dealt with as health and human services or policing issues. However, given citizens' concerns and the politics that follow, planners are often charged with inventing solutions that will offer reassurances of safety to community residents. In such cases, it is important that planners remember their duty to serve the public interest. This includes those citizens who are being targeted by such regulations. Care must be taken to ensure that these residents are not excluded from communities and that their rights are considered and protected. Such efforts may not be popular but are necessary in ensuring the long-term welfare and safety of all residents.

Discussion Prompts

- A successful procedural due process challenge is a trump card in land use litigation. Why?
- What are the primary differences between procedural and substantive due process?
- The two are often confused. How should a local government work to ensure that a local ordinance is both procedurally and substantively valid?

Bibliography

Salsich, Peter W. (1986). Group Homes, Shelters and Congregate Housing: Deinstitutionalization Policies and the NIMBY Syndrome. *Real Property, Probate and Trust Journal*, 21:413, 413–434.

Tassinary, L. G., Jourdan, D. E., and Parsons, R. (2010). Equal Protection and Aesthetic Zoning: A Possible Crack and a Preemptive Repair. *Urban Lawyer*, 42:2, 375–394.

Tekle, Asmura (2007). Privatizing Eminent Domain: The Delegation of a Very Public Power to Private, Non-Profit Corporations. *American University Law Review*, 56:455, 455–514.

9

POSSESSORY TAKINGS

The Fifth Amendment to the U.S. Constitution sits at the crux of the protection of private property rights and the local government's authority to regulate land development activities. The Fifth Amendment ensures that when the government formally dispossesses property owners from their land, even temporarily, they will be justly compensated for their losses.

Possessory Takings Wicked Problem

Bob James owns 100 acres of farmland in a rural part of a county in Eastern Kansas. His neighbor, Eli Homes, owns a similarly sized tract of land to the east of Bob's property. These properties are both dedicated to wheat production. The Sunflower Subdivision is situated adjacent to Eli Homes' parcel of property. Developed in 1955, the Sunflower Subdivision is also a 100-acre tract of land containing approximately 80 single-family homes of the same vintage. These homes are modest but well kept.

These three properties are bisected by a state highway. Until recently, there has been no discussion of new development in the area. However, county leaders have begun a dialogue with a sports franchise that seeks to set up operations in the county. Specifically, the franchise seeks to enter into a public-private partnership to build a regional entertainment complex in the county. Franchise representatives have told the county that they seek their assistance identifying and assembling a parcel of land large enough to host their operations. They have requested that the selected property is approximately 100 acres and immediately accessible from the highway.

County administrators identify the most suitable area for the redevelopment as the 300-acre area owned by James, Homes, and the residents of the Sunflower Subdivision. Eli Homes hears a rumor about the potential project and employs a financial advisor to assess the impact of the proposed development on his property. The advisor tells Mr. Homes that there is more money to be made if he initiates plans to develop his property to host the commercial uses that are typically ancillary to entertainment complexes of this magnitude. He immediately approaches county administrators with plans to build a large-scale commercial development on his property.

County administrators are excited to move to secure the franchiser's commitment for the public-private partnership. They, along with the franchiser, decide to locate the new facility on the site of the Sunflower Subdivision. The county begins to acquire the properties one by one using their eminent domain powers. Within a year, more than 35 households quickly accept the county's financial offers, which are slightly above

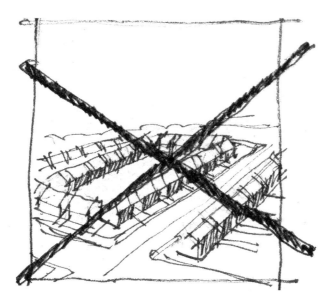

Figure 8 Credit: David D. Boeck

the market value of homes in the area during a period of extreme declining values brought on by the foreclosure crisis. Simultaneously, the remaining property owners seek to go to State Court to challenge the county's use of eminent domain to acquire their properties.

The primary basis of their claim is that the county is taking their properties for private rather than public use. The property owners living in the Sunflower Subdivision contend that the public-private partnership is a sham arrangement to get around the state's law following the *Kelo v. City of New London* case (discussed below) that local governments may no longer utilize eminent domain power for the sake of economic development activities spearheaded by private individuals.

Secondarily, the Sunflower Subdivision property owners maintain that the county is taking advantage of the mortgage crisis to dispossess them of their homes significantly below market value. While the county's financial offers are at present market value, those offers are reflective of a housing market that has been depressed by 30 percent over the last year.

Assess the veracity of the property owners' arguments. Before responding to the hypothetical above, read the material in the following sections. A response to this wicked problem is provided at the conclusion of these sections on the topic of possessory takings.

Cases

The following cases will be useful to you as you attempt to analyze this chapter's wicked problem:

Yee v. City of Escondito, 503 U.S. 519 (1992)

Loretto v. Teleprompter Manhattan CATV, 458 U.S. 419 (1982)
Kelo v. City of New London, 545 U.S. 469 (2005)

Yee v. City of Escondido

503 U.S. 519 (1992)

Facts
The city of Escondito passed a rent control ordinance upon mobile home park owners, artificially setting a maximum rental rate the landlords may charge lot tenants. The park owners sued, arguing the rate regulation amounted to a physical occupation entitling them to just compensation. The trial court dismissed the park owners' action and California's Court of Appeals confirmed.

Issue
Did the city's rent control ordinance amount to a physical taking requiring compensation?

Held
No. A physical taking only occurs when the state forces physical occupation upon property owners. The rent control ordinance did not force property owners to rent the mobile home sites or otherwise submit to occupation because landlords had already acquiesced to renting to mobile home tenants.

Discussion
The city of Escondito's rent control ordinance did not deprive the mobile home owners of the economic value of their sites. The ordinance merely regulated the use of the property. The *Yee* Court's holding found that governmental bodies may place caps on rent prices. Such a cap, in and of itself, did not constitute a taking.

Case Excerpt
Petitioners do not claim that the ordinary rent control statutes regulating housing throughout the country violate the Takings Clause. Brief for Petitioners 7, 10. Cf. *Pennell* v. *San Jose*, 485 U. S. 1, 12, n. 6 (1988); *Loretto, supra,* at 440. Instead, their argument is predicated on the unusual economic relationship between park owners and mobile home owners. Park owners may no longer set rents or decide who their tenants will be. As a result, according to petitioners, any reduction in the rent for a mobile home pad causes a corresponding increase in the value of a mobile home, because the mobile home owner now owns, in addition to a mobile home, the right to occupy a pad at a rent below the value that would be set by the free market. Cf. Hirsch & Hirsch, 35 UCLA L. Rev., at 425. Because under the California Mobilehome Residency Law the park owner cannot evict a mobile home owner or easily convert the property to other uses, the argument goes, the mobile home owner is effectively a perpetual tenant of the park, and the increase in the mobile home's value thus represents the right

to occupy a pad at below-market rent indefinitely. And because the Mobilehome Residency Law permits the mobile home owner to sell the mobile home in place, the mobile home owner can receive a premium from the purchaser corresponding to this increase in value. The amount of this premium is not limited by the Mobilehome Residency Law or the Escondido ordinance. As a result, petitioners conclude, the rent control ordinance has transferred a discrete interest in land – the right to occupy the land indefinitely at a submarket rent – from the park owner to the mobile home owner. Petitioners contend that what has been transferred from park owner to mobile home owner is no less than a right of physical occupation of the park owner's land.

This argument, while perhaps within the scope of our regulatory taking cases, cannot be squared easily with our cases on physical takings. The government effects a physical taking only where it *requires* the landowner to submit to the physical occupation of his land. "This element of required acquiescence is at the heart of the concept of occupation." *FCC* v. *Florida Power Corp.*, 480 U. S. 245, 252 (1987). Thus whether the government floods a landowner's property, *Pumpelly* v. *Green Bay Co.*, 13 Wall. 166 (1872), or does no more than require the landowner to suffer the installation of a cable, *Loretto, supra,* the Takings Clause requires compensation if the government authorizes a compelled physical invasion of property.

But the Escondido rent control ordinance, even when considered in conjunction with the California Mobile home Residency Law, authorizes no such thing. Petitioners voluntarily rented their land to mobile home owners. At least on the face of the regulatory scheme, neither the city nor the State compels petitioners, once they have rented their property to tenants, to continue doing so. To the contrary, the Mobile home Residency Law provides that a park owner who wishes to change the use of his land may evict his tenants, albeit with 6 or 12 months notice. Cal. Civ. Code Ann. § 798.56(g). Put bluntly, no government has required any physical invasion of petitioners' property. Petitioners' tenants were invited by petitioners, not forced upon them by the government. See *Florida Power, supra,* at 252–253. While the "right to exclude" is doubtless, as petitioners assert, "one of the most essential sticks in the bundle of rights that are commonly characterized as property," *Kaiser Aetna* v. *United States,* 444 U. S. 164, 176 (1979), we do not find that right to have been taken from petitioners on the mere face of the Escondido ordinance.

Petitioners suggest that the statutory procedure for changing the use of a mobile home park is in practice "a kind of gauntlet," in that they are not in fact free to change the use of their land. Reply Brief for Petitioners 10, n. 16. Because petitioners do not claim to have run that gauntlet, however, this case provides no occasion to consider how the procedure has been applied to petitioners' property, and we accordingly confine ourselves to the face of the statute. See *Keystone Bituminous Coal Assn.* v. *DeBenedictis,* 480 U. S. 470, 493–495 (1987). A different case would be presented were the statute, on its face or as applied, to compel a landowner over objection to rent his property or to refrain in perpetuity from terminating a tenancy. See *Florida Power, supra,* at 251–252, n. 6; see also *Nollan* v. *California Coastal Comm'n,* 483 U. S. 825, 831–832

(1987); *Fresh Pond Shopping Center, Inc.* v. *Callahan,* 464 U. S. 875, 877 (1983) (Rehnquist, J., dissenting).

On their face, the state and local laws at issue here merely regulate petitioners' *use* of their land by regulating the relationship between landlord and tenant. "This Court has consistently affirmed that States have broad power to regulate housing conditions in general and the landlord-tenant relationship in particular without paying compensation for all economic injuries that such regulation entails." *Loretto,* 458 U. S., at 440. See also *Florida Power, supra,* at 252 ("statutes regulating the economic relations of landlords and tenants are not *per se* takings"). When a landowner decides to rent his land to tenants, the government may place ceilings on the rents the landowner can charge, see, *e. g., Pennell, supra,* at 12, n. 6, or require the landowner to accept tenants he does not like, see, *e. g., Heart of Atlanta Motel, Inc.* v. *United States,* 379 U. S. 241, 261 (1964), without automatically having to pay compensation. See also *PruneYard Shopping Center* v. *Robins,* 447 U. S. 74, 82–84 (1980). Such forms of regulation are analyzed by engaging in the "essentially ad hoc, factual inquiries" necessary to determine whether a regulatory taking has occurred. *Kaiser Aetna, supra,* at 175. In the words of Justice Holmes, "while property may be regulated to a certain extent, if regulation goes too far it will be recognized as a taking." *Pennsylvania Coal Co.* v. *Mahon,* 260 U. S. 393, 415 (1922).

Petitioners emphasize that the ordinance transfers wealth from park owners to incumbent mobile home owners. Other forms of land use regulation, however, can also be said to transfer wealth from the one who is regulated to another. Ordinary rent control often transfers wealth from landlords to tenants by reducing the landlords' income and the tenants' monthly payments, although it does not cause a one-time transfer of value as occurs with mobile homes. Traditional zoning regulations can transfer wealth from those whose activities are prohibited to their neighbors; when a property owner is barred from mining coal on his land, for example, the value of his property may decline but the value of his neighbor's property may rise. The mobile home owner's ability to sell the mobile home at a premium may make this wealth transfer more *visible* than in the ordinary case, see Epstein, Rent Control and the Theory of Efficient Regulation, 54 Brooklyn L. Rev. 741, 758–759 (1988), but the existence 530*530 of the transfer in itself does not convert regulation into physical invasion.

Petitioners also rely heavily on their allegation that the ordinance benefits incumbent mobile home owners without benefiting future mobile home owners, who will be forced to purchase mobile homes at premiums. Mobile homes, like motor vehicles, ordinarily decline in value with age. But the effect of the rent control ordinance, coupled with the restrictions on the park owner's freedom to reject new tenants, is to increase significantly the value of the mobile home. This increased value normally benefits only the tenant in possession at the time the rent control is imposed. See Hirsch & Hirsch, 35 UCLA L. Rev., at 430–431. Petitioners are correct in citing the existence of this premium as a difference between the alleged effect of the Escondido ordinance and that of an ordinary apartment rent control statute. Most apartment tenants do not sell anything to their successors (and are often prohibited from charging "key money"), so a typical rent control statute will transfer wealth from the landlord to the incumbent tenant and all future tenants. By contrast, petitioners contend that the Escondido ordinance transfers wealth only to the incumbent mobile home owner. This effect might have some bearing on whether the ordinance causes a *regulatory* taking, as it may shed some light on whether there is a sufficient nexus between the effect of the ordinance and the objectives it is supposed to advance. See *Nollan* v. *California Coastal Comm'n, supra,* at 834–835. But it has nothing to do with whether the ordinance causes a *physical* taking. Whether the ordinance benefits only current mobile home owners or all mobile home owners, it does not require petitioners to submit to the physical occupation of their land.

The same may be said of petitioners' contention that the ordinance amounts to compelled physical occupation because it deprives petitioners of the ability to choose their incoming tenants. Again, this effect may be relevant to a regulatory taking argument, as it may be one factor a reviewing court would wish to consider in determining whether the ordinance unjustly imposes a burden on petitioners that should "be compensated by the government, rather than remain[ing] disproportionately concentrated on a few persons." *Penn Central Transportation Co.* v. *New York City,* 438 U. S., at 124. But it does not convert regulation into the unwanted physical occupation of land. Because they voluntarily open their property to occupation by others, petitioners cannot assert a *per se* right to compensation based on their inability to exclude particular individuals. See *Heart of Atlanta Motel, Inc.* v. *United States,* 379 U. S., at 261; see also *id.,* at 259 ("[A]ppellant has no 'right' to select its guests as it sees fit, free from governmental regulation"); *PruneYard Shopping Center* v. *Robins,* 447 U. S., at 82–84.

Petitioners' final line of argument rests on a footnote in *Loretto,* in which we rejected the contention that "the landlord could avoid the requirements of [the statute forcing her to permit cable to be permanently placed on her property] by ceasing to rent the building to tenants." We found this possibility insufficient to defeat a physical taking claim, because "a landlord's ability to rent his property may not be conditioned on his forfeiting the right to compensation for a physical occupation." *Loretto,* 458 U. S., at 439, n. 17. Petitioners argue that if they have to leave the mobile home park business in order to avoid the strictures of the Escondido 532*532 ordinance, their ability to rent their property has in fact been conditioned on such a forfeiture. This argument fails at its base, however, because there has simply been no compelled physical occupation giving rise to a right to compensation that petitioners could have forfeited. Had the city required such an occupation, of course, petitioners would have a right to compensation, and the city might then lack the power to condition petitioners' ability to run mobile home parks on their waiver of this right. Cf. *Nollan* v. *California Coastal Comm'n,* 483 U. S., at 837. But because the ordinance does not effect a physical taking in the first place, this footnote in *Loretto* does not help petitioners.

With respect to physical takings, then, this case is not far removed from *FCC* v. *Florida Power Corp.,* 480 U. S. 245 (1987), in which the respondent had voluntarily leased space on its utility poles to a cable television company for the installation of cables. The Federal Government, exercising its statutory authority to regulate pole attachment agreements, substantially reduced the annual rent. We rejected the respondent's claim that "it is a taking under *Loretto* for a tenant invited to lease at a rent of $7.15 to remain at the regulated rent of $1.79." *Id.*, at 252. We explained that "it is the invitation, not the rent, that makes the difference. The line which separates [this case] from *Loretto* is the unambiguous distinction between a ... lessee and an interloper with a government license." *Id.*, at 252–253. The distinction is equally unambiguous here. The Escondido rent control ordinance, even considered against the backdrop of California's Mobilehome Residency Law, does not authorize an unwanted physical occupation of petitioners' property. It is a regulation of petitioners' *use* of their property, and thus does not amount to a *per se* taking.

Loretto v. Teleprompter Manhattan CATV Corporation

458 U.S. 419 (1982)

Facts
With the previous owner's permission, Teleprompter installed cable lines and two cable boxes on the roof of the apartment building that was purchased by Loretto in 1971. In 1973, the State of New York enacted a law that prevented property owners from interfering with the installation of cable equipment on their properties. In 1976, Loretto filed a class action suit against Teleprompter on behalf of all New York owners of real property on which the company had installed equipment.

Issue
Does a state law requiring property owners to allow a cable television company to permanently install cable facilities on their property constitute a taking, requiring just compensation under the Fifth and Fourteenth Amendments?

Held
Yes. Regardless of the important public benefits the law might serve, permanent physical occupation by the government of private property is one of the most serious forms of invasion because it undermines all of a property owner's rights. The size of the physical occupation is irrelevant in the determination of a taking.

Discussion
The Court mused that if a state law required landlords to allow the construction of swimming pools on their property by a third party, it would clearly be a taking; despite the relative size of Teleprompter's cable equipment, it

constituted a physical taking that requires compensation under the Fifth Amendment.

Case Excerpt

The Court's recent Takings Clause decisions teach that *nonphysical* government intrusions on private property, such as zoning ordinances and other land-use restrictions, have become the rule rather than the exception. Modern government regulation exudes intangible "externalities" that may diminish the value of private property far more than minor physical touchings. Nevertheless, as the Court recognizes, it has "often upheld substantial regulation of an owner's use of his own property where deemed necessary to promote the public interest." *Ante,* at 426. See, *e. g., Agins* v. *City of Tiburon,* 447 U. S. 255 (1980); *Penn Central Transportation Co.* v. *New York City,* 438 U. S. 104, 124–125 (1978); *Village of Euclid* v. *Ambler Realty Co.,* 272 U. S. 365 (1926).

Precisely because the extent to which the government may injure private interests now depends so little on whether or not it has authorized a "physical contact," the Court has avoided *per se* takings rules resting on outmoded distinctions between physical and nonphysical intrusions. As one commentator has observed, a takings rule based on such a distinction is inherently suspect because "its capacity to distinguish, even crudely, between significant and insignificant losses is too puny to be taken seriously." Michelman, Property, Utility, and Fairness: Comments on the Ethical Foundations of "Just Compensation" Law, 80 Harv. L. Rev. 1165, 1227 (1967).

Surprisingly, the Court draws an even finer distinction today – between "temporary physical invasions" and "permanent physical occupations." When the government authorizes the latter type of intrusion, the Court would find "a taking without regard to the public interests" the regulation may serve. *Ante,* at 426. Yet an examination of each of the three words in the Court's "permanent physical occupation" formula illustrates that the newly created distinction is even less substantial than the distinction between physical and nonphysical intrusions that the Court already has rejected.

First, what does the Court mean by "permanent"? Since all "temporary limitations on the right to exclude" remain "subject to a more complex balancing process to determine whether they are a taking," *ante,* at 435, n. 12, the Court presumably describes a government intrusion that lasts forever. But as the Court itself concedes, § 828 does not require appellant to permit the cable installation forever, but only "[s]o long as the property remains residential and a CATV company wishes to retain the installation." *Ante,* at 439. This is far from "permanent."

The Court reaffirms that "States have broad power to regulate housing conditions in general and the landlord-tenant relationship in particular without paying compensation for all economic injuries that such regulation entails." *Ante,* at 440. Thus, § 828 merely defines one of the many statutory responsibilities that a New Yorker accepts when she enters the rental business. If appellant occupies her own building, or converts it into a commercial property, she becomes perfectly free to exclude **Teleprompter** from her one-eighth cubic foot of roof space. But once appellant chooses to use her property for rental purposes, she must comply with all reasonable government statutes regulating the landlord-tenant relationship. If § 828 authorizes a "permanent" occupation, and thus works a taking "without regard to the public interests that it may serve," then all other New York statutes that require a landlord to make physical attachments to his rental property also must constitute takings, even if they serve indisputably valid public interests in tenant protection and safety.

The Court denies that its theory invalidates these statutes, because they "do not require the landlord to suffer the physical occupation of a portion of his building by a third party." *Ante,* at 440. But surely this factor cannot be determinative, since the Court simultaneously recognizes that temporary invasions by third parties are not subject to a *per se* rule. Nor can the qualitative difference arise from the incidental fact that, under § 828, **Teleprompter,** rather than appellant or her tenants, owns the cable installation. Cf. *ante,* at 440, and n. 19. If anything, § 828 leaves appellant better off than do other housing statutes, since it ensures that her property will not be damaged esthetically or physically, see n. 4, *supra,* without burdening her with the cost of buying or maintaining the cable.

In any event, under the Court's test, the "third party" problem would remain even if appellant herself owned the cable. So long as **Teleprompter** continuously passed its electronic signal through the cable, a litigant could argue that the second element of the Court's formula – a "physical touching" by a stranger – was satisfied and that § 828 therefore worked a taking. Literally read, the Court's test opens the door to endless metaphysical struggles over whether or not an individual's property has been "physically" touched. It was precisely to avoid "permit[ting] technicalities of form to dictate consequences of substance," *United States* v. *Central Eureka Mining Co.,* 357 U. S. 155, 181 (1958) (Harlan, J., dissenting), that the Court abandoned a "physical contacts" test in the first place.

Third, the Court's talismanic distinction between a continuous "occupation" and a transient "invasion" finds no basis in either economic logic or Takings Clause precedent. In the landlord-tenant context, the Court has upheld against takings challenges rent control statutes permitting "temporary" physical invasions of considerable economic magnitude. See, *e. g., Block* v. *Hirsh,* 256 U. S. 135 (1921) (statute permitting tenants to remain in physical possession of their apartments for two years after the termination of their leases). Moreover, precedents record numerous other "temporary" officially authorized invasions by third parties that have intruded into an owner's enjoyment of property far more deeply than did **Teleprompter's** long-unnoticed cable. See, *e. g., PruneYard Shopping Center* v. *Robins,* 447 U. S. 74 (1980) (leafletting and demonstrating in busy shopping center); *Kaiser Aetna* v. *United States,* 444 U. S. 164 (1979) (public easement of passage to private pond); *United States* v. *Causby,* 328 U. S. 256 (1946) (noisy airplane flights over private land). While, under the Court's balancing test, some of these "temporary invasions" have been found to be takings, the Court has subjected none of them to the inflexible *per se* rule now adapted to analyze the far less obtrusive "occupation" at issue in the present case. Cf. *ante,* at 430–431, 432–435.

In sum, history teaches that takings claims are properly evaluated under a multifactor balancing test. By directing that all "permanent physical occupations" automatically are compensable, "without regard to whether the action achieves an important public benefit or has only minimal economic impact on the owner," *ante,* at 434–435, the Court does not further equity so much as it encourages litigants to manipulate their factual allegations to gain the benefit of its *per se* rule. Cf. n. 8, *supra.* I do not relish the prospect of distinguishing the inevitable flow of certiorari petitions attempting to shoehorn insubstantial takings claims into today's "set formula."

Kelo v. City of New London

545 U.S. 469 (2005)

Facts
The city of New London was economically distressed. In the late 1990s, the city authorized the New London Development Corporation (NLDC), a private non-profit group to assist with economic development by purchasing or acquiring properties as necessary. If an owner refused to sell, the city would acquire the property through eminent domain. Property obtained through eminent domain would ultimately be transferred to attractive commercial entities viewed as beneficial to New London's development plan. Nine petitioners who refused to sell brought suit when eminent domain proceedings were instituted against them for the purpose of transferring the property to a pharmaceutical company.

Issue
Did the city's condemnation of private properties for the purposes of economic development satisfy the "public use" requirement of the Takings Clause of the Fifth Amendment?

Held
Yes. The state may acquire private property through eminent domain so long as the reason for the taking was for public use. Here, "public use" was given a broader meaning of "public purpose," thereby including economic development as a valid public use.

Discussion
"Promoting economic development is a traditional and long-accepted function of government." Relying on precedent, the Court held that the goals of economic development demand that areas be considered not on a piecemeal basis, but in light of the entire plan, hence it was irrelevant that petitioners' properties were not themselves blighted.

Case Excerpt

We granted certiorari to determine whether a city's decision to take property for the purpose of economic development satisfies the "public use" requirement of the Fifth Amendment. 542 U. S. 965 (2004).

Two polar propositions are perfectly clear. On the one hand, it has long been accepted that the sovereign may not take the property of *A* for the sole purpose of transferring it to another private party *B*, even though *A* is paid just compensation. On the other hand, it is equally clear that a State may transfer property from one private party to another if future "use by the public" is the purpose of the taking; the condemnation of land for a railroad with common-carrier duties is a familiar example. Neither of these propositions, however, determines the disposition of this case.

As for the first proposition, the City would no doubt be forbidden from taking petitioners' land for the purpose of conferring a private benefit on a particular private party. See *Midkiff,* 467 U. S., at 245 ("A purely private taking could not withstand the scrutiny of the public use requirement; it would serve no legitimate purpose of government and would thus be void"); *Missouri Pacific R. Co.* v. *Nebraska,* 164 U. S. 403 (1896). Nor would the City be allowed to take property under the mere pretext of a public purpose, when its actual purpose was to bestow a private benefit. The takings before us, however, would be executed pursuant to a "carefully considered" development plan. 268 Conn., at 54, 843 A. 2d, at 536. The trial judge and all the members of the Supreme Court of Connecticut agreed that there was no evidence of an illegitimate purpose in this case. Therefore, as was true of the statute challenged in *Midkiff,* 467 U. S., at 245, the City's development plan was not adopted "to benefit a particular class of identifiable individuals."

On the other hand, this is not a case in which the City is planning to open the condemned land – at least not in its entirety – to use by the general public. Nor will the private lessees of the land in any sense be required to operate like common carriers, making their services available to all comers. But although such a projected use would be sufficient to satisfy the public use requirement, this "Court long ago rejected any literal requirement that condemned property be put into use for the general public." *Id.,* at 244. Indeed, while many state courts in the mid-19th century endorsed "use by the public" as the proper definition of public use, that narrow view steadily eroded over time. Not only was the "use by the public" test difficult to administer (*e. g.,* what proportion of the public need have access to the property? at what price?), but it proved to be impractical given the diverse and always evolving needs of society. Accordingly, when this Court began applying the Fifth Amendment to the States at the close of the 19th century, it embraced the broader and more natural interpretation of public use as "public purpose." See, *e. g., Fallbrook Irrigation Dist.* v. *Bradley,* 164 U. S. 112, 158–164 (1896). Thus, in a case upholding a mining company's use of an aerial bucket line to transport ore over property it did not own, Justice Holmes' opinion for the Court stressed "the inadequacy of use by the general public as a universal test." *Strickley* v. *Highland Boy Gold Mining Co.,* 200 U. S. 527, 531 (1906). We have repeatedly and consistently rejected that narrow test ever since.

The disposition of this case therefore turns on the question whether the City's development plan serves a "public purpose." Without exception, our cases have defined that concept broadly, reflecting our longstanding policy of deference to legislative judgments in this field.

In *Berman* v. *Parker,* 348 U. S. 26 (1954), this Court upheld a redevelopment plan targeting a blighted area of Washington, D. C., in which most of the housing for the area's 5,000 inhabitants was beyond repair. Under the plan, the area would be condemned and part of it utilized for the construction of streets, schools, and other public facilities. The remainder of the land would be leased or sold to private parties for the purpose of redevelopment, including the construction of low-cost housing.

The owner of a department store located in the area challenged the condemnation, pointing out that his store was not itself blighted and arguing that the creation of a "better balanced, more attractive community" was not a valid public use. *Id.,* at 31. Writing for a unanimous Court, Justice Douglas refused to evaluate this claim in isolation, deferring instead to the legislative and agency judgment that the area "must be planned as a whole" for the plan to be successful. *Id.,* at 34. The Court explained that "community redevelopment programs need not, by force of the Constitution, be on a piecemeal basis – lot by lot, building by building." *Id.,* at 35. The public use underlying the taking was unequivocally affirmed:

"We do not sit to determine whether a particular housing project is or is not desirable. The concept of the public welfare is broad and inclusive... The values it represents are spiritual as well as physical, aesthetic as well as monetary. It is within the power of the legislature to determine that the community should be beautiful as well as healthy, spacious as well as clean, well-balanced as well as carefully patrolled. In the present case, the Congress and its authorized agencies have made determinations that take into account a wide variety of values. It is not for us to reappraise them. If those who govern the District of Columbia decide that the Nation's Capital should be beautiful as well as sanitary, there is nothing in the Fifth Amendment that stands in the way." *Id.,* at 33.

In *Hawaii Housing Authority* v. *Midkiff,* 467 U. S. 229 (1984), the Court considered a Hawaii statute whereby fee title was taken from lessors and transferred to lessees (for just compensation) in order to reduce the concentration of land ownership. We unanimously upheld the statute and rejected the Ninth Circuit's view that it was "a naked attempt on the part of the state of Hawaii to take the property of A and transfer it to B solely for B's private use and benefit." *Id.,* at 235 (internal quotation marks omitted). Reaffirming *Berman*'s deferential approach to legislative judgments in this field, we concluded that the State's purpose of eliminating the "social and economic evils of a land oligopoly" qualified as a valid public use. 467 U. S., at 241–242. Our opinion also rejected the contention that the mere fact that the State immediately transferred the properties to private individuals upon condemnation somehow diminished the public character of the taking. "[I]t is only the taking's purpose, and not its mechanics," we explained, that matters in determining public use. *Id.,* at 244.

In that same Term we decided another public use case that arose in a purely economic context. In *Ruckelshaus* v. *Monsanto Co.*, 467 U. S. 986 (1984), the Court dealt with provisions of the Federal Insecticide, Fungicide, and Rodenticide Act under which the Environmental Protection Agency could consider the data (including trade secrets) submitted by a prior pesticide applicant in evaluating a subsequent application, so long as the second applicant paid just compensation for the data. We acknowledged that the "most direct beneficiaries" of these provisions were the subsequent applicants, *id.,* at 1014, but we nevertheless upheld the statute under *Berman* and *Midkiff.* We found sufficient Congress' belief that sparing applicants the cost of time-consuming research eliminated a significant barrier to entry in the pesticide market and thereby enhanced competition. 467 U. S., at 1015.

Viewed as a whole, our jurisprudence has recognized that the needs of society have varied between different parts of the Nation, just as they have evolved over time in response to changed circumstances. Our earliest cases in particular embodied a strong theme of federalism, emphasizing the "great respect" that we owe to state legislatures and state courts in discerning local public needs. See *Hairston* v. *Danville & Western R. Co.*, 208 U. S. 598, 606–607 (1908) (noting that these needs were likely to vary depending on a State's "resources, the capacity of the soil, the relative importance of industries to the general public welfare, and the long-established methods and habits of the people"). For more than a century, our public use jurisprudence has wisely eschewed rigid formulas and intrusive scrutiny in favor of affording legislatures broad latitude in determining what public needs justify the use of the takings power.

Those who govern the City were not confronted with the need to remove blight in the Fort Trumbull area, but their determination that the area was sufficiently distressed to justify a program of economic rejuvenation is entitled to our deference. The City has carefully formulated an economic development plan that it believes will provide appreciable benefits to the community, including – but by no means limited to – new jobs and increased tax revenue. As with other exercises in urban planning and development, the City is endeavoring to coordinate a variety of commercial, residential, and recreational uses of land, with the hope that they will form a whole greater than the sum of its parts. To effectuate this plan, the City has invoked a state statute that specifically authorizes the use of eminent domain to promote economic development. Given the comprehensive character of the plan, the thorough deliberation that preceded its adoption, and the limited scope of our review, it is appropriate for us, as it was in *Berman,* to resolve the challenges of the individual owners, not on a piecemeal basis, but rather in light of the entire plan. Because that plan unquestionably serves a public purpose, the takings challenged here satisfy the public use requirement of the Fifth Amendment.

To avoid this result, petitioners urge us to adopt a new bright-line rule that economic development does not qualify as a public use. Putting aside the unpersuasive suggestion that the City's plan will provide only purely economic benefits, neither precedent nor logic supports petitioners' proposal. Promoting economic development is a traditional and long-accepted function of government. There is, moreover, no principled way of distinguishing economic development from the other public purposes that we have recognized. In our cases upholding takings that facilitated agriculture and mining, for example, we emphasized the importance of those industries to the welfare of the States in question, see, *e. g., Strickley,* 200 U. S. 527; in *Berman,* we endorsed the purpose of transforming a blighted area into a "well-balanced" community through redevelopment, 348 U. S., at 33; in *Midkiff,* we upheld the interest in breaking up a land oligopoly that "created artificial deterrents to the normal functioning of the State's residential land market," 467 U. S., at 242; and in *Monsanto,* we accepted Congress' purpose of eliminating a "significant barrier to entry in the pesticide market," 467 U. S., at 1014–1015. It would be incongruous to hold that the City's interest in the economic benefits to be derived from the development of the Fort Trumbull area has less of a public character than any of those other interests. Clearly, there is no basis for exempting economic development from our traditionally broad understanding of public purpose.

Petitioners contend that using eminent domain for economic development impermissibly blurs the boundary between public and private takings. Again, our cases foreclose this objection. Quite simply, the government's pursuit of a public purpose will often benefit individual private parties. For example, in *Midkiff,* the forced transfer of property conferred a direct and significant benefit on those lessees who were previously unable to purchase their homes. In *Monsanto,* we recognized that the "most direct beneficiaries" of the data-sharing provisions were the subsequent pesticide applicants, but benefiting them in this way was necessary to promoting competition in the pesticide market. 467 U. S., at 1014. The owner of the department store in *Berman* objected to "taking from one businessman for the benefit of another businessman," 348 U. S., at 33, referring to the fact that under the redevelopment plan land would be leased or sold to private developers for redevelopment. Our rejection of that contention has particular relevance to the instant case: "The public end may be as well or better served through an agency of private enterprise than through a department of government – or so the Congress might conclude. We cannot say that public ownership is the sole method of promoting the public purposes of community redevelopment projects." *Id.,* at 33–34.

It is further argued that without a bright-line rule nothing would stop a city from transferring citizen *A*'s property to citizen *B* for the sole reason that citizen *B* will put the property to a more productive use and thus pay more taxes. Such a one-to-one transfer of property, executed outside the confines of an integrated development plan, is not presented in this case. While such an unusual exercise of government power would certainly raise a suspicion that a private purpose was afoot, the hypothetical cases posited by petitioners can be confronted if and when they arise. They do not warrant the crafting of an artificial restriction on the concept of public use.

Alternatively, petitioners maintain that for takings of this kind we should require a "reasonable certainty" that the expected public benefits will actually accrue. Such a rule, however, would represent an even greater departure from our precedent. "When the legislature's purpose is legitimate and its means are not irrational, our cases make clear that empirical debates over the wisdom of takings – no less than debates over the wisdom of other kinds of socioeconomic legislation – are not to be carried out in the federal courts." *Midkiff,* 467 U. S., at 242–243. Indeed, earlier this Term we explained why similar practical concerns (among others) undermined the use of the "substantially advances" formula in our regulatory takings doctrine. See *Lingle* v. *Chevron U. S. A. Inc.,* 544 U. S. 528, 544 (2005) (noting that this formula "would empower – and might often require – courts to substitute their predictive judgments for those of elected legislatures and expert agencies"). The disadvantages of a heightened form of review are especially pronounced in this type of case. Orderly implementation of a comprehensive redevelopment plan obviously requires that the legal rights of all interested parties be established before new construction can be commenced. A constitutional rule that required postponement of the judicial approval of every condemnation until the likelihood of success of the plan had been assured would unquestionably impose a significant impediment to the successful consummation of many such plans.

Just as we decline to second-guess the City's considered judgments about the efficacy of its development plan, we also decline to second-guess the City's determinations as to what lands it needs to acquire in order to effectuate the project. "It is not for the courts to oversee the choice of the boundary line nor to sit in review on the size of a particular project area. Once the question of the public purpose has been decided, the amount and character of land to be taken for the project and the need for a particular tract to complete the integrated plan rests in the discretion of the legislative branch." *Berman,* 348 U. S., at 35–36.

In affirming the City's authority to take petitioners' properties, we do not minimize the hardship that condemnations may entail, notwithstanding the payment of just compensation. We emphasize that nothing in our opinion precludes any State from placing further restrictions on its exercise of the takings power. Indeed, many States already impose "public use" requirements that are stricter than the federal baseline. Some of these requirements have been established as a matter of state constitutional law, while others are expressed in state eminent domain statutes that carefully limit the grounds upon which takings may be exercised. As the submissions of the parties and their *amici* make clear, the necessity and wisdom of using eminent domain to promote economic development are certainly matters of legitimate public debate. This Court's authority, however, extends only to determining whether the City's proposed condemnations are for a "public use" within the meaning of the Fifth Amendment to the Federal Constitution. Because over a century of our case law interpreting that provision dictates an affirmative answer to that question, we may not grant petitioners the relief that they seek.

Primer on Possessory Takings as an Issue for Planners

What is "Taking"?

The Fifth Amendment to the U.S. Constitution provides, in part: "Nor shall private property be taken for public use without just compensation." This amendment establishes two constitutional protections that are important to land use disputes: due process and takings. While we deal separately with the issue of due process in Chapter 8, a brief summary is appropriate here. The due process clause in the constitution prohibits Congress from passing laws that do not substantially advance legitimate state interests. This means that a land use regulation is invalid if it does not further a legitimate public purpose. For example, a regulation that is adopted to favor only the private interests of one individual may not be considered to further a legitimate public purpose. The due process clause also guarantees that property owners are entitled to proper notice and the right to participate in public hearings when a unit of government passes a law that has a direct impact on a parcel of private property. This includes the right to challenge that decision in the court system.

In this chapter, we will focus on the issue of takings. There are two types: possessory and regulatory. In this chapter, we will focus on possessory takings. The Fifth Amendment permits units of the federal government to acquire private property for the purpose of putting the land to a public use, such as the widening of a road or the construction of a new water treatment plant. The law entitles the affected property owner to the payment of just compensation for the taken property. The underlying premise is that a private property owner should not be asked to bear a disproportionate burden for something that is intended to benefit the public at large. Generally, courts will expect that just compensation will be nearly equivalent to a fair market valuation of the property. The Founding Fathers bequeathed the same rights to states to confiscate property in the Eleventh Amendment. All states have divested eminent domain powers to units of local government, i.e. cities, towns, etc. These entities use their eminent domain powers to promote the public health, safety, and general welfare as established by the state's zoning enabling legislation. The use of eminent domain is not without controversy and is often relied on as a tool to respond to a "wicked problem" such as the one identified at the beginning of this chapter. The sections that follow break down the legal requirements and issues that commonly arise in possessory takings disputes.

Public v. Private Property

Private property is property that is owned by a non-governmental legal entity, such as a homeowner, small business proprietor, or a corporation. Public property, by contrast, is property that is owned by a unit of government. The mere fact that the property is publicly owned does not mean that the general public has the right to access it. Typically, however, public property is either utilized or intended to be used for a governmental function. For example, a public park is owned, operated, and maintained by a governmental entity and its delegees. The general public is welcome to use the park for its intended purposes during the designated hours of operation. Public elementary schools are also owned by units of government, i.e. school districts. While these buildings are public, the use of these buildings is more restrictive than a public park, given concerns regarding the safety of schoolchildren and the staff who serve them. Governmental entities may also hold undeveloped land from which they typically exclude the general public. This land is often kept by the governmental entity as a placeholder for the development of future public facilities, like water treatment plants, fire stations, or other public infrastructure projects.

Public Use Defined

Private property may be taken by a governmental entity for the development of a public use. Courts have broadly interpreted the dimensions of public uses. One of the most expansive definitions of the term originated in *Berman v. Parker*, 348 U.S. 26 (1954). In *Berman*, the high court validated a local government's taking of a private property containing a viable department store. While the store itself was marginally profitable, the Court upheld the taking because of the blighted nature of the surrounding neighborhood. The plaintiffs argued that their property was viable and income producing. Further, the department store owner argued that the property could not be taken away from them and turned over to a private developer for redevelopment in the name of urban renewal. The owner contended that "a taking from one businessman for the benefit of another businessman" did not constitute a public use.

The Supreme Court unanimously ruled in favor of the Planning Commission by arguing that the problem of large-scale blight needed to be addressed with a large-scale integrated redevelopment plan. Justice Douglas opined: "If owner after owner were permitted to resist these redevelopment programs on the ground that his particular property was not being used against the public interest, integrated plans for redevelopment would suffer greatly." The High Court judged the practice of urban renewal to be well within a locality's eminent domain powers. The Court further ruled that the taking of unblighted parcels of property was acceptable when they were part of a larger redevelopment plan. The Court ultimately declined to address the specifics of the plan, saying that "[o]nce the question of the public purpose has been decided, the amount and character of the land to be taken for a particular tract to complete the integrated plan rests in the discretion of the legislative branch."

Until very recently, courts commonly validated possessory takings carried out in the name of economic development. However, this common practice changed subsequent to the Supreme Court's ruling in *Kelo v. City of New London* (2005). In a 5–4 decision, the Supreme Court held that a private redevelopment plan qualified as a "public use" under the Takings Clause of the Fifth Amendment because of the general community benefits conferred by the redevelopment scheme.

A brief discussion of the facts of this case is necessary to explain the Court's ruling, as well as the nationwide political response to this decision. In 1999, the New Development Corporation (NDC), a city-sponsored redevelopment corporation, began buying and tearing down homes in the Fort Trumbull neighborhood of Connecticut. Among the homes targeted for destruction was the infamous little pink house owned by Suzette Kelo. Ms. Kelo refused to accept the NDC's fair market value offer for her home. She went to court and challenged the possessory taking on the grounds that the transfer of property from one private owner to another in the name of urban redevelopment was not an appropriate "public use" pursuant to the Fifth Amendment of the U.S. Constitution.

The Kelo case reached the U.S. Supreme Court in 2005. The Court ruled against Ms. Kelo, finding that the taking was a part of a comprehensive and necessary scheme for the redevelopment of a blighted area. The Kelo decision sparked a nationwide conversation about the appropriate use of eminent domain, leading 43 state legislatures to modify their constitutions to limit the instances where eminent domain may be utilized as a tool to correct for blight. This decision has had a chilling effect on redevelopment efforts in an economic climate that might have otherwise benefited from the use of this tool. New London is just now beginning to recover from the fall-out of this case. Until very recently, the neighborhood surrounding Kelo's house sat barren. Pfizer, the corporate giant for which the NDC had assembled the land, walked away from the project.

Temporary v. Permanent Possessory Taking

The time scale of a taking is important in the calculation of just compensation. A possessory taking may be either temporary or permanent. A temporary taking occurs when a local government divests a property owner from his or her land for a short period of time. This might occur, for example, if the local government needs to store road building equipment on private property during a road widening project. While property owners may not be completely and permanently displaced from their land, they are entitled to just compensation for the portion of their land taken during the period it was occupied by the equipment. In the alternative, a property is permanently taken when the government seeks to occupy a private parcel of property, or a portion of it, for an indefinite period of time. Following the previous example, a local government permanently divests a property owner from his or her property when it takes the property and tears down the structures on it to build a new public road across it. In both instances, just compensation is appropriate. The value paid to the property owner is dependent on both the time and degree of the possessory taking.

Just Compensation

In the instance that the government has taken private property, the Fifth Amendment requires the payment of just compensation to the affected owner of the property. Typically, the government makes an offer to the property owner based on what it judges to be the market value of the property. There is not a bright line rule regarding the calculation of fair market value. The general principle that guides compensation is what a willing buyer would pay a willing seller for the property on the open market, *Olson v. United States*, 292 U.S. 246 (1934). Deviation from this general guideline is deemed appropriate "when market value has been too difficult to find, or when its application would result in manifest injustice to owner or public," *United States v. Commodities Trading Corp.*, 339 U.S. 121, 123 (1950). It is common for the affected property owner to reject the government's offer of fair market value. At this point, the matter is assigned to a court who will hear experts hired by both the government and the affected property owner. The court utilizes this information to establish the fair market value of the property. Unless appealed, the fair market value determination stands. The government must either pay that amount to the affected property owner or retract its offer to acquire the private property through the use of eminent domain.

Response to Wicked Problem

The wicked problem at the start of this chapter asks you to consider two issues: (1) Does the proposed use of the property as a regional entertainment venue constitute a public use?; and (2) if so, did the county unfairly capitalize on the economic downturn in making its fair market value offers to the affected property owners?

With respect to the first issue, it is important for you to have some historical context of the actual case upon which this hypothetical is based. This possessory takings wicked problem is roughly based on a real dispute that occurred in Wyandotte County, Kansas prior to the Supreme Court's decision in the *Kelo* case. The real issue involved the location of a NASCAR track and the commercial development surrounding it. The government of Wyandotte County, Kansas was desperate for the magnitude of development that comes with the location of a major regional sports stadium. Representatives from the speedway began negotiating with the county after the Kansas legislature agreed to allow the county to offer a series of tax incentives to the developer, including land assemblage by the county (Brinson, 2006).

Together, the county and the speedway representatives elected to locate the new race track near the intersection of Interstate 435 and Interstate 70, given the prime accessibility to the site. The selected site was not vacant. Rather, it was home to 136 single-family residences. Through the use of eminent domain, the county acquired the property for the speedway's construction. The use of eminent domain for the acquisition of property led to major litigation from the property owners who charged that the taking violated the Fifth Amendment to the U.S. Constitution because, while the land was assembled by the government, it was being turned over to a private entity for redevelopment.

Ultimately, the Kansas Supreme Court upheld the use of eminent domain to take private property for economic development purposes. The Court held that the Kansas Speedway was a valid project for public purposes and therefore ruled that eminent domain authority could be exercised. Construction began on the speedway's 1.5-mile oval track and 75,000-seat stadium in May 1999 (Caper, 2011). The project was completed in early 2001 and held its first event in June 2001, the NASCAR Winston West Series Kansas 150 (Caper, 2012).

The *Kelo* decision, in essence, validated the use of eminent domain for urban redevelopment projects spearheaded by private entities. Accordingly, a similarly situated court would likely find that the public use identified in the possessory takings wicked problem to be acceptable pursuant to the Fifth Amendment. However, many states have modified their constitutional provisions related to takings, including Kansas. This has made it difficult, if not impossible, for local governments to assemble private property to give over to a private developer in the name of economic redevelopment. In the absence of such legal authority, local governments have been forced to become creative about the ways in which they might facilitate large-scale urban revitalization projects, such as a regional entertainment venue.

One of the solutions to the limitation in powers resulting from the the post-*Kelo* legislation has been the creation of public-private partnerships. Rather than turning assembled property over to a private developer for revitalization, local governments have become co-developers in public-private partnerships. They retain ownership and, to some degree, control over these large-scale redevelopment processes. These partnerships will likely produce a more effective and integrated redevelopment scheme as private developers and municipalities work together to ensure the viability of such projects. In the meantime, public-private partnerships are a necessary relationship that ensures that large-scale economic redevelopment activities may continue in states that no longer allow for the use of land assembly to support privately spearheaded redevelopment activities.

With respect to the second issue identified in the possessory takings wicked problem, you are being asked to judge if the "fair market value" offered by the local government to the displaced property owners is, in fact, fair. Remember, there is no bright line rule about what constitutes "just compensation." If the general standard holds true, i.e. what a willing buyer would pay a willing seller on the open market, the government's offer must only reflect the value of an arm's length transaction at the time of the government's acquisition of the property. In this case, the property owner would be expected to bare the loss caused by the economic turmoil in the local housing market. However, a court might be sympathetic if it felt that the local government was unfairly using the opportunity to capitalize on the misfortune of the economic downturn.

As this wicked problem demonstrates, possessory takings are often necessary to facilitate large-scale economic redevelopment activities in some communities. At times, these revitalization schemes disproportionately impact private property owners in the name of the common good. The Fifth Amendment to the U.S. Constitution seeks to ensure, in these cases, that those who are harmed by such endeavors are compensated in a meaningful way. It is important for planners to understand, however, that financial compensation does not necessarily address the losses experienced by private property owners who are socially, emotionally, and nostalgically tied to their properties. Local governments should consider these more intangible factors before making the decision to divest property owners of their homesteads for the sake of the community as a whole.

Discussion Prompts

• What is a public use?
• How is economic development done in the post-*Kelo* legislative climate?

Bibliography

Brinson, N. (2006). Political, Economic, and Cultural Revival in Kansas City, Kansas. Thesis, Department of Geography and the Faculty of the Graduate School of the University of Kansas.

Caper, B. A. (2012). Big Changes in a Small County: A Case Study of Economic Development in Wyandotte County, Kansas. Thesis, University of Florida, available at: http://ufdcimages. uflib.ufl.edu/UF/E0/04/41/59/00001/CAPER_B.pdf (last accessed July 27, 2015).

Jacobs, Harvey M. and Bassett, Ellen M. (2010). All Sound, No Fury? Assessing the Impacts of State-based Kelo Laws on Planning Practice. Working Paper, Lincoln Institute of Land Policy.

Kanner, Gideon (2006). Kelo v. New London: Bad Law, Bad Policy, and Bad Judgment. *The Urban Lawyer*, 38: 2, 201–235, available at: www.americanbar.org/content/dam/aba/events/ real_property_trust_estate/joint_fall/2007/kelo_v_new_london_bad_law.authcheckdam.pdf (last accessed July 20, 2015).

López, Edward J., Jewell, R. Todd, and Campbell, Noel D. (2009). Pass a Law, Any Law, Fast! State Legislative Responses to the Kelo Backlash. *Review of Law and Economics*, 5:1, 101–135.

Salkin, P. (2014). Still an Issue: The Taking Issue at 40. *Touro Law Review*, 30, 245–254.

10

REGULATORY TAKINGS

Local regulations may constitute takings pursuant to the Fifth Amendment of the U.S. Constitution. An owner whose property is significantly devalued as a result of the passage of a local regulation may be compensated. Compensation may be given for both temporary and permanent takings.

Regulatory Takings Wicked Problem

You are the planner for a fictional town called Arid, a small town in the southeastern corner of Oklahoma with a population of 2,000. The town's population is stable but projected to double in the next two decades as a result of mineral exploration and extraction opportunities. Most of the current residents work in agricultural production or in the limited local service economy. The vitality of the town is strongly correlated with the productivity of the farming industry. The primary crop being produced is corn, which is a crop that requires significant irrigation from the town's aquifer system. The international market for this crop is strong and growing. There is equal pressure to convert undeveloped land in the town to the production of corn crops or, in the alternative, housing for the future population of residents. A small group of landowners is pushing for the rezoning of these underutilized lands for single-family residential and industrial land use activities. A doubling of population will necessitate the development of housing stock. Industrial zoning is important to support extraction efforts. Industrial activities utilize less water than farming corn, but water usage is still high.

This proposal has caused a rift between factions in the community. Farmers, understanding the limitation of water supply, are concerned that extraction activities will impact the quality and quantity of water available for the irrigation of crops. The environmentalists believe that intensive agriculture is hard on the natural habitat of the region. They are also concerned about the impact of extraction activities on the water supply. Large landowners in the area support the proposal to rezone as an opportunity to insert economic vitality into the failing local economy.

What is clear from a recent study of the aquifer system is that the groundwater reserves are diminishing and not recharging at expected rates. This is likely due not only to use but also as a result of drought conditions. If practices continue as they are, there is probably enough water in the aquifer for 50 years. More intensive land uses will shorten the period of available water supplies.

Figure 9 Credit: David D. Boeck

You are the town's sole planner. You have been directed by the mayor to draft a water concurrency ordinance for consideration by the town council, limiting future development to the availability of water supply. Pursuant to the ordinance, new development will not be permitted in town unless the applicant can demonstrate that there is sufficient water in the aquifer to support the new development for at least 25 years. For the purpose of this hypothetical, you need not concern yourself with anything beyond the 25-year period. The town council is looking into creating a 100-mile pipeline to bring in water from another region to meet the town's future needs.

All factions (farmers, environmentalists, and developers) are concerned about the development proposal. The farmers object to any new development that might limit the longevity of their farming activities. The environmentalists see this as a policy that does not preserve and protect water quality; instead, it seeks to deplete the resource in a "first come, first served" manner. On this issue, the developers are in agreement. They are already joining forces to challenge the ordinance you have been tasked with crafting. They believe that an ordinance of this nature will constitute a regulatory taking when applied to the undeveloped lands in the community. Are they correct?

Cases

The following cases will be useful to you as you attempt to analyze this chapter's wicked problem:

Penn Central Transportation Co. v. City of New York, 430 U.S. 104 (1978)
Lucas v. South Carolina Coastal Commission, 505 U.S. 1003 (1992)
First English Evangelical Lutheran Church of Glendale v. County of Los Angeles, 482
   U.S. 304 (1987)
Tahoe-Sierra Preservation Council, Inc. v. Tahoe Regional Planning Agency, 535 U.S.
   302 (2002)

Penn Central Transportation Co. v. City of New York

438 U.S. 104 (1978)

Facts

In the interest of historic preservation, New York City enacted a law that created a system for owners of designated buildings of historical importance to alter their properties. In 1968, Penn Central Transportation Company, owners of Grand Central Terminal, entered into a contract to build a multi-story office building above the Terminal, which was a designated landmark. After the Landmark Preservation Commission denied two successive applications submitted by Penn Central for construction, Penn Central filed suit, claiming that the denial constituted a taking.

Issue

Does the application of restrictions on development under the City's Landmark Preservation Law to Grand Central Terminal constitute a taking under the Fifth and Fourteenth Amendments?

Held

No. Determining whether a government action has constituted a taking depends on an assessment of the economic impact of the regulation on the property owner, the owner's distinct investment-backed expectations, and the character of the governmental action. The city's law did not transfer control of the property away from Penn Central, affect the present use of the terminal as it had been used for 65 years, prohibit Penn from submitting future applications for development, or prevent Penn transferring its air rights.

Discussion

The Supreme Court has repeatedly used its three-prong test established in *Penn Central* in assessing whether a government actor has created a regulatory taking requiring compensation under the Fifth and Fourteenth Amendments.

Case Excerpt

In contending that the New York City law has "taken" their property in violation of the Fifth and Fourteenth Amendments, appellants make a series of arguments, which, while tailored to the facts of this case, essentially urge that any substantial restriction imposed pursuant to a landmark law must be accompanied by just compensation if it is to be constitutional. Before considering these, we emphasize what is not in dispute. Because this Court has recognized, in a number of settings, that states and cities may enact land-use restrictions or controls to enhance the quality of life by preserving the character and desirable aesthetic features of a city, see *New Orleans* v. *Dukes,* 427 U. S. 297 (1976); *Young* v. *American Mini Theatres, Inc.,* 427 U. S. 50 (1976); *Village of Belle Terre* v. *Boraas,* 416 U. S. 1, 9–10 (1974); *Berman* v. *Parker,* 348 U. S. 26, 33 (1954); *Welch* v. *Swasey,* 214 U. S., at 108, appellants do not contest that New York City's objective of preserving structures and areas with special historic, architectural, or cultural significance is an entirely permissible governmental goal. They also do not dispute that the restrictions imposed on its parcel are appropriate means of securing the purposes of the New York City law. Finally, appellants do not challenge any of the specific factual premises of the decision below. They accept, for present purposes, both that the parcel of land occupied by Grand CentralTerminal must, in its present state, be regarded as capable of earning a reasonable return, and that the transferable development rights afforded appellants by virtue of the Terminal's designation as a landmark are valuable, even if not as valuable as the rights to construct above the Terminal. In appellants' view none of these factors derogate from their claim that New York City's law has affected a "taking."

They first observe that the airspace above the Terminal is a valuable property interest, citing *United States* v. *Causby, supra.* They urge that the Landmarks Law has deprived them of any gainful use of their "air rights" above the Terminal and that, irrespective of the value of the remainder of their parcel, the city has "taken" their right to this superjacent airspace, thus entitling them to "just compensation" measured by the fair market value of these air rights.

Apart from our own disagreement with appellants' characterization of the effect of the New York City law, see *infra,* at 134–135, the submission that appellants may establish a "taking" simply by showing that they have been denied the ability to exploit a property interest that they heretofore had believed was available for development is quite simply untenable. Were this the rule, this Court would have erred not only in upholding laws restricting the development of air rights, see *Welch* v. *Swasey, supra,* but also in approving those prohibiting both the subjacent, see *Goldblatt* v. *Hempstead,* 369 U. S. 590 (1962), and the lateral, see *Gorieb* v. *Fox,* 274 U. S. 603 (1927), development of particular parcels. "Taking" jurisprudence does not divide a single parcel into discrete segments and attempt to determine whether rights in a particular segment have been entirely abrogated. In deciding whether a particular governmental action has effected a taking, this Court focuses rather both on the character of the action and on the nature and extent of the interference with rights in the parcel as a whole – here, the city tax block designated as the "landmark site."

Secondly, appellants, focusing on the character and impact of the New York City law, argue that it affects a "taking" because its operation has significantly diminished the value of the Terminal site. Appellants concede that the decisions sustaining other land-use regulations, which, like the New York City law, are reasonably related to the promotion of the general welfare, uniformly reject the proposition that diminution in property value, standing alone, can establish a "taking," see *Euclid* v. *Ambler Realty Co.*, 272 U. S. 365 (1926) (75% diminution in value caused by zoning law); *Hadacheck* v. *Sebastian*, 239 U. S. 394 (1915) (87 1/2% diminution in value); cf. *Eastlake* v. *Forest City Enterprises, Inc.*, 426 U. S., at 674 n. 8, and that the "taking" issue in these contexts is resolved by focusing on the uses the regulations permit. See also *Goldblatt* v. *Hempstead, supra.* Appellants, moreover, also do not dispute that a showing of diminution in property value would not establish a "taking" if the restriction had been imposed as a result of historic-district legislation, see generally *Maher* v. *New Orleans*, 516 F. 2d 1051 (CA5 1975), but appellants argue that New York City's regulation of individual landmarks is fundamentally different from zoning or from historic-district legislation because the controls imposed by New York City's law apply only to individuals who own selected properties.

Stated baldly, appellants' position appears to be that the only means of ensuring that selected owners are not singled out to endure financial hardship for no reason is to hold that any restriction imposed on individual landmarks pursuant to the New York City scheme is a "taking" requiring the payment of "just compensation." Agreement with this argument would, of course, invalidate not just New York City's law, but all comparable landmark legislation in the Nation. We find no merit in it.

It is true, as appellants emphasize, that both historic district legislation and zoning laws regulate all properties within given physical communities whereas landmark laws apply only to selected parcels. But, contrary to appellants' suggestions, landmark laws are not like discriminatory or "reverse spot," zoning: that is, a land-use decision which arbitrarily singles out a particular parcel for different, less favorable treatment than the neighboring ones. See 2 A. Rathkopf, The Law of Zoning and Planning 26-4, and n. 6 (4th ed. 1978). In contrast to discriminatory zoning, which is the antithesis of land-use control as part of some comprehensive plan, the New York City law embodies a comprehensive plan to preserve structures of historic or aesthetic interest wherever they might be found in the city, and as noted, over 400 landmarks and 31 historic districts have been designated pursuant to this plan.

Equally without merit is the related argument that the decision to designate a structure as a landmark "is inevitably arbitrary or at least subjective, because it is basically a matter of taste," Reply Brief for Appellants 22, thus unavoidably singling out individual landowners for disparate and unfair treatment. The argument has a particularly hollow ring in this case. For appellants not only did not seek judicial review of either the designation or of the denials of the certificates of appropriateness and of no exterior effect, but do not even now suggest that the Commission's decisions concerning the Terminal were in any sense arbitrary or unprincipled. But, in any event, a landmark owner has a right to judicial review of any Commission decision, and, quite simply, there is no basis whatsoever for a conclusion that courts will have any greater difficulty identifying arbitrary or discriminatory action in the context of landmark regulation than in the context of classic zoning or indeed in any other context.

Next, appellants observe that New York City's law differs from zoning laws and historic-district ordinances in that the Landmarks Law does not impose identical or similar restrictions on all structures located in particular physical communities. It follows, they argue, that New York City's law is inherently incapable of producing the fair and equitable distribution of benefits and burdens of governmental action which is characteristic of zoning laws and historic-district legislation and which they maintain is a constitutional requirement if "just compensation" is not to be afforded. It is, of course, true that the Landmarks Law has a more severe impact on some landowners than on others, but that in itself does not mean that the law affects a "taking." Legislation designed to promote the general welfare commonly burdens some more than others. The owners of the brickyard in *Hadacheck*, of the cedar trees in *Miller* v. *Schoene*, and of the gravel and sand mine in *Goldblatt* v. *Hempstead*, were uniquely burdened by the legislation sustained in those cases. Similarly, zoning laws often affect some property owners more severely than others but have not been held to be invalid on that account. For example, the property owner in *Euclid* who wished to use its property for industrial purposes was affected far more severely by the ordinance than its neighbors who wished to use their land for residences.

In any event, appellants' repeated suggestions that they are solely burdened and unbenefited are factually inaccurate. This contention overlooks the fact that the New York City law applies to vast numbers of structures in the city in addition to the Terminal – all the structures contained in the 31 historic districts and over 400 individual landmarks, many of which are close to the Terminal. Unless we are to reject the judgment of the New York City Council that the preservation of landmarks benefits all New York citizens and all structures, both economically and by improving the quality of life in the city as a whole – which we are unwilling to do – we cannot conclude that the owners of the Terminal have in no sense been benefited by the Landmarks Law. Doubtless appellants believe they are more burdened than benefited by the law, but that must have been true, too, of the property owners in *Miller, Hadacheck, Euclid,* and *Goldblatt*.

Appellants' final broad-based attack would have us treat the law as an instance, like that in *United States* v. *Causby*, in which government, acting in an enterprise capacity, has appropriated part of their property for some strictly governmental purpose. Apart from the fact that *Causby* was a case of invasion of airspace that destroyed the use of the farm beneath and this New York City law has in noway impaired the present use of the Terminal, the Landmarks Law neither exploits appellants' parcel for city purposes nor facilitates nor arises from any entrepreneurial operations of the city. The situation is not remotely like that in *Causby* where the airspace above the property was in the flight pattern for military aircraft. The Landmarks Law's effect is simply to prohibit appellants or anyone else from occupying portions of the airspace above the Terminal, while permitting appellants to use the remainder of the parcel in a gainful fashion. This is no more an appropriation of property by government for its own uses than is a zoning law prohibiting, for "aesthetic" reasons, two or more adult theaters within a specified area, see *Young* v. *American Mini Theatres, Inc.*, 427 U. S. 50 (1976), or a safety regulation prohibiting excavations below a certain level. See *Goldblatt* v. *Hempstead*.

Rejection of appellants' broad arguments is not, however, the end of our inquiry, for all we have established thus far is that the New York City law is not rendered invalid by its failure to provide "just compensation" whenever a landmark owner is restricted in the exploitation of property interests, such as air rights, to a greater extent than provided for under applicable zoning laws. We now must consider whether the interference with appellants' property is of such a magnitude that "there must be an exercise of eminent domain and compensation to sustain [it]." *Pennsylvania Coal Co.* v. *Mahon,* 260 U. S., at 413. That inquiry may be narrowed to the question of the severity of the impact of the law on appellants' parcel, and its resolution in turn requires a careful assessment of the impact of the regulation on the Terminal site.

Unlike the governmental acts in *Goldblatt, Miller, Causby, Griggs,* and *Hadacheck,* the New York City law does not interfere in any way with the present uses of the Terminal. Its designation as a landmark not only permits, but contemplates, that appellants may continue to use the property precisely as it has been used for the past 65 years: as a railroad terminal containing office space and concessions. So the law does not interfere with what must be regarded as Penn Central's primary expectation concerning the use of the parcel. More importantly, on this record, we must regard the New York City law as permitting Penn Centralnot only to profit from the Terminal but also to obtain a "reasonable return" on its investment.

Appellants, moreover, exaggerate the effect of the law on their ability to make use of the air rights above the Terminal in two respects. First, it simply cannot be maintained, on this record, that appellants have been prohibited from occupying *any* portion of the airspace above the Terminal. While the Commission's actions in denying applications to construct an office building in excess of 50 stories above the Terminal may indicate that it will refuse to issue a certificate of appropriateness for any comparably sized structure, nothing the Commission has said or done suggests an intention to prohibit *any* construction above the Terminal. The Commission's report emphasized that whether construction would be allowed depended upon whether the proposed addition "would harmonize in scale, material, and character with [the Terminal]." Record 2251. Since appellants have not sought approval for the construction of a smaller structure, we do not know that appellants will be denied any use of any portion of the airspace above the Terminal.

Second, to the extent appellants have been denied the right to build above the Terminal, it is not literally accurate to say that they have been denied *all* use of even those pre-existing air rights. Their ability to use these rights has not been abrogated; they are made transferable to at least eight parcels in the vicinity of the Terminal, one or two of which have been found suitable for the construction of new office buildings. Although appellants and others have argued that New York City's transferable development-rights program is far from ideal, the New York courts here supportably found that, at least in the case of the Terminal, the rights afforded are valuable. While these rights may well not have constituted "just compensation" if a "taking" had occurred, the rights nevertheless undoubtedly mitigate whatever financial burdens the law has imposed on appellants and, for that reason, are to be taken into account in considering the impact of regulation. Cf. *Goldblatt* v. *Hempstead*, 369 U. S., at 594 n. 3.

On this record, we conclude that the application of New York City's Landmarks Law has not affected a "taking" of appellants' property. The restrictions imposed are substantially related to the promotion of the general welfare and not only permit reasonable beneficial use of the landmark site but also afford appellants opportunities further to enhance not only the Terminal site proper but also other properties.

Lucas v. South Carolina Coastal Commission

505 U.S. 1003 (1992)

Facts
In 1986, Lucas bought two lots on a barrier island near Charleston for the price of $975,000 with the intent of erecting single-family residences, similar to those on adjacent lots. Two years later, South Carolina passed the Beachfront Management Act as a way of preserving the state's delicate coastal resource. When applied to his property, the act barred Lucas from erecting any permanent habitable structures on his lots, leaving his property nearly worthless.

Issue
Did the Beachfront Management Act so substantially diminish the value of the Lucas property that it constituted a taking under the Fifth and Fourteenth Amendments?

Held
Yes. The act was an exercise of the state's police powers to mitigate the perceived harm that continued development, such as Lucas' proposed development, would have on "critical" coastal lands. Any newly legislated regulation that deprives a private property owner of all economically beneficial use of their land must have its origins in the state's private nuisance laws.

Discussion
Precedent had already maintained that the regulatory takings could be divided into two categories: physical invasion of private property and complete denial of all economically beneficial or productive use of private property by the owner. *Lucas* established the Court's "total takings" test.

Case Excerpt
Prior to Justice Holmes's exposition in *Pennsylvania Coal Co.* v. *Mahon*, 260 U. S. 393 (1922), it was generally thought that the Takings Clause reached only a "direct appropriation" of property, *Legal Tender Cases*, 12 Wall. 457, 551 (1871), or the functional equivalent of a "practical ouster of [the owner's]

116

possession," *Transportation Co. v. Chicago,* 99 U. S. 635, 642 (1879). See also *Gibson v. United States,* 166 U. S. 269, 275–276 (1897). Justice Holmes recognized in *Mahon,* however, that if the protection against physical appropriations of private property was to be meaningfully enforced, the government's power to redefine the range of interests included in the ownership of property was necessarily constrained by constitutional limits. 260 U. S., at 414–415. If, instead, the uses of private property were subject to unbridled, uncompensated qualification under the police power, "the natural tendency of human nature [would be] to extend the qualification more and more until at last private property disappear[ed]." *Id.,* at 415. These considerations gave birth in that case to the oft-cited maxim that, "while property may be regulated to a certain extent, if regulation goes too far it will be recognized as a taking." *Ibid.*

Nevertheless, our decision in *Mahon* offered little insight into when, and under what circumstances, a given regulation would be seen as going "too far" for purposes of the Fifth Amendment. In 70-odd years of succeeding "regulatory takings" jurisprudence, we have generally eschewed any "set formula" for determining how far is too far, preferring to "engag[e] in … essentially ad hoc, factual inquiries." *Penn Central Transportation Co. v. New York City,* 438 U. S. 104, 124 (1978) (quoting *Goldblatt v. Hempstead,* 369 U. S. 590, 594 (1962)). See Epstein, Takings: Descent and Resurrection, 1987 S. Ct. Rev. 1, 4. We have, however, described at least two discrete categories of regulatory action as compensable without case-specific inquiry into the public interest advanced in support of the restraint. The first encompasses regulations that compel the property owner to suffer a physical "invasion" of his property. In general (at least with regard to permanent invasions), no matter how minute the intrusion, and no matter how weighty the public purpose behind it, we have required compensation. For example, in *Loretto v. Teleprompter Manhattan CATV Corp.,* 458 U. S. 419 (1982), we determined that New York's law requiring landlords to allow television cable companies to emplace cable facilities in their apartment buildings constituted a taking, *id.,* at 435–440, even though the facilities occupied at most only 1 12 cubic feet of the landlords' property, see *id.,* at 438, n. 16. See also *United States v. Causby,* 328 U. S. 256, 265, and n. 10 (1946) (physical invasions of airspace); cf. *Kaiser Aetna v. United States,* 444 U. S. 164 (1979) (imposition of navigational servitude upon private marina).

The second situation in which we have found categorical treatment appropriate is where regulation denies all economically beneficial or productive use of land. See *Agins,* 447 U. S., at 260; see also *Nollan v. California Coastal Comm'n,* 483 U. S. 825, 834 (1987); *Keystone Bituminous Coal Assn. v. DeBenedictis,* 480 U. S. 470, 495 (1987); *Hodel v. Virginia Surface Mining & Reclamation Assn., Inc.,* 452 1016*1016 U. S. 264, 295–296 (1981). As we have said on numerous occasions, the Fifth Amendment is violated when land-use regulation "does not substantially advance legitimate state interests *or denies an owner economically viable use of his land.*" *Agins, supra,* at 260 (citations omitted) (emphasis added).

We have never set forth the justification for this rule. Perhaps it is simply, as Justice Brennan suggested, that total deprivation of beneficial use is, from the landowner's point of view, the equivalent of a physical appropriation. See *San Diego Gas & Electric Co.* v. *San Diego*, 450 U. S., at 652 (dissenting opinion). "[F]or what is the land but the profits thereof[?]" 1 E. Coke, Institutes, ch. 1, § 1 (1st Am. ed. 1812). Surely, at least, in the extraordinary circumstance when *no* productive or economically beneficial use of land is permitted, it is less realistic to indulge our usual assumption that the legislature is simply "adjusting the benefits and burdens of economic life," *Penn Central Transportation Co.*, 438 U. S., at 124, in a manner that secures an "average reciprocity of advantage" to everyone concerned, *Pennsylvania Coal Co.* v. *Mahon*, 260 U. S., at 415. And the *functional* basis for permitting the government, by regulation, to affect property values without compensation – that "Government hardly could go on if to some extent values incident to property could not be diminished without paying for every such change in the general law," *id.*, at 413 – does not apply to the relatively rare situations where the government has deprived a landowner of all economically beneficial uses.

On the other side of the balance, affirmatively supporting a compensation requirement, is the fact that regulations that leave the owner of land without economically beneficial or productive options for its use – typically, as here, by requiring land to be left substantially in its natural state – carry with them a heightened risk that private property is being pressed into some form of public service under the guise of mitigating serious public harm. See, *e. g.*, *Annicelli* v. *South Kingstown*, 463 A. 2d 133, 140–141 (R. I. 1983) (prohibition on construction adjacent to beach justified on twin grounds of safety and "conservation of open space"); *Morris County Land Improvement Co.* v. *Parsippany-Troy Hills Township*, 40 N. J.539, 552–553, 193 A. 2d 232, 240 (1963) (prohibition on filling marshlands imposed in order to preserve region as water detention basin and create wildlife refuge). As Justice Brennan explained: "From the government's point of view, the benefits flowing to the public from preservation of open space through regulation may be equally great as from creating a wildlife refuge through formal condemnation or increasing electricity production through a dam project that floods private property." *San Diego Gas & Elec. Co., supra*, at 652 (dissenting opinion). The many statutes on the books, both state and federal, that 1019*1019 provide for the use of eminent domain to impose servitudes on private scenic lands preventing developmental uses, or to acquire such lands altogether, suggest the practical equivalence in this setting of negative regulation and appropriation. See, *e. g.*, 16 U. S. C. § 410ff-1(a) (authorizing acquisition of "lands, waters, or interests [within Channel Islands National Park] (including but not limited to scenic easements)"); § 460aa-2(a) (authorizing acquisition of "any lands, or lesser interests therein, including mineral interests and scenic easements" within Sawtooth National Recreation Area); §§ 3921–3923 (authorizing acquisition of wetlands); N. C. Gen. Stat. § 113A-38 (1990) (authorizing acquisition of, *inter alia*, "'scenic easements'" within the North Carolina natural and scenic rivers system); Tenn. Code Ann.

§§ 11-15-101 to 11-15-108 (1987) (authorizing acquisition of "protective easements" and other rights in real property adjacent to State's historic, architectural, archaeological, or cultural resources).

We think, in short, that there are good reasons for our frequently expressed
belief that when the owner of real property has been called upon to sacrifice *all*
economically beneficial uses in the name of the common good, that is, to leave
his property economically idle, he has suffered a taking.

...The "total taking" inquiry we require today will ordinarily entail (as the
application of state nuisance law ordinarily entails) analysis of, among other
things, the degree of harm to public lands and resources, or adjacent private
property, posed by the claimant's proposed activities, see, *e. g.,* Restatement
(Second) of Torts §§ 826, 827, the social value of the claimant's activities
and their suitability to the locality in question, see, *e. g., id.,* §§ 828(a) and
(b), 831, and the relative ease with which the alleged harm can be avoided
through measures taken by the claimant and the government (or adjacent
private landowners) alike, see, *e. g., id.,* §§ 827(e), 828(c), 830. The fact that
a particular use has long been engaged in by similarly situated owners ordinarily imports a lack of any common-law prohibition (though changed circumstances or new knowledge may make what was previously permissible
no longer so, see *id.,* § 827, Comment g. So also does the fact that other
landowners, similarly situated, are permitted to continue the use denied to
the claimant.

It seems unlikely that common-law principles would have prevented the
erection of any habitable or productive improvements on petitioner's land;
they rarely support prohibition of the "essential use" of land, *Curtin* v. *Benson,*
222 U. S. 78, 86 (1911). The question, however, is one of state law to be dealt
with on remand. We emphasize that to win its case South Carolina must do
more than proffer the legislature's declaration that the uses Lucas desires are
inconsistent with the public interest, or the conclusory assertion that they
violate a common-law maxim such as *sic utere tuo ut alienum non laedas.* As
we have said, a "State, by *ipse dixit,* may not transform private property into
public property without compensation ..." *Webb's Fabulous Pharmacies, Inc.*
v. *Beckwith,* 449 U. S. 155, 164 (1980). Instead, as it would be required to
do if it sought to restrain Lucasin a commonlaw action for public nuisance,
South Carolina must identify background principles of nuisance and property
law that prohibit the uses he now intends in the circumstances in which the
property is presently found. Only on this showing can the State fairly claim
that, in proscribing all such beneficial uses, the Beach front Management Act
is taking nothing.

First English Evangelical Lutheran Church of Glendale v. County of Los Angeles

482 U.S. 304 (1987)

Facts

The First Evangelical Church owned acreage situated alongside the Mill Creek Canyon in the Angeles National Forest, which was used as a retreat center and recreational area known as "Lutherglen." In 1978, a year after a forest fire created serious flood hazards in the area, a flood ravaged Lutherglen and destroyed all of its buildings. The following year, Los Angeles County passed an interim ordinance prohibiting the construction of any buildings within Mill Creek Canyon in the interest of public health and safety. First Evangelical filed a complaint that the ordinance denied them all use of Lutherglen.

Issue

Does the Fifth Amendment require compensation for temporary regulatory takings?

Held

Yes. Regulatory takings, whether permanent or temporary, require compensation if the said regulation prohibits practical use of the property. After a court has found a taking, subsequent invalidation or amendment of the regulation or exercise of eminent domain does not relieve the government of its obligation to compensate for the period of time the owner was deprived of its property.

Discussion

Although the Court had repeatedly held that governmental regulatory takings require compensation under the constitution, it had yet to decide whether or not temporary but complete deprivations of property were compensable. In *First English*, the Court acknowledged the impact that the Court's holding could have on municipal governments' flexibility when drafting and enacting land use regulations, but that the constitution required such limits.

Case Excerpt

... the compensation question must begin with direct reference to the language of the Fifth Amendment, which provides in relevant part that "private property [shall not] be taken for public use, without just compensation." As its language indicates, and as the Court has frequently noted, this provision does not prohibit the taking of private property, but instead places a condition on the exercise of that power. See *Williamson County*, 473 U. S., at 194; *Hodel* v. *Virginia Surface Mining & Reclamation Assn., Inc.*, 452 U. S. 264, 297, n. 40 (1981); *Hurley* v. *Kincaid*, 285 U. S. 95, 104 (1932); *Monongahela Navigation Co.* v. *United States*, 148 U. S. 312, 336 (1893); *United States* v. *Jones*, 109 U. S. 513, 518 (1883). This basic understanding of the Amendment makes clear that it is designed not to limit the governmental interference with property rights *per se*, but rather to secure *compensation* in the event of otherwise proper interference amounting to a taking. Thus, government action that works a taking of property rights necessarily implicates the "constitutional obligation to pay just compensation." *Armstrong* v. *United States,* 364 U. S. 40, 49 (1960).

We have recognized that a landowner is entitled to bring an action in inverse condemnation as a result of "the self-executing character of the constitutional provision with respect to compensation ..." *United States* v. *Clarke,* 445 U. S. 253, 257 (1980), quoting 6 P. Nichols, Eminent Domain § 25.41 (3d rev. ed. 1972). As noted in JUSTICE BRENNAN's dissent in *San Diego Gas & Electric Co.,* 450 U. S., at 654–655, it has been established at least since *Jacobs* v. *United States,* 290 U. S. 13 (1933), that claims for just compensation are grounded in the Constitution itself:

"The suits were based on the right to recover just compensation for property taken by the United States for public use in the exercise of its power of eminent domain. *That right was guaranteed by the Constitution.* The fact that condemnation proceedings were not instituted and that the right was asserted in suits by the owners did not change the essential nature of the claim. The form of the remedy did not qualify the right. It rested upon the Fifth Amendment. Statutory recognition was not necessary. A promise to pay was not necessary. Such a promise was implied because of the duty to pay imposed by the Amendment. *The suits were thus founded upon the Constitution of the United States." Id.,* at 16. (Emphasis added.)

Jacobs, moreover, does not stand alone for the Court has frequently repeated the view that, in the event of a taking, the compensation remedy is required by the Constitution. See, *e. g., Kirby Forest Industries, Inc.* v. *United States,* 467 U. S. 1, 5 (1984); *United States* v. *Causby,* 328 U. S. 256, 267 (1946); *Seaboard Air Line R. Co.* v. *United States,* 261 U. S. 299, 304–306 (1923); *Monongahela Navigation, supra,* at 327.

It has also been established doctrine, at least since Justice Holmes' opinion for the Court in *Pennsylvania Coal Co.* v. *Mahon,* 260 U. S. 393 (1922), that "[t]he general rule at least is, that while property may be regulated to a certain extent, if regulation goes too far it will be recognized as a taking." *Id.,* at 415. While the typical taking occurs when the government acts to condemn property in the exercise of its power of eminent domain, the entire doctrine of inverse condemnation is predicated on the proposition that a taking may occur without such formal proceedings. In *Pumpelly* v. *Green Bay Co.,* 13 Wall. 166, 177–178 (1872), construing a provision in the Wisconsin Constitution identical to the Just Compensation Clause, this Court said:

"It would be a very curious and unsatisfactory result, if... it shall be held that if the government refrains from the absolute conversion of real property to the uses of the public it can destroy its value entirely, can inflict irreparable and permanent injury to any extent, can, in effect, subject it to total destruction without making any compensation, because, in the narrowest sense of that word, it is not *taken* for the public use."

Later cases have unhesitatingly applied this principle. See, *e. g., Kaiser Aetna* v. *United States,* 444 U. S. 164 (1979); *United States* v. *Dickinson,* 331 U. S. 745, 750 (1947); *United States* v. *Causby, supra.*

While the California Supreme Court may not have actually disavowed this general rule in *Agins,* we believe that it has truncated the rule by disallowing damages that occurred prior to the ultimate invalidation of the challenged regulation. The California Supreme Court justified its conclusion at length in the *Agins* opinion, concluding that:

"In combination, the need for preserving a degree of freedom in the land-use planning function, and the inhibiting financial force which inheres in the inverse condemnation remedy, persuade us that on balance mandamus or declaratory relief rather than inverse condemnation is the appropriate relief under the circumstances." 24 Cal. 3d, at 276–277, 598 P. 2d, at 31.

We, of course, are not unmindful of these considerations, but they must be evaluated in the light of the command of the Just Compensation Clause of the Fifth Amendment. The Court has recognized in more than one case that the government may elect to abandon its intrusion or discontinue regulations. See, *e. g., Kirby Forest Industries, Inc.* v. *United States, supra; United States* v. *Dow,* 357 U. S. 17, 26 (1958). Similarly, a governmental body may acquiesce in a judicial declaration that one of its ordinances has affected an unconstitutional taking of property; the landowner has no right under the Just Compensation Clause to insist that a "temporary" taking be deemed a permanent taking. But we have not resolved whether abandonment by the government requires payment of compensation for the period of time during which regulations deny a landowner all use of his land.

In considering this question, we find substantial guidance in cases where the government has only temporarily exercised its right to use private property. In *United States* v. *Dow, supra,* at 26, though rejecting a claim that the Government may not abandon condemnation proceedings, the Court observed that abandonment "results in an alteration in the property interest taken – from [one of] full ownership to one of temporary use and occupation... In such cases compensation would be measured by the principles normally governing the taking of a right to use property temporarily. See *Kimball Laundry Co.* v. *United States,* 338 U. S. 1 [1949]; *United States* v. *Petty Motor Co.,* 327 U. S. 372 [1946]; *United States* v. *General Motors Corp.,* 323 U. S. 373 [1945]." Each of the cases cited by the *Dow* Court involved appropriation of private property by the United States for use during World War II. Though the takings were in fact "temporary," see *United States* v. *Petty Motor Co.,* 327 U. S. 372, 375 (1946), there was no question that compensation would be required for the Government's interference with the use of the property; the Court was concerned in each case with determining the proper measure of the monetary relief to which the property holders were entitled. See *Kimball Laundry Co.* v. *United States,* 338 U. S. 1, 4–21 (1949); *Petty Motor Co., supra,* at 377–381; *United States* v. *General Motors Corp.,* 323 U. S. 373, 379–384 (1945).

These cases reflect the fact that "temporary" takings which, as here, deny a landowner all use of his property, are not different in kind from permanent takings, for which the Constitution clearly requires compensation. Cf. *San Diego Gas & Electric Co.*, 450 U. S., at 657 (BRENNAN, J., dissenting) ("Nothing in the Just Compensation Clause suggests that 'takings' must be permanent and irrevocable"). It is axiomatic that the Fifth Amendment's just compensation provision is "designed to bar Government from forcing some people alone to bear public burdens which, in all fairness and justice, should be borne by the public as a whole." *Armstrong v. United States*, 364 U. S., at 49. See also *Penn Central Transportation Co. v. New York City*, 438 U. S. 104, 123–125 (1978); *Monongahela Navigation Co. v. United States*, 148 U. S., at 325. In the present case the interim ordinance was adopted by the County of Los Angeles in January 1979, and became effective immediately. Appellant filed suit within a month after the effective date of the ordinance and yet when the California Supreme Court denied a hearing in the case on October 17, 1985, the merits of appellant's claim had yet to be determined. The United States has been required to pay compensation for leasehold interests of shorter duration than this. The value of a leasehold interest in property for a period of years may be substantial, and the burden on the property owner in extinguishing such an interest for a period of years may be great indeed. See, *e. g., United States v. General Motors, supra.* Where this burden results from governmental action that amounted to a taking, the Just Compensation Clause of the Fifth Amendment requires that the government pay the landowner for the value of the use of the land during this period. Cf. *United States v. Causby*, 328 U. S., at 261 ("It is the owner's loss, not the taker's gain, which is the measure of the value of the property taken"). Invalidation of the ordinance or its successor ordinance after this period of time, though converting the taking into a "temporary" one, is not a sufficient remedy to meet the demands of the Just Compensation Clause.

Appellee argues that requiring compensation for denial of all use of land prior to invalidation is inconsistent with this Court's decisions in *Danforth v. United States*, 308 U. S. 271 (1939), and *Agins v. Tiburon*, 447 U. S. 255 (1980). In *Danforth*, the landowner contended that the "taking" of his property had occurred prior to the institution of condemnation proceedings, by reason of the enactment of the Flood Control Act itself. He claimed that the passage of that Act had diminished the value of his property because the plan embodied in the Act required condemnation of a flowage easement across his property. The Court held that in the context of condemnation proceedings a taking does not occur until compensation is determined and paid, and went on to say that "[a] reduction or increase in the value of property may occur by reason of legislation for or the beginning or completion of a project," but "[s]uch changes in value are incidents of ownership. They cannot be considered as a 'taking' in the constitutional sense." *Danforth, supra*, at 285. *Agins* likewise rejected a claim that the city's preliminary activities constituted a taking, saying that "[m]ere fluctuations in value during the process of governmental decisionmaking, absent extraordinary delay, are 'incidents of ownership.'" See 447 U. S., at 263, n. 9.

But these cases merely stand for the unexceptional proposition that the valuation of property which has been taken must be calculated as of the time of the taking, and that depreciation in value of the property by reason of preliminary activity is not chargeable to the government. Thus, in *Agins,* we concluded that the preliminary activity did not work a taking. It would require a considerable extension of these decisions to say that no compensable regulatory taking may occur until a challenged ordinance has ultimately been held invalid.

Nothing we say today is intended to abrogate the principle that the decision to exercise the power of eminent domain is a legislative function "'for Congress and Congress alone to determine.'" *Hawaii Housing Authority* v. *Midkiff,* 467 U. S. 229, 240 (1984), quoting *Berman v. Parker,* 348 U. S. 26, 33 (1954). Once a court determines that a taking has occurred, the government retains the whole range of options already available – amendment of the regulation, withdrawal of the invalidated regulation, or exercise of eminent domain. Thus we do not, as the Solicitor General suggests, "permit a court, at the behest of a private person, to require the ... Government to exercise the power of eminent domain ..." Brief for United States as *Amicus Curiae* 22. We merely hold that where the government's activities have already worked a taking of all use of property, no subsequent action by the government can relieve it of the duty to provide compensation for the period during which the taking was effective.

We also point out that the allegation of the complaint which we treat as true for purposes of our decision was that the ordinance in question denied appellant all use of its property. We limit our holding to the facts presented, and of course do not deal with the quite different questions that would arise in the case of normal delays in obtaining building permits, changes in zoning ordinances, variances, and the like which are not before us. We realize that even our present holding will undoubtedly lessen to some extent the freedom and flexibility of land-use planners and governing bodies of municipal corporations when enacting land-use regulations. But such consequences necessarily flow from any decision upholding a claim of constitutional right; many of the provisions of the Constitution are designed to limit the flexibility and freedom of governmental authorities, and the Just Compensation Clause of the Fifth Amendment is one of them. As Justice Holmes aptly noted more than 50 years ago, "a strong public desire to improve the public condition is not enough to warrant achieving the desire by a shorter cut than the constitutional way of paying for the change." *Pennsylvania Coal Co.* v. *Mahon,* 260 U. S., at 416.

Here we must assume that the Los Angeles County ordinance has denied appellant all use of its property for a considerable period of years, and we hold that invalidation of the ordinance without payment of fair value for the use of the property during this period of time would be a constitutionally insufficient remedy. The judgment of the California Court of Appeal is therefore reversed, and the case is remanded for further proceedings not inconsistent with this opinion.

Tahoe-Sierra Preservation Council, Inc.
v. Tahoe Regional Planning Agency

535 U.S. 302 (2002)

Facts

As development in the Lake Tahoe Basin began to burgeon in the 1960s, increased impervious surface created runoff issues that affected the lake's renowned clarity. In an effort to create a comprehensive land use plan that would protect the area, the Tahoe Regional Planning Authority (TRPA) enacted two moratoria on development, virtually prohibiting all expansion within their jurisdiction for a period of 32 months. The Tahoe-Sierra Preservation Council, a non-profit organization representing local property owners, brought suit claiming that the moratoria had the effect of a regulatory taking.

Issue

Does a moratorium on residential development while a comprehensive land use plan is enacted constitute a per se taking of property under the Fifth Amendment?

Held

No. The moratorium enacted by TRPA did not constitute a taking because it did not deprive property owners of all economic benefit. While the Fifth Amendment distinguishes between physical and regulatory takings, the majority argued only physical takings need be compensated for. The Court refused to craft a new rule to determine whether or not a taking had occurred and instead, pointed to the *Penn Central Transportation Co. v. City of New York* three-prong test.

Discussion

Municipalities frequently use moratoria while crafting permanent land use development strategies. As a matter of sound policy, the Court refused to hold that any deprivation of all economic use, no matter how brief, would constitute a taking because it would undermine well-established police powers.

Case Excerpt

Considerations of "fairness and justice" arguably could support the conclusion that TRPA's moratoria were takings of petitioners' property based on any of seven different theories. First, even though we have not previously done so, we might now announce a categorical rule that, in the interest of fairness and justice, compensation is required whenever government temporarily deprives an owner of all economically viable use of her property. Second, we could craft a narrower rule that would cover all temporary land use restrictions except those "normal delays in obtaining building permits, changes in zoning ordinances, variances, and the like" which were put to one side in our opinion in *First English*, 482 U. S., at 321. Third, we could adopt a rule like the one suggested by an *amicus* supporting petitioners that would "allow a short fixed period for deliberations to take place without compensation – say maximum one year – after which the just compensation requirements" would "kick in." Fourth, with the benefit of hindsight, we might characterize the successive actions of TRPA as a "series of rolling moratoria" that were the functional equivalent of a permanent taking. Fifth, were it not for the findings of the District Court that TRPA acted diligently and in good faith, we might have concluded that the agency was stalling in order to avoid promulgating the environmental threshold carrying capacities and regional plan mandated by the 1980 Compact. Cf. *Monterey* v. *Del Monte Dunes at Monterey, Ltd.*, 526 U. S. 687, 698 (1999). Sixth, apart from the District Court's finding that TRPA's actions represented a proportional response to a serious risk of harm to the lake, petitioners might have argued that the moratoria did not substantially advance a legitimate state interest, see *Agins* and *Monterey*. Finally, if petitioners had challenged the application of the moratoria to their individual parcels, instead of making a facial challenge, some of them might have prevailed under a *Penn Central* analysis.

As the case comes to us, however, none of the last four theories is available. The "rolling moratoria" theory was presented in the petition for certiorari, but our order granting review did not encompass that issue, 533 U. S. 948 (2001); the case was tried in the District Court and reviewed in the Court of Appeals on the theory that each of the two moratoria was a separate taking, one for a 2-year period and the other for an 8-month period. 216 F. 3d, at 769. And, as we have already noted, recovery on either a bad faith theory or a theory that the state interests were insubstantial is foreclosed by the District Court's unchallenged findings of fact. Recovery under a *Penn Central* analysis is also foreclosed both because petitioners expressly disavowed that theory, and because they did not appeal from the District Court's conclusion that the evidence would not support it. Nonetheless, each of the three *per se* theories is fairly encompassed within the question that we decided to answer.

With respect to these theories, the ultimate constitutional question is whether the concepts of "fairness and justice" that underlie the Takings Clause will be better served by one of these categorical rules or by a *Penn Central* inquiry into all of the relevant circumstances in particular cases. From that perspective, the extreme categorical rule that any deprivation of all economic use, no matter how brief, constitutes a compensable taking surely cannot be sustained. Petitioners' broad submission would apply to numerous "normal delays in obtaining building permits, changes in zoning ordinances, variances, and the like," 482 U. S., at 321, as well as to orders temporarily prohibiting access to crime scenes, businesses that violate health codes, fire-damaged buildings, or other areas that we cannot now foresee. Such a rule would undoubtedly require changes in numerous practices that have long been considered permissible exercises of the police power. As Justice Holmes warned in *Mahon*, "[g]overnment hardly could go on if to some extent values incident to property could not be diminished without paying for every such change in the general law." 260 U. S., at 413. A rule that required compensation for every delay in the use of property would render routine government processes prohibitively expensive or encourage hasty decisionmaking. Such an important change in the law should be the product of legislative rulemaking rather than adjudication.

More importantly, for reasons set out at some length by Justice O'Connor in her concurring opinion in *Palazzolo* v. *Rhode Island*, 533 U. S., at 636, we are persuaded that the better approach to claims that a regulation has effected a temporary taking "requires careful examination and weighing of all the relevant circumstances." In that opinion, Justice O'Connor specifically considered the role that the "temporal relationship between regulatory enactment and title acquisition" should play in the analysis of a takings claim. *Id.*, at 632. We have no occasion to address that particular issue in this case, because it involves a different temporal relationship – the distinction between a temporary restriction and one that is permanent. Her comments on the "fairness and justice" inquiry are, nevertheless, instructive:

"Today's holding does not mean that the timing of the regulation's enactment relative to the acquisition of title is immaterial to the *Penn Central* analysis. Indeed, it would be just as much error to expunge this consideration from the takings inquiry as it would be to accord it exclusive significance. Our polestar instead remains the principles set forth in *Penn Central* itself and our other cases that govern partial regulatory takings. Under these cases, interference with investment-backed expectations is one of a number of factors that a court must examine…

"The Fifth Amendment forbids the taking of private property for public use without just compensation. We have recognized that this constitutional guarantee is 'designed to bar Government from forcing some people alone to bear public burdens which, in all fairness and justice, should be borne by the public as a whole.' *Penn Central*, [438 U. S.], at 123–124 (quoting *Arm- strong* v. *United States*, 364 U. S. 40, 49 (1960)). The concepts of 'fairness and justice' that underlie the Takings Clause, of course, are less than fully determinate. Accordingly, we have eschewed 'any "set formula" for determining when "justice and fairness" require that economic injuries caused by public action be compensated by the government, rather than remain disproportionately concentrated on a few persons.' *Penn Central, supra,* at 124 (quoting *Goldblatt* v. *Hemp- stead,* 369 U. S. 590, 594 (1962)). The outcome instead 'depends largely "upon the particular circumstances [in that] case."' *Penn Central, supra,* at 124 (quoting *United States* v. *Central Eureka Mining Co.,* 357 U. S. 155, 168 (1958))." *Id.,* at 633.

In rejecting petitioners' *per se* rule, we do not hold that the temporary nature of a land-use restriction precludes finding that it effects a taking; we simply recognize that it should not be given exclusive significance one way or the other.

A narrower rule that excluded the normal delays associated with processing permits, or that covered only delays of more than a year, would certainly have a less severe impact on prevailing practices, but it would still impose serious financial constraints on the planning process. Unlike the "extraordinary circumstance" in which the government deprives a property owner of all economic use, *Lucas,* 505 U. S., at 1017, moratoria like Ordinance 81–5 and Resolution 83–21 are used widely among land-use planners to preserve the status quo while formulating a more permanent development strategy. In fact, the consensus in the planning community appears to be that moratoria, or "interim development controls" as they are often called, are an essential tool of successful development. Yet even the weak version of petitioners' categorical rule would treat these interim measures as takings regardless of the good faith of the planners, the reasonable expectations of the landowners, or the actual impact of the moratorium on property values.

The interest in facilitating informed decisionmaking by regulatory agencies counsels against adopting a *per se* rule that would impose such severe costs on their deliberations. Otherwise, the financial constraints of compensating property owners during a moratorium may force officials to rush through the planning process or to abandon the practice altogether. To the extent that communities are forced to abandon using moratoria, landowners will have incentives to develop their property quickly before a comprehensive plan can be enacted, thereby fostering inefficient and ill-conceived growth. A finding in the 1980 Compact itself, which presumably was endorsed by all three legislative bodies that participated in its enactment, attests to the importance of that concern. 94 Stat. 3243 ("The legislatures of the States of California and Nevada find that in order to make effective the regional plan as revised by the agency, it is necessary to halt temporarily works of development in the region which might otherwise absorb the entire capability of the region for further development or direct it out of harmony with the ultimate plan").

As Justice Kennedy explained in his opinion for the Court in *Palazzolo,* it is the interest in informed decisionmaking that underlies our decisions imposing a strict ripeness requirement on landowners asserting regulatory takings claims:

"These cases stand for the important principle that a landowner may not establish a taking before a land use authority has the opportunity, using its own reasonable procedures, to decide and explain the reach of a challenged regulation. Under our ripeness rules a takings claim based on a law or regulation which is alleged to go too far in burdening property depends upon the landowner's first having followed reasonable and necessary steps to allow regulatory agencies to exercise their full discretion in considering development plans for the property, including the opportunity to grant any variances or waivers allowed by law. As a general rule, until these ordinary processes have been followed the extent of the restriction on property is not known and a regulatory taking has not yet been established. See *Suitum* [v. *Tahoe Regional Planning Agency,* 520 U. S. 725, 736, and n. 10 (1997)] (noting difficulty of demonstrating that 'mere enactment' of regulations restricting land use effects a taking)." 533 U. S., at 620–621.

We would create a perverse system of incentives were we to hold that landowners must wait for a takings claim to ripen so that planners can make well-reasoned decisions while, at the same time, holding that those planners must compensate landowners for the delay.

Indeed, the interest in protecting the decisional process is even stronger when an agency is developing a regional plan than when it is considering a permit for a single parcel. In the proceedings involving the Lake Tahoe Basin, for example, the moratoria enabled TRPA to obtain the benefit of comments and criticisms from interested parties, such as the petitioners, during its deliberations. Since a categorical rule tied to the length of deliberations would likely create added pressure on decisionmakers to reach a quick resolution of land-use questions, it would only serve to disadvantage those landowners and interest groups who are not as organized or familiar with the planning process. Moreover, with a temporary ban on development there is a lesser risk that individual landowners will be "singled out" to bear a special burden that should be shared by the public as a whole. *Nollan* v. *California Coastal Comm'n*, 483 U. S. 825, 835 (1987). At least with a moratorium there is a clear "reciprocity of advantage," *Mahon*, 260 U. S., at 415, because it protects the interests of all affected landowners against immediate construction that might be inconsistent with the provisions of the plan that is ultimately adopted. "While each of us is burdened somewhat by such restrictions, we, in turn, benefit greatly from the restrictions that are placed on others." *Keystone*, 480 U. S., at 491. In fact, there is reason to believe property values often will continue to increase despite a moratorium. See, *e. g., Growth Properties, Inc.* v. *Klingbeil Holding Co.*, 419 F. Supp. 212, 218 (Md. 1976) (noting that land values could be expected to increase 20% during a 5-year moratorium on development). Cf. *Forest Properties, Inc.* v. *United States*, 177 F. 3d 1360, 1367 (CA Fed. 1999) (record showed that market value of the entire parcel increased despite denial of permit to fill and develop lake-bottom property). Such an increase makes sense in this context because property values throughout the Basin can be expected to reflect the added assurance that Lake Tahoe will remain in its pristine state. Since in some cases a 1-year moratorium may not impose a burden at all, we should not adopt a rule that assumes moratoria always force individuals to bear a special burden that should be shared by the public as a whole.

It may well be true that any moratorium that lasts for more than one year should be viewed with special skepticism. But given the fact that the District Court found that the 32 months required by TRPA to formulate the 1984 Regional Plan was not unreasonable, we could not possibly conclude that every delay of over one year is constitutionally unacceptable. Formulating a general rule of this kind is a suitable task for state legislatures. In our view, the duration of the restriction is one of the important factors that a court must consider in the appraisal of a regulatory takings claim, but with respect to that factor as with respect to other factors, the "temptation to adopt what amount to *per se* rules in either direction must be resisted." *Palazzolo*, 533 U. S., at 636 (O'Connor, J., concurring). There may be moratoria that last longer than one year which interfere with reasonable investment-backed expectations, but as the District Court's opinion illustrates, petitioners' proposed rule is simply "too blunt an instrument" for identifying those cases. *Id.*, at 628. We conclude, therefore, that the interest in "fairness and justice" will be best served by relying on the familiar *Penn Central* approach when deciding cases like this, rather than by attempting to craft a new categorical rule.

Primer on Regulatory Takings

Non-Trespassory Invasions

While case law pertaining to possessory takings requires physical occupation of a parcel of property by a governmental entity, regulatory takings law does not. Regulatory takings cases typically focus on challenges to local regulations that go too far. In

Pennsylvania Coal Co. v. Mahon, 260 U.S. 393 (1922), the U.S. Supreme Court held "that while property may be regulated to a certain extent, if a regulation goes too far it will be recognized as a taking." Like possessory takings, an injured party may receive just compensation for damages.

"Substantially" Advances No More

In 1980, the Supreme Court issued an opinion that has led to more than two decades of confusion relating to regulatory takings. In *Agins v. City of Tiburon*, 447 U.S. 255 (1980), the High Court held that a regulatory taking could occur if a local regulation did not substantially advance a legitimate state interest or, in the alternative, if it denied the property owner all economically viable uses of his or her land.

Neither prong of this test was unfamiliar to land use planners or attorneys. The second part of this test originated in the *Lucas* case, when the High Court held that a South Carolina Coastal Commission rule that completely precluded a landowner from developing on his coastal property was a compensable regulatory taking, *Lucas v. South Carolina Coastal Commission*, 505 U.S. 1003 (1992). In that case, the regulation left Lucas with two undevelopable, sand-covered lots, in a sea of previously developed homes. The state purchased the lots for $850,000 and sold them to private developers. If you search the Internet for a photograph of the undeveloped lots, you will not find them. Instead, you find photographs of the houses that were subsequently built. In the end, many worthwhile regulations are simply too expensive to implement given the strength of the property rights guaranteed by the Fifth Amendment.

The "substantially advances" language in *Agins* was rather an anomaly to takings law. This language is, however, common to first amendment and due process claims. It is often perceived as inappropriate for determining if a regulatory taking has occurred, and was invalided by the Supreme Court in *Lingle v. Chevron USA Inc.*, 544 U.S. 528 (2005). In this case, the High Court was asked to consider a Hawaii state statute that attempted to cap the rent oil companies might charge to those who sell their products. There, the Court ruled that the "substantially advances" language was not a takings test. The Court held:

> [The] "substantially advances" inquiry reveals nothing about the magnitude or character of the burden a particular regulation imposes upon private property rights. Nor does it provide any information about how any regulatory burden is distributed among property owners.

Total Deprivation

Those alleging regulatory takings must demonstrate that the regulation causes the owner to be deprived of all "economically beneficial use" of the property, *Lucas v. South Carolina Coastal Commission*, 505 U.S. 1003 (1992). This test, like so many others in the realm of land use law, recognizes the need for local regulation of land use activities so long as they do not go "too far." The courts have not drawn a line in the sand to demarcate what this means. Instead, these decisions are made on a case-by-case basis. Generally, courts do not find a taking when there is still some reasonable use to which a property may be put. The law does not guarantee property owners the highest and best use of their lands.

Multi-Factor Test

Historically, the Supreme Court has reviewed most regulatory takings cases utilizing the multi-factor test originating from the holding in *Penn Central Transp. Co. v. New York City*, 438 U.S. 104 (1978). In *Penn Central*, the owner of Grand Central Terminal challenged a city's landmark law. The landmark law precluded the demolition of historically significant buildings listed on the city's local register. Working with Penn Central Railroad, architect Marcel Breuer submitted two designs for the site to the New York Landmarks Preservation Commission. The first was a 55-story office building to be constructed over the existing structure. The Commission rejected both proposals and Penn Central's subsequent request for a Certificate of Appropriateness.

Understanding the economic impacts of such regulations on private property interests in a growing metropolis, the Commission offered Penn Central the right to transfer the development rights to which they were entitled as a result of the landmarks ordinance. The bequest of transfer of development rights would have allowed Penn Central to sell their rights to develop the airspace above the historic train station to other developers in an area of town where density was a priority. Penn Central challenged the transfer of development rights scheme on the grounds that this tool did not provide adequate compensation for their loss.

Upon hearing, the trial court ruled that the landmarks law, as applied to the plaintiffs' property, was unconstitutional, and the court enjoined the city from using the landmarks law to impede construction of any structure that might otherwise lawfully be constructed at the site of the Grand Central Terminal. On January 21, 1975, the Supreme Court of New York reversed the decision of trial court in favor of the City of New York. This decision was affirmed by the New York Court of Appeals.

The U.S. Supreme Court sought to consider whether the ordinance, as applied to Penn Central's property, was a compensable taking within the meaning of the Fifth Amendment. The Court concluded that the application of New York City's Landmarks Law was not a "taking" of Penn Central's property. The Court reasoned that: "The restrictions imposed are substantially related to the promotion of the general welfare, and not only permit reasonable beneficial use of the landmark site, but also afford appellants opportunities further to enhance not only the Terminal site proper but also other properties" (Supreme Court of the United States, 1978, p. 18).

The Court reached the decision in *Penn Central* by applying a multi-factor test that has subsequently shaped the way in which the High Court has reviewed regulatory takings cases. These factors include the following: (1) whether the land use regulation furthers a legitimate state interest; (2) whether the regulation has an adverse economic effect on the property with no alternative or offsetting reciprocal benefits; and (3) whether the character of the government action places a disproportionate burden upon a single landowner when it should more properly be borne by the community (Bohlen, p. 163). The High Court quickly found that the landmarks law furthered a legitimate public interest related to historic preservation. It is important to note, however, that this factor was eliminated from consideration in the *Lingle* case in 2005. With respect to the "adverse economic effect" of the landmarks law on Penn Central, the Supreme Court ruled that the transfer of development rights provision was adequate to offset the costs associated with the preservation of the train station in its historic form. This provision, according to the Court, ensured that the burden of the preservation regulation did not fall disproportionately on the property owner.

Temporal Issues and Moratoria

A regulation does not have to permanently deprive a property owner all viable use of his or her property in order to be considered a taking. A temporary deprivation of property rights, in some cases, is enough to amount to a compensable taking.

In *First English Evangelical Lutheran Church of Glendale v. County of Los Angeles*, 482 U.S. 304 (1987), First English owned a camp for children with disabilities in the Angeles National Forest. A forest fire left the area vulnerable and a subsequent flood destroyed the buildings on the church's campground. In response, the county passed an interim ordinance temporarily preventing construction in a flood zone. The ordinance was vague and did not set a time frame for lifting the ordinance.

The church unsuccessfully sued the county in the California Superior Court. The California Appellate Court affirmed the trial court's decision in favor of the county. The Supreme Court of California refused to hear the case. The church appealed. The U.S. Supreme Court was left to determine if an interim ordinance rose to the level of a compensable taking under the Fifth Amendment. The Supreme Court ruled in favor of the church and remanded the case for a trial regarding temporary damages sustained by the church during the period when the ordinance was in place. The High Court reasoned that temporary takings were the same as permanent takings when the land is reduced to having no development potential.

The Supreme Court revisited the issue of temporary takings in *Tahoe-Sierra Preservation Council, Inc. v. Tahoe Regional Planning Association*, 535 U.S. 302 (2002). In 1968, Nevada and California signed a compact that established the Tahoe Regional Planning Agency (TRPA) to coordinate and regulate development and conserve natural resources in the area surrounding Lake Tahoe. In 1980, the TRPA commenced efforts to create a regional plan for the area. The TRPA adopted a moratorium to halt development in the area during the planning process. The moratorium lasted for 32 months.

A group of developers in the area challenged the moratorium as a compensable taking. The District Court found that the moratorium was a categorical taking as under *Lucas*. The Ninth Circuit Court of Appeals reversed the trial court's decision, holding that the regulations only had a temporary impact on fee interest and, thus, a categorical taking had not occurred. The Supreme Court was asked to ascertain if the moratorium enacted by the TRPA to halt development while a comprehensive regional plan was created constituted a taking under the standards set forth by *Lucas v. South Carolina Coastal Council*. The High Court ruled that a per se taking had not occurred because landowners had not been completely deprived of all economically viable use of their land, as previously established in *Penn Central*.

The Supreme Court reached different conclusions in these two very similar cases. Why? The answer lies in the planning process. In both instances, the local government was attempting to remedy an environmental crisis. However, in *Tahoe*, the

TRPA set a time limit for the moratorium, not in months or years, but in activity. In that case, the moratorium was slated to expire when: (1) the consultant had completed a study of development practices in the area and their impacts on the lake and (2) the regional planning authority had subsequently issued a new set of building requirements to ensure that future development did not negatively impact the water quality in the lake. There was no such timeline associated with the moratorium in *First Evangelical*. From these cases, an inference can be drawn about the importance of connecting moratoria to an active planning process where best efforts are made to study a problem and develop an appropriate solution to the identified problem. If this process is followed, only unnecessary delay may result in a finding of a compensable taking.

Response to Wicked Problem

The outraged local residents will likely challenge the water concurrency ordinance as a facial taking. The lawsuit will find that the ordinance constitutes a taking by merely reading the ordinance. This is a high threshold to overcome. In this case, the residents will argue that no one knows how much water is presently available or, in the alternative, how much water each household, built now or in the future, will actually use. Further, they will argue that it is difficult to predict how much precipitation will fall in the future, particularly in the face of climate change, to recharge the aquifer. The residents will argue that it is impossible for the local government to fairly determine development rights now and into the future. They will conclude by suggesting that the ordinance unfairly rewards those who develop first, regardless of the quality of those developments.

The city will respond to the residents' argument suggesting that the ordinance is not a taking on its face. They will argue that growth management is an acceptable tool that promotes the restriction of development rights based on the availability of resources. The city will provide evidence that it has a good handle on the contents of the aquifer and water use rates. They will contend that this measure is necessary to ensure that there is enough water available to meet current and future needs with reasonable growth projections in mind.

A court reviewing the challenge brought to Arid's water concurrency ordinance would likely apply the multi-factor test established by the Court in *Penn Central* and modified in *Lingle*. As you will recall, it is no longer important for the Court to decide whether the land use regulation furthers a legitimate state interest per the Supreme Court's decision in *Lingle*. Instead, the reviewing court will consider the character of the governmental action and the economic effect of the regulation on the property. In this case, the Court will be attempting to determine if the water concurrency regulation places an undue burden on future development in favor of existing development. In addition, the Court will be asked to consider the economic effect of the regulation on future development within the community.

The Court is likely to find in favor of the city. First, the Court is likely to note that a facial taking has not occurred. Water concurrency regulations are a natural extension of growth management practices. The ordinance, on its face, does not currently deprive any property owner of the right to develop. The Court will remind the residents that the law does not favor land speculation. It will encourage the residents to pursue land development in an orderly and appropriate fashion in order to vest the rights to develop while the water supply is adequate and available.

In reality, it might make more sense for the parties challenging the ordinance to wait to file their challenge until after the ordinance has been enacted and applied to a development proposal as applied challenges of this nature provide more clarity to the courts about the economic impacts associated with a particular ordinance on a parcel of property. A developer who is not able to build his sustainable, mixed use, infill development because suburban developers have previously claimed all of the water rights may have a good claim for a compensable as applied, regulatory taking.

Discussion Prompts

- What is the relevance of the terms facial or as applied when discussing regulatory takings claims?
- Many of the regulatory takings cases that have found their way before the U.S. Supreme Court involve coastal properties. Why is that?
- How does the possibility of regulatory takings challenges squelch the ability of local governments to plan for adaptation to an impending sea level rise?

Bibliography

Bohlen, Edward G. (2002). Palazzolo Remand: There Was No Taking Under Penn Central. *Boston College Environmental Affairs Law Review*, 30:1, 163–169.

Hiatt, Michael A. (2007–2008). Come Hell or High Water: Reexamining the Takings Clause in a Climate Changed Future. *Duke Environmental Law and Policy Forum*, 18, 371–398.

Lucero, L. and Soule, J. (2002). A Win for Lake Tahoe: The Supreme Court Validates Moratoriums in a Path-Breaking Decision. *Planning*, 69:6, 4–7.

Miceli, Thomas J. and Segerson, Kathleen (1994). Regulatory Takings: When Should Compensation Be Paid? *Journal of Legal Studies*, 23:2, 749–776.

Nolon, J. R. (2005–2006). Historical Overview of the American Land Use System: A Diagnostic Approach to Evaluating Governmental Land Use Control. *Pace Environmental Law Review*, 23, 821–852.

Wolf, M. A. (1999–2000). Taking Regulatory Takings Personally: The Perils of (Mis)Reasoning by Analogy. *Alabama Law Review*, 51, 1355–1379.

11

THE FIRST AMENDMENT

The First Amendment to the U.S. Constitution guarantees freedom of speech and religion, among other promises. These protections are relevant to planners and are often of special concern when decisions are made affecting the regulation of signs, adult entertainment establishments, and religious institutions. These First Amendment protections do not insulate these land uses from regulation. However, local regulators must take special care to justify such efforts to restrict these protected land uses.

First Amendment Wicked Problem

The town of Katsburg has never had any type of sexually oriented business. The town's zoning code permits adult entertainment in two places: by special use permit in the town's historic downtown and along the frontage road on the outskirts of town. In both instances, the town will only issue a permit for the operation of a sexually oriented business if it is more than 500 feet from churches, parks, schools, and residences. This spatial requirement, while not intentional, is a barrier to the development of any adult entertainment establishments in the entire town for two reasons. First, the town's historic downtown contains many residences, parks, schools, and churches. There is no place to develop or operate an adult entertainment establishment more than 500 feet from these protected land uses. There is also a problem with locating along the frontage road. Nearly all of the land is occupied by commercial enterprises, such as big box retail, car dealers, chain restaurants, and mega churches. Only one site is available for development. This site is 501 feet away from the mega church.

   The owner of XXX Corporation has acquired the property along the frontage road next to the mega church. XXX's application to operate the Pussy Cat Club is pending before the town council. In its application, XXX Corporation explains that the primary entertainment on the site will be nude dancing. Alcohol will not be served. The design for the building will be relatively innocuous with tinted glass windows. Proposed signage for the facility will be limited, with only one pole sign directing traffic to the business. The sign, crafted out of neon, will say Pussy Cat Club and depict a hissing black cat with its back arched and tail raised. As with all special use permits, the town council seeks to condition the grant of permits to operate adult entertainment establishments. In this case, the town council seeks to require the company to

135

Figure 10 Credit: David D. Boeck

remove the depiction of the cat from the sign. The council reasons that this makes sense to prevent children from being interested in the property.

(1) XXX seeks to challenge the condition of the permit related to the sign. Draft XXX's best argument explaining why the permit condition pertaining to the sign violates the First Amendment.
(2) The mega church is preparing to challenge the issuance of the permit to XXX to operate the Pussy Cat Club. They complain that the spirit of the buffer requirement should preclude XXX from operating the club 501 feet away from the church. How likely is the mega church to prevail in this matter?

Cases

The following cases will be useful to you as you attempt to analyze this chapter's wicked problem:

City of Ladue v. Gilleo, 512 U.S. 43 (1994)
Metromedia, Inc. v. City of San Diego, 453 U.S. 490 (1981)
City of Renton v. Playtime Theatres, Inc., 475 U.S. 41 (1986)

City of Ladue v. Gilleo

512 U.S. 43 (1994)

Facts
The city of Ladue enacted a sign ordinance banning all residential signs, with a limited number of exemptions, in order to reduce visual clutter. In 1990, Gilleo, a Ladue resident, posted a sign on her front lawn protesting the Gulf War, which promptly disappeared. After reporting the incident, Gilleo was informed by the police that such signs were prohibited. The city denied Ladue a variance.

Issue
Did the city of Ladue's ordinance limiting residential signs violate a resident's constitutional right to free speech?

Held
Yes. Municipalities have the authority to regulate physical characteristics of signs, but may not use regulation as a means of censorship. Although the ordinance's purpose was to minimize the visual clutter associated with signs, the city's ordinance clearly favored commercial speech over non-commercial speech. Furthermore, Ladue's prohibition of residential signs left residents without a meaningful substitute form of communication.

Discussion
Although the First Amendment's Free Speech Clause protects signs, they can create problems that are subject to municipal police powers. Residential signs are an inexpensive form of communication for individuals to convey desired political, religious, and personal messages to the public, making them an important tool in modern society.

Case Excerpt
Under the Court of Appeals' content discrimination rationale, the City might theoretically remove the defects in its ordinance by simply repealing all of the exemptions. If, however, the ordinance is also vulnerable because it prohibits too much speech, that solution would not save it. Moreover, if the prohibitions in Ladue's ordinance are impermissible, resting our decision on its exemptions would afford scant relief for respondent Gilleo. She is primarily concerned not with the scope of the exemptions available in other locations, such as commercial areas and on church property; she asserts a constitutional right to display an antiwar sign at her own home. Therefore, we first ask whether Ladue may properly *prohibit* Gilleo from displaying her sign, and then, only if necessary, consider the separate question whether it was improper for the City simultaneously to *permit* certain other signs. In examining the propriety of Ladue's near total prohibition of residential signs, we will assume, *arguendo*, the validity of the City's submission that the various exemptions are free of impermissible content or viewpoint discrimination.

In *Linmark* we held that the city's interest in maintaining a stable, racially integrated neighborhood was not sufficient to support a prohibition of residential "For Sale" signs. We recognized that even such a narrow sign prohibition would have a deleterious effect on residents' ability to convey important information because alternatives were "far from satisfactory." 431 U. S., at 93. Ladue's sign ordinance is supported principally by the City's interest in minimizing the visual clutter associated with signs, an interest that is concededly valid but certainly no more compelling than the interests at stake in *Linmark*. Moreover, whereas the ordinance in *Linmark* applied only to a form of commercial speech, Ladue's ordinance covers even such absolutely pivotal speech as a sign protesting an imminent governmental decision to go to war.

The impact on free communication of Ladue's broad sign prohibition, moreover, is manifestly greater than in *Linmark*. Gilleo and other residents of Ladue are forbidden to display virtually any "sign" on their property. The ordinance defines that term sweepingly. A prohibition is not always invalid merely because it applies to a sizeable category of speech; the sign ban we upheld in *Vincent*, for example, was quite broad. But in *Vincent* we specifically noted that the category of speech in question – signs placed on public property – was not a "uniquely valuable or important mode of communication," and that there was no evidence that "appellees' ability to communicate effectively is threatened by ever-increasing restrictions on expression." 466 U. S., at 812.

Here, in contrast, Ladue has almost completely foreclosed a venerable means of communication that is both unique and important. It has totally foreclosed that medium to political, religious, or personal messages. Signs that react to a local happening or express a view on a controversial issue both reflect and animate change in the life of a community. Often placed on lawns or in windows, residential signs play an important part in political campaigns, during which they are displayed to signal the resident's support for particular candidates, parties, or causes. They may not afford the same opportunities for conveying complex ideas as do other media, but residential signs have long been an important and distinct medium of expression.

Our prior decisions have voiced particular concern with laws that foreclose an entire medium of expression. Thus, we have held invalid ordinances that completely banned the distribution of pamphlets within the municipality, *Lovell* v. *City of Griffin*, 303 U. S. 444, 451–452 (1938); handbills on the public streets, *Jamison* v. *Texas*, 318 U. S. 413, 416 (1943); the door-to-door distribution of literature, *Martin* v. *City of Struthers*, 319 U. S. 141, 145–149 (1943); *Schneider* v. *State (Town of Irvington)*, 308 U. S. 147, 164–165 (1939), and live entertainment, *Schad* v. *Mount Ephraim*, 452 U. S. 61, 75–76 (1981). See also *Frisby* v. *Schultz*, 487 U. S. 474, 486 (1988) (picketing focused upon individual residence is "fundamentally different from more generally directed means of communication that may not be completely banned in residential areas"). Although prohibitions foreclosing entire media may be completely free of content or viewpoint discrimination, the danger they pose to the freedom of speech is readily apparent – by eliminating a common means of speaking, such measures can suppress too much speech.

Ladue contends, however, that its ordinance is a mere regulation of the "time, place, or manner" of speech because residents remain free to convey their desired messages by other means, such as *hand-held* signs, "letters, handbills, flyers, telephone calls, newspaper advertisements, bumper stickers, speeches, and neighborhood or community meetings." Brief for Petitioners 41. However, even regulations that do not foreclose an entire medium of expression, but merely shift the time, place, or manner of its use, must "leave open ample alternative channels for communication." *Clark* v. *Community for Creative Non-Violence,* 468 U. S. 288, 293 (1984). In this case, we are not persuaded that adequate substitutes exist for the important medium of speech that Ladue has closed off.

Displaying a sign from one's own residence often carries a message quite distinct from placing the same sign someplace else, or conveying the same text or picture by other means. Precisely because of their location, such signs provide information about the identity of the "speaker." As an early and eminent student of rhetoric observed, the identity of the speaker is an important component of many attempts to persuade. A sign advocating "Peace in the Gulf" in the front lawn of a retired general or decorated war veteran may provoke a different reaction than the same sign in a 10-year-old child's bedroom window or the same message on a bumper sticker of a passing automobile. An espousal of socialism may carry different implications when displayed on the grounds of a stately mansion than when pasted on a factory wall or an ambulatory sandwich board.

Residential signs are an unusually cheap and convenient form of communication. Especially for persons of modest means or limited mobility, a yard or window sign may have no practical substitute. Cf. *Vincent,* 466 U. S., at 812–813, n. 30; *Anderson* v. *Celebrezze,* 460 U. S. 780, 793–794 (1983); *Martin* v. *City of Struthers,* 319 U. S., at 146; *Milk Wagon Drivers* v. *Meadowmoor Dairies, Inc.,* 312 U. S. 287, 293 (1941). Even for the affluent, the added costs in money or time of taking out a newspaper advertisement, handing out leaflets on the street, or standing in front of one's house with a hand-held sign may make the difference between participating and not participating in some public debate. Furthermore, a person who puts up a sign at her residence often intends to reach *neighbors,* an audience that could not be reached nearly as well by other means.

A special respect for individual liberty in the home has long been part of our culture and our law, see, *e. g., Payton* v. *New York,* 445 U. S. 573, 596–597, and nn. 44–45 (1980); that principle has special resonance when the government seeks to constrain a person's ability to *speak* there. See *Spence* v. *Washington,* 418 U. S. 405, 406, 409, 411 (1974) *(per curiam).* Most Americans would be understandably dismayed, given that tradition, to learn that it was illegal to display from their window an 8- by 11-inch sign expressing their political views. Whereas the government's need to mediate among various competing uses, including expressive ones, for public streets and facilities is constant and unavoidable, see *Cox* v. *New Hampshire,* 312

U. S. 569, 574, 576 (1941); see also *Widmar* v. *Vincent*, 454 U. S. 263, 278 (1981) (Stevens, J., concurring in judgment), its need to regulate temperate speech from the home is surely much less pressing, see *Spence*, 418 U. S., at 409.

Our decision that Ladue's ban on almost all residential signs violates the First Amendment by no means leaves the City powerless to address the ills that may be associated with residential signs. It bears mentioning that individual residents themselves have strong incentives to keep their own property values up and to prevent "visual clutter" in their own yards and neighborhoods – incentives markedly different from those of persons who erect signs on others' land, in others' neighborhoods, or on public property. Residents' self-interest diminishes the danger of the "unlimited" proliferation of residential signs that concerns the City of Ladue. We are confident that more temperate measures could in large part satisfy Ladue's stated regulatory needs without harm to the First Amendment rights of its citizens. As currently framed, however, the ordinance abridges those rights.

Metromedia, Inc. v. City of San Diego

453 U.S. 490 (1981)

Facts
The city of San Diego passed an ordinance that prohibited off-site outdoor advertising display signs, with a limited number of exceptions including, primarily, on-site commercial advertisements. The ordinance was enacted for the purpose of eliminating the hazards that such signs presented to motorists and pedestrians and enhancing the appearance of the city. Metromedia and several other companies who owned a vast number of outdoor advertising signs at the time the ordinance asked the court to enjoin the city from enforcing the ordinance, arguing that the ordinance would effectively eliminate outdoor advertising in San Diego.

Issue
Did San Diego's outdoor sign ordinance infringe on the First Amendment rights of those who utilized off-site outdoor advertisement signage as a means of communication?

Held
Yes. The ordinance is unconstitutional on its face because the allowance of on-site commercial signage discriminated against non-commercial interests. Potential owners of non-commercial signs faced very limited options for outdoor advertisement.

Discussion
While billboards provide an important medium for political, social, and commercial expression, as large, immobile, and permanent structures, they create unique problems for those charged with land use regulation.

Case Excerpt
This Court has often faced the problem of applying the broad principles of the First Amendment to unique forums of expression. See, *e. g., Consolidated Edison Co.* v. *Public Service Comm'n*, 447 U. S. 530 (1980) (billing envelope inserts); *Carey* v. *Brown*, 447 U. S. 455 (1980) (picketing in residential areas); *Schaumburg* v. *Citizens for a Better Environment*, 444 U. S. 620 (1980) (door-to-door and on-street solicitation); *Greer* v. *Spock*, 424 U. S. 828 (1976) (Army bases); *Erznoznik* v. *City of Jacksonville*, 422 U. S. 205 (1975) (outdoor movie theaters); *Lehman* v. *City of Shaker Heights*, 418 U. S. 298 (1974) (advertising space within city-owned transit system). Even a cursory reading of these opinions reveals that at times First Amendment values must yield to other societal interests. These cases support the cogency of Justice Jackson's remark in *Kovacs* v. *Cooper*, 336 U. S. 77, 97 (1949): Each method of communicating ideas is "a law unto itself" and that law must reflect the "differing natures, values, abuses and dangers" of each method. We deal here with the law of billboards.

Billboards are a well-established medium of communication, used to convey a broad range of different kinds of messages. As Justice Clark noted in his dissent below:

"The outdoor sign or symbol is a venerable medium for expressing political, social and commercial ideas. From the poster or 'broadside' to the billboard, outdoor signs have played a prominent role throughout American history, rallying support for political and social causes." 26 Cal. 3d, at 888, 610 P. 2d, at 430–431.

The record in this case indicates that besides the typical commercial uses, San Diego billboards have been used "to publicize the 'City in motion' campaign of the City of San Diego, to communicate messages from candidates for municipal, state and national offices, including candidates for judicial office, to propose marriage, to seek employment, to encourage the use of seat belts, to denounce the United Nations, to seek support for Prisoners of War and Missing in Action, to promote the United Crusade and a variety of other charitable and socially-related endeavors and to provide directions to the traveling public."

But whatever its communicative function, the billboard remains a "large, immobile, and permanent structure which like other structures is subject to … regulation." *Id.*, at 870, 610 P. 2d, at 419. Moreover, because it is designed to stand out and apart from its surroundings, the billboard creates a unique set of problems for land-use planning and development.

Billboards, then, like other media of communication, combine communicative and noncommunicative aspects. As with other media, the government has legitimate interests in controlling the noncommunicative aspects of the medium,

Kovacs v. *Cooper, supra,* but the First and Fourteenth Amendments foreclose a similar interest in controlling the communicative aspects. Because regulation of the noncommunicative aspects of a medium often impinges to some degree on the communicative aspects, it has been necessary for the courts to reconcile the government's regulatory interests with the individual's right to expression. "'[A] court may not escape the task of assessing the First Amendment interest at stake and weighing it against the public interest allegedly served by the regulation.'" *Linmark Associates, Inc.* v. *Willingboro,* 431 U. S. 85, 91 (1977), quoting *Bigelow* v. *Virginia,* 421 U. S. 809, 826 (1975). Performance of this task requires a particularized inquiry into the nature of the conflicting interests at stake here, beginning with a precise appraisal of the character of the ordinance as it affects communication.

As construed by the California Supreme Court, the ordinance restricts the use of certain kinds of outdoor signs. That restriction is defined in two ways: first, by reference to the structural characteristics of the sign; second, by reference to the content, or message, of the sign. Thus, the regulation only applies to a "permanent structure constituting, or used for the display of, a commercial or other advertisement to the public." 26 Cal. 3d, at 856, n. 2, 610 P. 2d, at 410, n. 2. Within that class, the only permitted signs are those (1) identifying the premises on which the sign is located, or its owner or occupant, or advertising the goods produced or services rendered on such property and (2) those within one of the specified exemptions to the general prohibition, such as temporary political campaign signs. To determine if any billboard is prohibited by the ordinance, one must determine how it is constructed, where it is located, and what message it carries.

Thus, under the ordinance (1) a sign advertising goods or services available on the property where the sign is located is allowed; (2) a sign on a building or other property advertising goods or services produced or offered elsewhere is barred; (3) noncommercial advertising, unless within one of the specific exceptions, is everywhere prohibited. The occupant of property may advertise his own goods or services; he may not advertise the goods or services of others, nor may he display most noncommercial messages.

City of Renton v. Playtime Theatres, Inc.

475 U.S. 41 (1986)

Facts

The city of Renton enacted an ordinance prohibiting adult motion picture theaters from being located within 1,000 feet of specified land uses, including residential zones, single- or multi-family dwellings, churches, parks, or within one mile of any school. One year after the ordinance's enactment, Playtime Theatres acquired two existing theaters in downtown Renton for the purpose of showing adult films. Playtime Theatres filed suit, alleging that the ordinance violated its First and Fourteenth Amendments rights.

Issue
Did Renton's zoning ordinance regulating the placement of adult movie theaters violate Playtime Theatres' First Amendment rights?

Held
No. Renton's ordinance did not place an outright ban on adult theaters, but rather sought to control their placement within the community, constituting a time, place, and manner regulation. The ordinance's goal was not to restrict the content of adult movie theaters, which would inherently violate the First Amendment, but to control the secondary effects that such theaters have on the surrounding community, by, for example, preventing crime, maintaining surrounding property values, and preserving the quality of urban life.

Discussion
Renton's ordinance was a valid response to the problems associated with adult theaters. According to the Court, Renton had a substantial governmental interest in regulating the location of adult theaters within the community and by leaving more than 5 percent of the land area within the city as permissible locations for such theaters, the city provided Playtime Theaters ample opportunity to maintain a presence in the community.

Case Excerpt
In our view, the resolution of this case is largely dictated by our decision in *Young v. American Mini Theatres, Inc., supra.* There, although five Members of the Court did not agree on a single rationale for the decision, we held that the city of Detroit's zoning ordinance, which prohibited locating an adult theater within 1,000 feet of any two other "regulated uses" or within 500 feet of any residential zone, did not violate the First and Fourteenth Amendments. *Id.,* at 72–73 (plurality opinion of STEVENS, J., joined by BURGER, C. J., and WHITE and REHNQUIST, JJ.); *id.,* at 84 (POWELL, J., concurring). The Renton ordinance, like the one in *American Mini Theatres,* does not ban adult theaters altogether, but merely provides that such theaters may not be located within 1,000 feet of any residential zone, single- or multiple-family dwelling, church, park, or school. The ordinance is therefore properly analyzed as a form of time, place, and manner regulation. *Id.,* at 63, and n. 18; *id.,* at 78–79 (POWELL, J., concurring).

Describing the ordinance as a time, place, and manner regulation is, of course, only the first step in our inquiry. This Court has long held that regulations enacted for the purpose of restraining speech on the basis of its content presumptively violate the First Amendment. See *Carey* v. *Brown,* 447 U. S. 455, 462–463, and n. 7 (1980); *Police Dept. of Chicago* v. *Mosley,* 408 U. S. 92, 95, 98–99 (1972). On the other hand, so-called "content-neutral" time, place, and manner regulations are acceptable so long as they are designed to serve a substantial governmental interest and do not unreasonably limit alternative avenues of communication. See *Clark* v. *Community for Creative Non-Violence*, 468 U. S. 288, 293 (1984); City *Council of Los Angeles* v. *Taxpayers for Vincent*, 466 U. S. 789, 807 (1984); *Heffron* v. *International Society for Krishna Consciousness, Inc.*, 452 U. S. 640, 647–648 (1981).

At first glance, the Renton ordinance, like the ordinance in *American Mini Theatres*, does not appear to fit neatly into either the "content-based" or the "content-neutral" category. To be sure, the ordinance treats theaters that specialize in adult films differently from other kinds of theaters. Nevertheless, as the District Court concluded, the Renton ordinance is aimed not at the *content* of the films shown at "adult motion picture theatres," but rather at the *secondary effects* of such theaters on the surrounding community. The District Court found that the City Council's "*predominate* concerns" were with the secondary effects of adult theaters, and not with the content of adult films themselves. App. to Juris. Statement 31a (emphasis added). But the Court of Appeals, relying on its decision in *Tovar* v. *Billmeyer*, 721 F. 2d 1260, 1266 (CA9 1983), held that this was not enough to sustain the ordinance. According to the Court of Appeals, if "*a motivating factor*" in enacting the ordinance was to restrict respondents' exercise of First Amendment rights the ordinance would be invalid, apparently no matter how small a part this motivating factor may have played in the City Council's decision. 748 F. 2d, at 537 (emphasis in original). This view of the law was rejected in *United States* v. *O'Brien*, 391 U. S., at 382–386, the very case that the Court of Appeals said it was applying:

"It is a familiar principle of constitutional law that this Court will not strike down an otherwise constitutional statute on the basis of an alleged illicit legislative motive...

...

"... What motivates one legislator to make a speech about a statute is not necessarily what motivates scores of others to enact it, and the stakes are sufficiently high for us to eschew guesswork." *Id.*, at 383–384.

The District Court's finding as to "predominate" intent, left undisturbed by the Court of Appeals, is more than adequate to establish that the city's pursuit of its zoning interests here was unrelated to the suppression of free expression. The ordinance by its terms is designed to prevent crime, protect the city's retail trade, maintain property values, and generally "protec[t] and preserv[e] the quality of [the city's] neighborhoods, commercial districts, and the quality of urban life," not to suppress the expression of unpopular views. See App. to Juris. Statement 90a. As JUSTICE POWELL observed in *American Mini Theatres*, "[i]f [the city] had been concerned with restricting the message purveyed by adult theaters, it would have tried to close them or restrict their number rather than circumscribe their choice as to location." 427 U. S., at 82, n. 4.

In short, the Renton ordinance is completely consistent with our definition of "content-neutral" speech regulations as those that "are *justified* without reference to the content of the regulated speech." *Virginia Pharmacy Board* v. *Virginia*

Citizens Consumer Council, Inc., 425 U. S. 748, 771 (1976) (emphasis added); *Community for Creative Non-Violence, supra,* at 293; *International Society for Krishna Consciousness, supra,* at 648. The ordinance does not contravene the fundamental principle that underlies our concern about "content-based" speech regulations: that "government may not grant the use of a forum to people whose views it finds acceptable, but deny use to those wishing to express less favored or more controversial views." *Mosley, supra,* at 95–96....

The appropriate inquiry in this case, then, is whether then Renton ordinance is designed to serve a substantial governmental interest and allows for reasonable alternative avenues of communication. See *Community for Creative Non-Violence,* 468 U. S., at 293; *International Society for Krishna Consciousness,* 452 U. S., at 649, 654. It is clear that the ordinance meets such a standard. As a majority of this Court recognized in *American Mini Theatres,* a city's "interest in attempting to preserve the quality of urban life is one that must be accorded high respect." 427 U. S., at 71 (plurality opinion); see *id.,* at 80 (POWELL, J., concurring) ("Nor is there doubt that the interests furthered by this ordinance are both important and substantial"). Exactly the same vital governmental interests are at stake here....

We hold that Renton was entitled to rely on the experiences of Seattle and other cities, and in particular on the "detailed findings" summarized in the Washington Supreme Court's *Northend Cinema* opinion, in enacting its adult theater zoning ordinance. The First Amendment does not require a city, before enacting such an ordinance, to conduct new studies or produce evidence independent of that already generated by other cities, so long as whatever evidence the city relies upon is reasonably believed to be relevant to the problem that the city addresses. That was the case here...

We also find no constitutional defect in the method chosen by Renton to further its substantial interests. Cities may regulate adult theaters by dispersing them, as in Detroit, or by effectively concentrating them, as in Renton. "It is not our function to appraise the wisdom of [the city's] decision to require adult theaters to be separated rather than concentrated in the same areas... [T]he city must be allowed a reasonable opportunity to experiment with solutions to admittedly serious problems." *American Mini Theatres,* 427 U. S., at 71 (plurality opinion). Moreover, the Renton ordinance is "narrowly tailored" to affect only that category of theaters shown to produce the unwanted secondary effects, thus avoiding the flaw that proved fatal to the regulations in *Schad* v. *Mount Ephraim,* 452 U. S. 61 (1981), and *Erznoznik* v. *City of Jacksonville,* 422 U. S. 205 (1975)...

Finally, turning to the question whether the Renton ordinance allows for reasonable alternative avenues of communication, we note that the ordinance leaves some 520 acres, or more than five percent of the entire land area of Renton, open to use as adult theater sites. The District Court found, and the Court of Appeals did not dispute the finding, that the 520 acres of land consists of "[a]mple, accessible real estate," including "acreage in all stages of development from raw land to developed, industrial, warehouse, office, and shopping space that is criss-crossed by freeways, highways, and roads." App. to Juris. Statement 28a.

Respondents argue, however, that some of the land in question is already occupied by existing businesses, that "practically none" of the undeveloped land is currently for sale or lease, and that in general there are no "commercially viable" adult theater sites within the 520 acres left open by the Renton ordinance. Brief for Appellees 34–37. The Court of Appeals accepted these arguments, concluded that the 520 acres was not truly "available" land, and therefore held that the Renton ordinance "would result in a substantial restriction" on speech. 748 F. 2d, at 534.

We disagree with both the reasoning and the conclusion of the Court of Appeals. That respondents must fend for themselves in the real estate market, on an equal footing with other prospective purchasers and lessees, does not give rise to a First Amendment violation…

In sum, we find that the Renton ordinance represents a valid governmental response to the "admittedly serious problems" created by adult theaters. See *id.*, at 71 (plurality opinion). Renton has not used "the power to zone as a pretext for suppressing expression," *id.*, at 84 (POWELL, J., concurring), but rather has sought to make some areas available for adult theaters and their patrons, while at the same time preserving the quality of life in the community at large by preventing those theaters from locating in other areas. This, after all, is the essence of zoning. Here, as in *American Mini Theatres*, the city has enacted a zoning ordinance that meets these goals while also satisfying the dictates of the First Amendment.

Primer on the First Amendment as an Issue for Planners

Signs

Drivers travelling down any commercial strip in the United States will pass by a litany of types of signage, from the McDonald's Golden Arches on a pole sign, to purple inflatable gorillas perched atop car dealerships, and temporary signs advertising sales. While residential streets are typically free from commercial advertisements, it is not atypical for homeowners to attempt to display their political thoughts through the display of signs in their yards, such as election signs or war protests. The messages conveyed on both types of sign are protected by the First Amendment to the U.S. Constitution as free speech. However, the degree of protection varies according to the message conveyed, with political speech receiving a higher degree of protection than commercial messages.

The founding fathers sought to protect future citizens of the United States from being governed by laws which would "abridge" their freedom of speech. Even then, this did not mean that a private citizen could say anything he or she wished. The freedom of speech does not protect hate speech, speech that will result in violence, or speech which is knowingly false, among a number of other unprotected forms of free speech.

The type of political speech which is afforded a high degree of protection is the kind of speech as issue in *City of Ladue v. Gilleo*, 512 U.S. 43 (1994). At issue in this case was a sign that Ms. Gilleo posted on her front lawn in which she objected to the Persian Gulf war. At the time, a city ordinance banned all signs in residential areas except for address markers and for sale signs. Ms. Gilleo sought and was denied a variance to post this same sign on her lawn. She sued, claiming that the ordinance violated her First Amendment rights to free speech. At all levels, the courts found that the ordinance violated Ms. Gilleo's free speech rights because it was content-based. The city could not overcome the fact that it permitted other sign types in residential neighborhoods and that it also allowed political signs in the city's commercial districts. While the Court agreed that regulating signs on the basis of controlling for visual blight was a legitimate reason for regulating sings, it found that this reason was not a "sufficiently compelling" basis to justify a ban on political speech signs in residential neighborhoods. Furthermore, the regulation had almost completely foreclosed Ms. Gilleo's opportunity to share her political beliefs at her home, the only place she was truly free to post her beliefs.

The holding in *Ladue* does not prevent cities from regulating political signs. It merely limits the scope of such regulations. For instance, cities may legitimately regulate the length of time in which campaign signs can be displayed in neighborhoods. In some communities, political signs must be removed within 10 days of the election date. Signs that are not taken down are removed by the city at a cost to the candidate or campaign. However, municipalities are wise to take care to craft regulations that are both content and viewpoint neutral. It is particularly important that such regulations are not crafted to favor one political message over another.

Commercial speech is protected under the First Amendment to the U.S. Constitution. In *Bigelow v. Virginia*, 421 U.S. 809 (1975), the High Court held that the fact that speech is commercial in natures does not justify the narrowing of First Amendment protections. The next term went further to characterize the nature and importance of commercial communications in *Virginia Pharmacy Board v. Virginia Consumer Council*, 425 U.S. 748 (1976). The High Court reinforced "the right of a commercial advertiser to share his message and the right of a potential consumer to receive it." The Court steadfastly held that "The free flow of commercial speech should be considered … an instrument to enlighten public decision making in a democracy" (ibid. at 766).

In 1980, the High Court developed its first "test" applicable to the regulation of commercial advertising displays. In *Central Hudson Gas & Electric Company v. Public Service Commission*, 447 U.S. 557 (1980), the Court found invalid a state statute preventing companies from promoting their products through advertising utilizing a four-pronged test referred to as the Central Hudson factors. According to the High Court, commercial speech is protected by the First Amendment if:

(1) it at least concerns lawful activity and is not misleading;
(2) the asserted government interest is substantial;
(3) the regulation directly advances the governmental interest asserted; and
(4) the regulation is not more extensive than is necessary to serve that interest (ibid. at 566).

The term "governmental interest" remains undefined. Courts have deferred to the discretion of local governments to determine what activities fall within the scope of this term. With respect to signs, regulations are typically justified in the name of police powers like aesthetics and traffic safety. Courts have rarely delved into these justifications. However, this is beginning to change as more research has been produced that questions these claims, especially with respect to traffic safety.

The U.S. Supreme Court was again asked to review the state of the law with respect to the regulation of commercial signs, both on and off premise, in *Metromedia v. City of San Diego*, 453 U.S. 490 (1981). Outdoor advertising companies challenged the city of San Diego's off-premise sign code which, among other components, banned off-premise billboard signs. The ordinance exempted on-premise signs from this blanket ban. The Court's decision in this case was split with the justices issuing five separate opinions. Ultimately, the court upheld the ban on off-premise signs. No conclusion was definitively reached with respect to the regulation on on-premise signs. Yet, many localities reach to the dicta of this case to justify their sign codes provisions relating to the regulation of on-premise signs.

The Court's most recent decision with respect to the regulation of signs was issued in 2001. In *Lorillard Tobacco Co. v. Reilly*, 533 U.S. 525 (2001), the Supreme Court invalided a state statute that restricted tobacco companies from advertising their products within 1,000 feet of schools and playgrounds. The regulation further required indoor advertising to occur at least five feet off the floor. The Court ruled that the burden on commercial speech was disproportionate to the value to children's health, reminding governments that such regulations must be narrowly tailed. *Lorillard* is also important for sign law because it markets a "potential shift in the level of scrutiny applied in challenges to on-premise sign ordinances from intermediate to strict scrutiny when regulations are content specific."

The state of the law pertaining to the regulation of commercial and political signs is less than clear. Planners are wise to work with their city attorneys to assess the legality of the code provisions they seek to enforce. It is also prudent that such regulations are developed with input from the business community and sign makers themselves. Signs are the primary way businesses communicate with their customers. If commercial areas are not adequately identified, business vitality will be impacted. This sort of decline can lead to a major impact on the economic welfare of all or part of a city.

Adult Entertainment

The term adult entertainment establishment refers to land uses that allow for the depiction of sexually explicit materials. This often includes strip clubs, bookstores, massage parlors, and movie theaters. The mere proposal of the development of one of these land uses typically causes great concern and even activism at the local level. Most communities, with some limited exceptions, would simply like to exclude adult entertainment establishments from locating within city boundaries.

What is the underlying cause of the local reaction to the development of adult entertainment businesses? Some list the potential dimunition of property values as their primary concern. For these individuals, they fear that the presence of the adult entertainment establishment will cause their property values to decline. There is some validity to this concern. Concern about the secondary impacts of these businesses on neighborhood conditions is the most common concern. Secondary impacts include problems such as increased criminal activities associated with the operation of adult entertainment establishments, especially when they are concentrated in an area or situated next to businesses that sell alcohol.

In *Young v. American Mini Theatres, Inc.*, 427 U.S. 50 (1976), the Supreme Court first upheld a municipal regulation on adult entertainment activities. In this case the court suggested that a 1,000-foot spacing requirement for such land uses and a 500-foot buffer requirement between adult entertainment activities and residential areas did not violate the First Amendment rights of the theater. The High Court ruled that the city's interest in preserving quality of life was sufficient to justify a regulation that would limit, but not preclude, the location of adult entertainment establishments.

The Supreme Court has heard more than a dozen cases dealing with municipal regulations that impact either the location or operation of sexually oriented businesses. In the majority of instances, these regulations have been upheld so long as they do not preclude the operation of some degree of adult entertainment within the community, even if that location is undesirable from a market perspective.

Religious Uses

Along with expression and speech, religious freedom is a fundamental tenet of the U.S. Constitution due to the fact that early colonists fled to America to avoid religious persecution. In order to understand why municipalities regulate places of worship, it is important to understand how the placement of these institutions in communities, in terms of both form and location, has changed overtime.

The church began as a fixture of the vibrant downtown. Area residents were able to walk to the church. However, as the number and type of places of worship increased, so, too, did the locations they inhabited. Many of these new churches moved into residential neighborhoods. In the early days, the presence of these churches in residential neighborhoods was welcome. However, as churches began expanding their parking lots, adding soup kitchens to serve the homeless, and adding stadium lighting to adjacent ball fields, these institutions became less desirable neighbors. Cities began enacting ordinances that sought to relocate churches to places that were previously abandoned, such as historic downtowns and empty commercial strip malls. The advent of the mega church brought with it the need to locate these very large facilities in places with good access. In all cases, these institutions seemed to find their way to commercial areas where land taxes were highest. This was not a problem for most religious institutions because they were deemed tax exempt by federal tax codes. This did, however, become a problem for localities that were losing a significant amount of tax revenue. At this point in recent history, local governments began seeking new ways to limit the impacts of places of worship on neighborhoods, commercial districts, and local economies.

Congress tried to intervene with the passage of the Religious Freedom Restoration Act (commonly referred to as RFRA). Declared unconstitutional by the U.S. Supreme Court in *City of Boerne v. Flores*, 521 U.S. 507 (1997), Congress again attempted to codify the extent to which state and local governments could regulate places of worship with the passage of the Religious Land Uses and Institutionalized Persons Act of 2001. Under this act (42 U.S.C. Section 20000cc(a)(1)), a local government may not pass a law that:

Imposes a substantial burden on the religious exercise of a person, including a religious assembly or institution, unless the government demonstrates the imposition of the burden on that person, assembly, or institution (a) is in furtherance of a compelling governmental interest; and (b) is the least restrictive means of furthering that compelling governmental interest.

While undefined in the law, a regulation may be considered a substantial burden if the requirement forces the applicant to choose between his or her religious beliefs and government benefits. Zoning restrictions rarely rise to this level.

Response to Wicked Problem

It is possible to own and operate adult entertainment establishments in Katsburg. The town's code allows for the construction of these facilities by special use permit in two designated districts: the downtown historic district and along the frontage road. Within these two areas, there exists a buffering requirement that prevents these establishments from being located within 500 feet of any school, church, park, or residence. The buffering requirement, relatively conservative in scope, is also legally acceptable as a result of opinions such as the one rendered in *Renton*. While the mega church may be unhappy about its location a mere 501 feet away, the Pussy Cat Club is legally entitled to operate where it is situated. Its argument about the spirit of the law is not legally persuasive.

XXX has a good case against the town council's proposed condition on its sign. Katsburg permits the operation of adult entertainment establishments by special use permit. Special use permits may be used to empower the local government to exercise additional controls over land uses that would otherwise be deemed impermissible in some or all locations. In this case, the town council seeks to restrict the content of XXX's sign. As a condition of the special use permit, the town council has asked XXX to remove the hissing black cat from its sign. The justification given is a concern that the sign will attract children's attention. While it is permissible for a local government to restrict the design and operation of adult entertainment establishments, this particularly condition oversteps the legal bounds of the First Amendment as it applies to the regulation of commercial signs. More specifically, the condition also violates the federal Lantham Act which prohibits governments from passing laws interfering with the use of trademarks. The hissing black cat is XXX's trademark and its use must be permitted. While unable to remove the trademark black cat from the sign, the town council may condition its approval of the special use permit to require a different type of sign that does not attract so much attention or restrict the hours in which the sign may be illuminated.

Discussion Prompts

• Planners have a love-hate relationship with signs. Adequate, legible signage is important for wayfinding within a community. However, too much signage can lead to visual blight and also result in traffic safety issues. How might a city craft an ordinance that promotes wayfinding without infringing on businesses' rights to communicate with potential customers?

- Adult entertainment establishments are one of the most controversial land uses. These land uses receive special protections under the First Amendment. How far can a city go in regulating adult entertainment activities? Where is the best place for these land uses to be situated in a community?
- Mega churches are becoming increasingly popular. Why are these churches problematic from the perspectives of zoning and taxation? Where are these religious land uses best located?

Bibliography

Jourdan, D. (2013) A Response to Mandelker's Free Speech Law for On Premise Signs. *Planning and Environmental Law*, 65:4, 3–32.

Jourdan, D., Hurd, K., Hawkins, W. Gene, and Geideman, K. Winson (2014). Evidence Based Sign Regulation: Regulating Signage on the Basis of Empirical Wisdom. *The Urban Lawyer*, 45:2, 327–348.

Tucker, Dana M. (1996–7). Preventing the Secondary Effects of Adult Entertainment Establishments: Is Zoning the Solution? *Journal of Land Use and Environmental Law*, 12, 383.

12

AFFORDABLE HOUSING

Housing affordability is a critical issue throughout the United States. While the costs and associated issues vary state by state, it is clear that zoning regulations may either inhibit or enhance the supply of affordable housing units. Zoning schemes should be removed of barriers to the production of affordable housing and, to the extent possible, be crafted to be inclusionary.

Affordable Housing Wicked Problem

The town of Edwards (population 50,000) is a relatively affluent community that is positioned 30 miles outside a larger city with a population of 500,000 inhabitants. Due to a number of factors, including the quality of inner-city schools, many poor and working-class families are seeking opportunities to relocate to Edwards. Fearing that the town might absorb a disproportionate share of families, the Edwards Town Council passes an ordinance, which establishes a baseline for how many units of affordable housing may be built based on current demand. By ordinance, the town of Edwards is committed to producing five units of affordable housing for every thousand residents. Simultaneously, the town has designated additional areas of the town as appropriate for the development of affordable housing. The majority of these areas are located in places zoned for mixed use and industrial development. None of these newly designated areas are located next to the town's best schools.

Based on the facts set forth above, respond to the following questions:

(1) Is the city providing its regional fair share of housing pursuant to *Mt. Laurel* (see Cases section)?
(2) Give an example of how the town might redraft its housing policies to support a more inclusionary approach to zoning.

Cases

The following cases will be useful to you as you attempt to analyze this chapter's wicked problem:

Southern Burlington County NAACP v. Township of Mount Laurel, 67 N.J. 151 (1975)

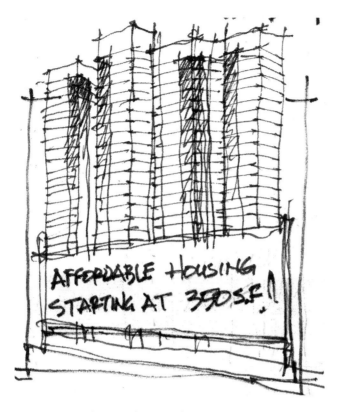

Figure 11 Credit: David D. Boeck

Southern Burlington County NAACP v. Township of Mount Laurel, 92 N.J. 158 (1983)
Village of Arlington Heights v. Metropolitan Housing Development Corporation, 429 U.S. 252 (1977)

Southern Burlington County NAACP v. Township of Mount Laurel (Mount Laurel I)

67 N.J. 151 (1975)

Facts

Mount Laurel experienced a population boom after World War II. In 1964, the township adopted a zoning ordinance that limited residential development to single-family residences, with the result that only persons with middle-class incomes could afford to live there. Due to its proximity to Camden and Philadelphia, Mount Laurel was a highly desirable residential community for urban workers.

Issue

Is it permissible for Mount Laurel to use zoning as a means of making affordable housing impossible and thereby exclude persons of low to moderate income from living there?

Held

No. The Supreme Court of New Jersey held that every municipality, including Mount Laurel, must aim their land use regulations at creating housing options and must use such regulations to give those on low to moderate incomes the opportunity to live there. In order to be a valid exercise of police power, zoning must be used to promote general welfare; Mount Laurel's ordinance, which made it physically and economically impossible to provide affordable housing, was an inappropriate use of its police power.

Discussion

To be valid, zoning is a tool to serve the people of a community, not to raise its tax revenue. Since the need for affordable housing is constant and widespread, *Mount Laurel* established the doctrine that municipalities are responsible for providing their "fair share" of regional affordable housing.

Case Excerpt

The legal question before us, as earlier indicated, is whether a developing municipality like Mount Laurel may validly, by a system of land use regulation, make it physically and economically impossible to provide low and moderate income housing in the municipality for the various categories of persons who need and want it and thereby, as Mount Laurel has, exclude such people from living within its confines because of the limited extent of their income and resources. Necessarily implicated are the broader questions of the right of such municipalities to limit the kinds of available housing and of any obligation to make possible a variety and choice of types of living accommodations.

We conclude that every such municipality must, by its land use regulations, presumptively make realistically possible an appropriate variety and choice of housing. More specifically, it cannot foreclose the opportunity of the classes of people mentioned for low and moderate income housing and in its regulations must affirmatively afford that opportunity, at least to the extent of the municipality's fair share of the present and prospective regional need therefor. These obligations must be met unless the particular municipality can sustain the heavy burden of demonstrating peculiar circumstances which dictate that it should not be required so to do.

...

It is plain beyond dispute that proper provision for adequate housing of all categories of people is certainly an absolute essential in promotion of the general welfare required in all local land use regulation. Further the universal and constant need for such housing is so important and of such broad public interest that the general welfare which developing municipalities like Mount Laurel must consider extends beyond their boundaries and cannot be parochially confined to the claimed good of the particular municipality. It has to follow that, broadly speaking, the presumptive obligation arises for each such municipality affirmatively to plan and provide, by its land use regulations, the reasonable opportunity for an appropriate variety and choice of housing, including, of course, low and moderate cost housing, to meet the needs, desires and resources of all categories of people who may desire to live within its boundaries. Negatively, it may not adopt regulations or policies which thwart or preclude that opportunity.

...

By way of summary, what we have said comes down to this. As a developing municipality, Mount Laurel must, by its land use regulations, make realistically possible the opportunity for an appropriate variety and choice of housing for all categories of people who may desire to live there, of course including those of low and moderate income. It must permit multifamily housing, without bedroom or similar restrictions, as well as small dwellings on very small lots, low cost housing of other types and, in general, high density zoning, without artificial and unjustifiable minimum requirements as to lot size, building size and the like, to meet the full panoply of these needs. Certainly when a municipality zones for industry and commerce for local tax benefit purposes, it without question must zone to permit adequate housing within the means of the employees involved in such uses. (If planned unit developments are authorized, one would assume that each must include a reasonable amount of low and moderate income housing in its residential 'mix,' unless opportunity for such housing has already been realistically provided for elsewhere in the municipality.) The amount of land removed from residential use by allocation to industrial and commercial purposes must be reasonably related to the present and future potential for such purposes. In other words, such municipalities must zone primarily for the living welfare of people and not for the benefit of the local tax rate.

Southern Burlington County NAACP v. Township of Mount Laurel (Mount Laurel II)

92 N.J. 158 (1983)

Facts
Eight years after the Supreme Court of New Jersey decided *Mount Laurel I*, Mount Laurel and other municipalities in the state had failed to rectify their exclusionary zoning practices that precluded persons of low- to moderate-income from living there because of the lack of affordable housing options.

Issue
In the absence of legislative initiative, may the court intervene to create a more effective system for municipalities to comply with the *Mount Laurel I* doctrine of providing realistic opportunities to meet their fair share of regional housing needs?

Held

Yes. Although the New Jersey Supreme Court maintained its position that its holding in *Mount Laurel I* requiring municipalities to meet their fair share of regional affordable housing needs was sound policy, it recognized municipal noncompliance as a continued barrier to affordable housing in New Jersey.

Discussion

The court acknowledged that it was not the judicial system's duty to build homes, but rather, to enforce the Constitution; any zoning ordinance that is exclusionary, such as those commonly found in New Jersey, is an unconstitutional exercise of police powers. *Mount Laurel II* clarified affirmative measures municipalities could enact to ensure they met their regional fair share of affordable housing, including the use of incentive zoning, requiring developers to include lower income housing in their projects, and drafting ordinances to allow for more types of low cost housing to be built.

Case Excerpt

D. *Meeting the Mount Laurel Obligation*

1. Removing Excessive Restrictions and Exactions

In order to meet their Mount Laurel obligations, municipalities, at the very least, must remove all municipally created barriers to the construction of their fair share of lower income housing. Thus, to the extent necessary to meet their prospective fair share and provide for their indigenous poor (and, in some cases, a portion of the region's poor), municipalities must remove zoning and subdivision restrictions and exactions that are not necessary to protect health and safety...

2. Using Affirmative Measures

Despite the emphasis in *Mount Laurel I* on the *affirmative* nature of the fair share obligation, the obligation has been sometimes construed (after *Madison*) as requiring in effect no more than a theoretical, rather than realistic, opportunity. As noted later, the alleged realistic opportunity for lower income housing in [Mount Laurel Township] is provided through three zones owned entirely by three individuals. There is absolutely no assurance that there is anything realistic in this "opportunity": the individuals may, for many different reasons, simply not desire to build lower income housing. They may not want to build any housing at all, they may want to use the land for industry, for business, or just leave it vacant. It was never intended in *Mount Laurel I* that this awesome constitutional obligation, designed to give the poor a fair chance for housing, be satisfied by meaningless amendments to zoning or other ordinances. "Affirmative," in the *Mount Laurel* rule, suggests that the *municipality* is going to do something, and "realistic opportunity" suggests that what it is going to do will make it *realistically* possible for lower income housing to be built. Satisfaction of the *Mount Laurel* doctrine cannot depend on the inclination of developers to help the poor. It has to depend on affirmative inducements to make the opportunity real.

It is equally unrealistic, even where the land is owned by a developer eager to build, simply to rezone that land to permit the construction of lower income housing if the construction of other housing is permitted on the same land and the latter is more profitable than lower income housing. One of the new zones in Mount Laurel provides a good example. The developer there intends to build housing out of the reach of the lower income group. After creation of the new zone, he still is allowed to build such housing but now has the "opportunity" to build lower income housing to the extent of 10 percent of the units. There is absolutely no reason why he should take advantage of this opportunity if, as seems apparent, his present housing plans will result in a higher profit. There is simply no inducement, no reason, nothing affirmative, that makes this opportunity "realistic." For an opportunity to be "realistic" it must be one that is at least sensible for someone to use.

Therefore, unless removal of restrictive barriers will, without more, afford a realistic opportunity for the construction of the municipality's fair share of the region's lower income housing need, affirmative measures will be required.

There are two basic types of affirmative measures that a municipality can use to make the opportunity for lower income housing realistic: (1) encouraging or requiring the use of available state or federal housing subsidies, and (2) providing incentives for or requiring private developers to set aside a portion of their developments for lower income housing. Which, if either, of these devices will be necessary in any particular municipality to assure compliance with the constitutional mandate will be initially up to the municipality itself. Where necessary, the trial court overseeing compliance may require their use...

The most commonly used inclusionary zoning techniques are incentive zoning and mandatory set-asides. The former involves offering economic incentives to a developer through the relaxation of various restrictions of an ordinance (typically density limits) in exchange for the construction of certain amounts of low and moderate income units. The latter, a mandatory set-aside, is basically a requirement that developers include a minimum amount of lower income housing in their projects.

(i) Incentive Zoning

Incentive zoning is usually accomplished either through a sliding scale density bonus that increases the permitted density as the amount of lower income housing provided is increased, or through a set bonus for participation in a lower income housing program. See Fox & Davis, 3 Hastings Const. L.Q. 1015, 1060–62 (1977).

Incentive zoning leaves a developer free to build only upper income housing if it so chooses. Fox and Davis, in their survey of municipalities using inclusionary devices, found that while developers sometimes profited through density bonuses, they were usually reluctant to cooperate with incentive zoning programs; and that therefore those municipalities that relied exclusively on such programs were not very successful in actually providing lower income housing. Id. at 1067…

(ii) Mandatory Set-Asides

A more effective inclusionary device that municipalities must use if they cannot otherwise meet their fair share obligations is the mandatory set-aside…

The use of mandatory set-asides is not without its problems: dealing with the scarcity of federal subsidies, maintaining the rent or sales price of lower income units at lower income levels over time, and assuring developers an adequate return on their investments. Fox and Davis found that the scarcity of federal subsidies has greatly undermined the effectiveness of mandatory set-asides where they are triggered only when a developer is able to obtain such subsidies. Where practical, a municipality should use mandatory set-asides even where subsidies are not available…

Because a mandatory set-aside program usually requires a developer to sell or rent units at below their full value so that the units can be affordable to lower income people, the owner of the development or the initial tenant or purchaser of the unit may be induced to re-rent or re-sell the unit at its full value.

This problem, which municipalities *must* address in order to assure that they continue to meet their fair share obligations, can be dealt with in [several] ways… [The] more common approach for dealing with the re-sale or re-rent problem is for the municipality to require that re-sale or re-rent prices be kept at lower income levels… A more sophisticated approach, considered by Princeton Township, would have established disposition covenants…, binding the owners and renters of such units to sell or rent only at lower income levels…

In addition to the mechanisms we have just described, municipalities and trial courts must consider such other affirmative devices as zoning substantial areas for mobile homes and for other types of low cost housing and establishing maximum square footage zones, i.e., zones where the developers cannot build units with *more* than a certain footage or build anything other than lower income housing or housing that includes a specified portion of lower income housing. In some cases, a realistic opportunity to provide the municipality's fair share may require over-zoning, i.e., zoning to allow for *more* than the fair share if it is likely, as it usually is, that not all of the property made available for lower income housing will actually result in such housing.

Although several of the defendants concede that simply removing restrictions and exactions is unlikely to result in the construction of lower income housing, they maintain that requiring the municipality to use affirmative measures is beyond the scope of the courts' authority. We disagree…

The contention that generally these devices are beyond the municipal power because they are "socio-economic" is particularly inappropriate. The very basis for the constitutional obligation underlying *Mount Laurel* is a belief, fundamental, that excluding a class of citizens from housing on an economic basis (one that substantially corresponds to a socio-economic basis) distinctly disserves the general welfare. That premise is essential to the conclusion that such zoning ordinances are an abuse of the zoning power and are therefore unconstitutional.

It is nonsense to single out inclusionary zoning (providing a realistic opportunity for the construction of lower income housing) and label it "socio-economic" if that is meant to imply that other aspects of zoning are not. Detached single family residential zones, high-rise multi-family zones of any kind, factory zones, "clean" research and development zones, recreational, open space, conservation, and agricultural zones, regional shopping mall zones, indeed practically any significant kind of zoning now used, has a substantial socio-economic impact and, in some cases, a socio-economic motivation. It would be ironic if inclusionary zoning to encourage the construction of lower income housing were ruled beyond the power of a municipality because it is "socio-economic" when its need has arisen from the socio-economic zoning of the past that excluded it.

We find the distinction between the exercise of the zoning power that is "directly tied to the physical use of the property," *Madison*, and its exercise tied to the income level of those who use the property artificial in connection with the *Mount Laurel* obligation, although it obviously troubled us in *Madison*. The prohibition of this kind of affirmative device seems unfair when we have for so long allowed large lot single family residence districts, a form of zoning keyed, in effect, to income levels. The constitutional obligation itself is not to build three bedroom units, or single family residences on very small lots, or high-rise multi-family apartments, but rather to provide through the zoning ordinance a realistic opportunity to construct *lower income housing*. All of the physical uses are simply a means to this end. We see no reason why the municipality cannot exercise its zoning power to achieve that end directly rather than through a mass of detailed regulations governing the "physical use" of land, the sole purpose of which is to provide housing within the reach of lower income families. We know of no governmental purpose relating to zoning that is served by requiring a municipality to ingeniously design detailed land use regulations, purporting to be "directly tied to the physical use of the property," but actually aimed at accommodating lower income families, while not allowing it directly to require developers to construct lower income units. Indirection of this kind has no more virtue where its goal is to achieve that which is permitted – indeed, constitutionally mandated – than it has in achieving that which is prohibited.

3. Zoning for Mobile Homes

As the cost of ordinary housing skyrockets for purchasers and renters, mobile homes become increasingly important as a source of low cost housing... Therefore, subject to the qualifications noted hereafter, we rule that municipalities that cannot otherwise meet their fair share obligations must provide zoning for low-cost mobile homes as an affirmative device in their zoning ordinances...

E. *Judicial Remedies*

If a trial court determines that a municipality has not met its *Mount Laurel* obligation, it shall order the municipality to revise its zoning ordinance within a set time period to comply with the constitutional mandate; if the municipality fails adequately to revise its ordinance within that time, the court shall implement the remedies for noncompliance outlined below; and if plaintiff is a developer, the court shall determine whether a builder's remedy should be granted.

Village of Arlington Heights v. Metropolitan Housing Development Corporation

429 U.S. 252 (1977)

Facts
Metropolitan Housing Development Corporation (MHDC), an experienced non-profit developer, was hired by a religious group to build nearly 200 townhouse units in the Chicago suburb of Arlington Heights for low- and moderate-income tenants. Under federal subsidies, the development would be racially integrated. After a series of public meetings, the village denied MHDC's petition to rezone the property in question from single- to multi-family housing on the grounds that the area had always been zoned for single-family residences and that the village's policy of using multi-family housing as a buffer between single-family and commercial or industrial uses would not be met. MHDC brought suit, alleging that the village's denial of its rezoning request was racially discriminatory and violated the Fourteenth Amendment.

Issue
Did Arlington Heights violate the Equal Protection Clause of the Fourteenth Amendment when it denied MHDC's application to rezone?

Held
No. Although Arlington Heights' action would arguably bear a more serious consequence for racial minorities in the Chicago area, government action is not considered unconstitutional solely because it results in a racially disproportionate impact. In order to sustain a violation of the Fourteenth Amendment, proof of racially discriminatory intent or purpose is necessary. MHDC was unable to meet its burden.

Discussion
The Court never addressed the village's policy of using multi-family development to serve as a buffer between single-family residences and uses deemed incompatible with single-family housing, such as commercial or manufacturing uses.

Case Excerpt
Our decision last Term in *Washington v. Davis*, 426 U. S. 229 (1976), made it clear that official action will not be held unconstitutional solely because it results in a racially disproportionate impact. "Disproportionate impact is not irrelevant, but it is not the sole touchstone of an invidious racial discrimination." *Id.*, at 242. Proof of racially discriminatory intent or purpose is required to show a violation of the Equal Protection Clause. Although some contrary indications

160

may be drawn from some of our cases, the holding in *Davis* reaffirmed a principle well established in a variety of contexts. *E. g., Keyes* v. *School Dist. No. 1, Denver, Colo.,* 413 U. S. 189, 208 (1973) (schools); *Wright* v. *Rockefeller,* 376 U. S. 52, 56–57 (1964) (election districting); *Akins* v. *Texas,* 325 U. S. 398, 403–404 (1945) (jury selection).

Davis does not require a plaintiff to prove that the challenged action rested solely on racially discriminatory purposes. Rarely can it be said that a legislature or administrative body operating under a broad mandate made a decision motivated solely by a single concern, or even that a particular purpose was the "dominant" or "primary" one. In fact, it is because legislators and administrators are properly concerned with balancing numerous competing considerations that courts refrain from reviewing the merits of their decisions, absent a showing of arbitrariness or irrationality. But racial discrimination is not just another competing consideration. When there is a proof that a discriminatory purpose has been a motivating factor in the decision, this judicial deference is no longer justified.

Determining whether invidious discriminatory purpose was a motivating factor demands a sensitive inquiry into such circumstantial and direct evidence of intent as may be available. The impact of the official action – whether it "bears more heavily on one race than another," *Washington* v. *Davis, supra,* at 242 – may provide an important starting point. Sometimes a clear pattern, unexplainable on grounds other than race, emerges from the effect of the state action even when the governing legislation appears neutral on its face. *Yick Wo* v. *Hopkins,* 118 U. S. 356 (1886); *Guinn* v. *United States,* 238 U. S. 347 (1915); *Lane* v. *Wilson,* 307 U. S. 268 (1939); *Gomillion* v. *Lightfoot,* 364 U. S. 339 (1960). The evidentiary inquiry is then relatively easy. But such cases are rare. Absent a pattern as stark as that in *Gomillion* or *Yick Wo,* impact alone is not determinative, and the Court must look to other evidence.

...This case was tried in the District Court and reviewed in the Court of Appeals before our decision in *Washington* v. *Davis, supra.* The respondents proceeded on the erroneous theory that the Village's refusal to rezone carried a racially discriminatory effect and was, without more, unconstitutional. But both courts below understood that at least part of their function was to examine the purpose underlying the decision. In making its findings on this issue, the District Court noted that some of the opponents of Lincoln Green who spoke at the various hearings might have been motivated by opposition to minority groups. The court held, however, that the evidence "does not warrant the conclusion that this motivated the defendants." 373 F. Supp., at 211.

On appeal the Court of Appeals focused primarily on respondents' claim that the Village's buffer policy had not been consistently applied and was being invoked with a strictness here that could only demonstrate some other underlying motive. The court concluded that the buffer policy, though not always applied with perfect consistency, had on several occasions formed the basis for the Board's decision to deny other rezoning proposals. "The evidence does not necessitate a finding that Arlington Heights administered this policy in a discriminatory manner." 517 F. 2d, at 412. The Court of Appeals therefore approved the District Court's findings concerning the Village's purposes in denying rezoning to MHDC.

We also have reviewed the evidence. The impact of the Village's decision does arguably bear more heavily on racial minorities. Minorities constitute 18% of the Chicago area population, and 40% of the income groups said to be eligible for Lincoln Green. But there is little about the sequence of events leading up to the decision that would spark suspicion. The area around the Viatorian property has been zoned R-3 since 1959, the year when Arlington Heights first adopted a zoning map. Single-family homes surround the 80-acre site, and the Village is undeniably committed to single-family homes as its dominant residential land use. The rezoning request progressed according to the usual procedures. The Plan Commission even scheduled two additional hearings, at least in part to accommodate MHDC and permit it to supplement its presentation with answers to questions generated at the first hearing.

The statements by the Plan Commission and Village Board members, as reflected in the official minutes, focused almost exclusively on the zoning aspects of the MHDC petition, and the zoning factors on which they relied are not novel criteria in the Village's rezoning decisions. There is no reason to doubt that there has been reliance by some neighboring property owners on the maintenance of single-family zoning in the vicinity. The Village originally adopted its buffer policy long before MHDC entered the picture and has applied the policy too consistently for us to infer discriminatory purpose from its application in this case. Finally, MHDC called one member of the Village Board to the stand at trial. Nothing in her testimony supports an inference of invidious purpose.

In sum, the evidence does not warrant overturning the concurrent findings of both courts below. Respondents simply failed to carry their burden of proving that discriminatory purpose was a motivating factor in the Village's decision. This conclusion ends the constitutional inquiry. The Court of Appeals' further finding that the Village's decision carried a discriminatory "ultimate effect" is without independent constitutional significance.

Primer on Affordable Housing as an Issue for Planners

The Affordable Housing Problem

Americans have long associated the term "affordable housing" with housing for the poor. However, the United States Department of Housing and Urban Development suggests that a home is affordable if its occupants pay less than 30 percent of their gross annual income on rents or mortgages, including taxes, insurance and utility costs. As such, even middle and upper income Americans may experience a shortage of affordable housing if they pay more to occupy their homes.

Even in cases where there is an "adequate" supply of affordable units, or even a surplus, an affordable housing crisis may continue to exist. This can occur when the existing housing stock is replete with physically inadequate structures. These homes may not comply with local public and electrical codes. They may be poorly insulated, requiring occupants to pay exorbitant prices for heating and cooling. Rarely are there public or private funds available to bring these properties up to code because, in market terms, the cost of repairs commonly exceeds the value of the structures. These structures may also be physically inadequate because they are not large enough to accommodate the occupants, such as large families or multiple tenants who choose to live together to keep costs low.

Units deemed affordable are also commonly located in socially and physically distressed neighborhoods. Affordable housing is often clustered in areas of high poverty, particularly in the urban core. Families living in these units experience the issues associated with areas of concentrated poverty such as lack of access to quality jobs, food deserts, and substandard schools and other amenities.

Exclusionary Zoning

Areas of concentrated poverty are the result of both exclusionary zoning practices and market forces. Prior to the 1950s, zoning ordinances and private covenants, as well as redlining practices by lenders, were used to prevent racial and economic integration.

Changes in the law removed these barriers to the production of affordable housing. However, market forces, including consumer choice, perpetuated the problems associated with exclusionary zoning, as demonstrated in *Mount Laurel I* and *II*.

The Mount Laurel Doctrine

The legal battle for affordable housing was famously found in Mount Laurel, New Jersey. This small town, located close to Camden and Philadelphia, experienced rapid population growth between 1950 and 1970. In those 20 years, the town's population grew from 2,817 to 11,221 as a result of highway expansion. Responding to growth pressures, the local government modified its zoning ordinance. It rezoned more than 4,000 acres to industrial use. The remaining 10,000 acres of undeveloped land was zoned for single-family residential development. Simultaneously, the city began condemning and demolishing dilapidated housing, much of which was occupied by African American families.

Mount Laurel I arose out of the city's denial of a non-profit group's proposal to build 36 affordable garden apartments for families being displaced by urban renewal activities. Ethel Lawrence and the Southern Burlington County NAACP on behalf of the town's black and Hispanic residents, filed a class action lawsuit against Mount Laurel Township for making it physically and economically impossible to build low and moderate income housing in the area.

This case eventually reached the New Jersey Supreme Court who considered the question: Can land use regulations be employed to make it impossible to build low and moderate income housing opportunities for those who need it? The State Supreme Court ruled, among other holdings, that a zoning ordinance must make possible the development of a variety of types of housing opportunities in an effort to meet the township's regional fair share of affordable housing except where infeasible. The High Court stated its expectation that Mount Laurel permit the development of multi-family housing in sufficient quantities to house local and regional workers. The court gave the township 90 days to revise its zoning ordinance in accordance with its opinion. In its parting words, the court stated: "Should Mount Laurel not perform as we expect, further judicial action may be sought" (p. 734).

The township did not make sufficient progress in amending its zoning code as specified by the New Jersey Supreme Court. The township rezoned three tracts of land, roughly 20 acres, to allow for the development of affordable housing. The first parcel was located in an industrial park and had been purchased for the construction of a transit stop. The second was located in a filled wetland that was a significant distance from existing public water and sewer lines. The third tract of land was located within a planned unit development that limited the number of children who could live in units constructed there.

Nearly a decade later, the parties found themselves back in court for round two. In *Mount Laurel II*, the New Jersey Supreme Court made clear that it intended to rid any ambiguities left by its first decision. The court wrote:

> We have learned from experience, however, that unless a strong judicial hand is used, Mount Laurel will not result in housing, but in paper, process, witnesses, trials, and appeals. We intend by this decision to strengthen it, clarify it, and make it easier for public officials, including judges, to apply it.
>
> (p. 410)

In this opinion, the court clarified what it meant by regional fair share. While the court did not specifically define the term, it suggested that local governments had a limited affirmative duty to provide incentives to encourage the construction of affordable housing in an amount sufficient to house those employed there and in the surrounding region. This court prescribed that communities consider implementing a litany of incentives to encourage the production of affordable housing, including: subsidies, set asides, and zoning for mobile homes.

The High Court anticipated that it would be difficult to ensure that communities were meeting the regional fair share requirement for affordable housing. In an unprecedented act, the court established a three-panel court charged with reviewing claims made by developers who sought to, but were precluded from, constructing affordable housing within New Jersey communities. The court created a builder's remedy to encourage developers to challenge local barriers to the production of affordable housing.

It is important to understand that the type of jurisprudence coming from the *Mount Laurel* case is not common. Some contend that the *Mount Laurel* decision represents a violation of the separation of powers clause which precludes courts from acting like legislatures. The state's legislature eventually responded to the Court's challenge and created the State's Council on Affordable Housing. This entity crafts the state's affordable housing plan and helps local governments calculate their regional fair shares of affordable housing. The agency also helps arbitrate challenges surrounding barriers to the construction of affordable housing.

Ironically, the *Mount Laurel* cases did very little in terms of the generation of affordable housing units within the township. However, these cases started a national conversation about issues related to housing affordability. This conversation continues. More information on this litigation and more current legal challenges is available at: http://fairsharehousing.org.

NIMBYism

NIMBYism ("Not In My Backyard") continues to prevail as one of the most difficult obstacles to overcome in the construction of affordable housing. In some instances, local zoning regulations are still used to accomplish exclusionary purposes.

LIMITATIONS ON MANUFACTURED HOMES

Many zoning ordinances seek to prevent or limit the construction of manufactured homes. While there are arguably some good reasons for doing so, including structural integrity in regions prone to severe storms, this housing type is one of the most affordable options for lower income families.

LIMITED OPPORTUNITIES FOR THE CONSTRUCTION OF MULTI-FAMILY HOUSING

Other zoning ordinances seek to place limits on the number and location of multi-family units (apartments, townhouses, duplexes, etc.) that can be constructed in a community or particular area of a city. Multi-family housing, particularly that which is available for rent, is often the best available option for low-income families. However, property owners, particularly those in areas zoned for single-family residential development, commonly block proposals to allow multi-family development to happen within or in the immediate surrounds of these neighborhoods.

THE CREATION OF HOLDING ZONES

In some communities, undeveloped land is classified as agricultural land. Typically, zoning requirements in these areas prevent the development of multi-family housing. In the alternative, it allows the construction of housing on 10- to 20-acre plots of land. The construction of affordable housing is infeasible under such conditions given the land costs.

The same is true with respect of land use configurations that reserve an over-supply of undeveloped lands for future industrial development. While it is certainly appropriate for communities to anticipate future needs and location for industrial land uses, the reservation of "too much" land is unrealistic and often done to control the supply of land available for the construction of affordable housing.

Even more insidiously, some communities have sought to establish minimum square footage requirements for single-family homes. These ordinances offer home buyers the guarantee that all homes constructed within a particular area will be about the same size. This is done to alleviate fears that small homes will be constructed and diminish property values in these areas. Some courts have found that such practices amount to exclusionary zoning practices.

UNRELATED PERSONS ORDINANCES

Finally, many communities place limitations on the number of unrelated persons who may live together in a dwelling. This is most common in college towns where property owners, particularly in single-family neighborhoods located near campuses, are worried that houses will be rented to groups of college students who will not care for their properties, resulting in a diminution of property values. Rather than utilizing code enforcement to deal with infractions such as litter, noise, and maintenance issues, unrelated persons ordinances are utilized to limit the number of non-family members who can share a household together. While typically legally defensible, these ordinances often produce results that are exclusionary. For example, an ordinance preventing more than three unrelated persons from living together would allow the same three-bedroom home to be occupied by three unrelated college students or a family with two biological parents and six children. As a matter of public policy, these laws presuppose that a family, regardless of size, would take better care of its home than an unrelated set of college students or working professionals, as the case may be.

Inclusionary Zoning

Ideally, affordable housing units would be integrated into neighborhoods throughout cities. Inclusionary zoning would accomplish a number of purposes at the heart of good planning and zoning. First, inclusionary zoning practices would ensure that lower income households are no longer segregated in parts of cities that lack adequate infrastructure to support a good quality of life for these residents. In addition, inclusionary zoning could also be used as a tool that would help counteract the impacts of sprawl. Affordable housing could be produced in existing neighborhoods through infill development opportunities. This would accomplish both integration and density.

Inclusionary Zoning Tools

SET ASIDES

Set asides are the most commonly utilized tool to incentivize the construction of affordable housing. Cities, particularly those experiencing growth, may require developers of residential units to reserve a percentage of the units they construct as affordable housing. These units may be made available for sale or rental as long as the developer has worked with the city to ensure that the price of these units is kept affordable relative to the land market. Ordinances requiring set asides for affordable housing are typically time limited, allowing the developer to recapture any loss experienced after the expiration of the period set by the ordinance. In many cases, these units, particularly rental units, must remain affordable for 10 to 15 years. This does not mean that the developer cannot raise rents for this term. Rather, rents must be set in accordance with market fluctuations.

COST OFFSETS

Set asides are often accompanied with cost offsets, such as density bonuses, impact fee waivers, flexible design requirements, or expedited permitting. The city may offer a developer who is willing to build affordable housing units the opportunity to build more densely if he or she agrees to set aside a percentage of the units constructed for affordable housing. The grant of a density bonus typically increases the developer's short- and long-term profit margins.

IMPACT FEE WAIVERS

Cities that are experiencing growth pressures commonly adopt impact fees to ensure that new development pays for the burden it places on urban infrastructure, such as water, sewer, and road systems. As discussed more fully in Chapter 13 on growth management, impact fees can raise the cost of development. These added costs often interfere with the construction of affordable housing. As such, waivers of these fees are often necessary to incentivize the construction of affordable units.

FLEXIBLE DESIGN REQUIREMENTS

Bulk requirements in zoning codes can also interfere with the production of affordable housing units. Simple requirements such as setbacks and lot size restrictions can raise the costs of development or make small properties unusable for development. Suspension of these requirements, such as allowing an affordable house to be built with a zero lot line, is useful in helping create a climate conducive to the construction of affordable housing.

EXPEDITED PERMITTING

Developers commonly cite the burdens associated with the planning process as one of the most expensive barriers to the construction of affordable housing. Even in the absence of a lengthy and contested rezoning process, developers who are willing to build affordable housing often do not because of the expenses associated with holding a piece of property while it is reviewed by staff. In response, many cities have created expedited permitting processes for developers who will construct affordable units.

ALTERNATIVE TO ON-SITE UNITS

Some developers are not willing to build affordable units as a part of their developments because, in their opinion, these units are not appropriate in the context of surrounding development. Sympathetic to these concerns, some communities have crafted inclusionary zoning ordinances that allow developers to make "in lieu of payments." These payments are calculated by estimating the cost of producing affordable housing units. The developer pays the city this amount and leaves it to the city to arrange for the construction of affordable housing units in other locations of the city where demand is higher for affordable housing. While this does not promote integration of the units, in lieu of payments ensure that there is funding to build affordable housing.

Response to the Wicked Problem

In *Mount Laurel I* and *II*, the New Jersey Supreme Court expressly held that every municipality (except those who were near full build out) must provide "a realistic opportunity for decent housing." This promise was made as part of a legal doctrine that required all cities to provide their regional fair share of affordable housing. While the Court offered no specific formula for meeting this obligation, the expectation was clear. This pair of cases requires the removal of all zoning restrictions that impede the production of affordable housing. The *Mount Laurel II* Court went a step further in requiring communities to create incentives to spur the development of low and moderate income housing. The *Mount Laurel* cases were brought in response to the zoning ordinances of Mount Laurel.

In the hypothetical above, the town of Edwards has responded to the *Mount Laurel* charge by creating its own fair share housing scheme. This ordinance requires the production of five affordable housing units for every 1,000 residents. Further, the ordinance has expanded the number of zoning categories where affordable housing units can be located to include all mixed use and industrial zones.

In response to question 1, there is no way to tell if the new ordinance will aid Edwards in producing its regional fair share of affordable housing. The town has not demonstrated, based on market demand or demographics, that this ordinance will generate the amount of units demanded. In order to survive judicial scrutiny under the *Mount Laurel* cases, the town of Edwards must demonstrate that it can meet current and future demands for affordable housing within the community and as a part of the region. Given statements made by the town council at the public hearing on this ordinance, it is likely that standard was drafted conservatively in an effort to prevent an influx of poor and working-class families from settling in the town.

This ordinance may also be susceptible to a legal challenge as a result of locational requirements. The ordinance has directed the production of new units of affordable housing to areas that are mixed use and industrial. The hypothetical reveals that these zones are not located in the same areas as the town's best schools. As such, there may be an *Arlington Heights*-type claim based on patterns of discrimination. While such a claim is not likely to prevail, this is a common predicament in towns that seek to allow the production of affordable housing in areas that are less affluent.

While the town council may not need to repeal its affordable housing ordinance, it should direct planning staff to conduct an empirical analysis of affordable housing demands for the jurisdiction and its surrounds. In the absence of good data on the same, the town should look to the state's affordable housing study to estimate its current and future needs for affordable housing. Beyond calculating supply and demand of units, town planners should be mindful of the location of current units. New units should be distributed in a way that encourages inclusionary zoning. These efforts will ensure a heightened quality of life for all town residents by giving access to better schools, jobs, and amenities to residents of all economic thresholds.

Discussion Prompts

- What is affordable housing? What are the primary differences between public housing, affordable housing, and workforce housing?
- Why is affordable housing often treated like a NIMBY issue?
- Why hasn't the readjustment in the housing market eliminated previous supply constraints for affordable housing?
- Some scholars suggest that the affordable housing problem must be planned for regionally. Why? What are the constraints to this type of planning effort?

Bibliography

Berger, L. (1991). Inclusionary Zoning Devices as Takings: The Legacy of the Mount Laurel Cases. *Nebraska Law Review*, 70:186, 186–288.

Bogart, W. T. (1993) "What Big Teeth You Have!": Identifying the Motivations for Exclusionary Zoning. *Urban Studies*, 30: December, 1669–1681.

Duany, Andres, Plater-Zyberk, Elizabet, and Speck, Jeff (2000). *Suburban Nation: The Rise of Sprawl and the Decline of the American Dream*. New York: North Point Press.

Iglesias, Tim and Lento, Rochelle E. (2006). *The Legal Guide to Affordable Housing Development*. Chicago: American Bar Association.

13

GROWTH MANAGEMENT

The growth management movement emerged in the 1970s. Growth management strategies do not seek to stop growth or even slow it. Instead, growth management seeks to control the timing, location, amount, and character of development within the context of a given community. These strategies are typically related to the adequacy of available infrastructure, often shifting to developers the burden to pay for the expansion or creation of new infrastructure.

Growth Management Wicked Problem

The city of Nostalgia has had a small and stable population for 30 years, hovering at or around 10,000. However, the recent discovery of mineral deposits will likely result in substantial population growth due to the expansion of the oil and gas industry. Industry experts estimate that the town's population will double in the next 10 years. City officials are worried about how they will accommodate this potential growth and are uninterested in welcoming the types of lower income residents often occupying positions in the industry. The city passes a moratorium on all new residential development in the community to plan for the growth. The moratorium lasts for nine months. In that time, no experts are hired to study the problem. Fearing that the development community might bring a lawsuit if something is not done, the City Council considers two options:

- The city could pass a rate of development ordinance, limiting new residential development to 50 residential units per year. Only 10 percent of those units could be developed as multi-family housing.
- The city could pass an adequate public facilities ordinance, which would only permit new multi-family developments where the developers were willing to pay to install the water and sewerage infrastructure necessary to service those properties. The city would continue to pay for connecting infrastructure to new single family units.

1. What must the city do to justify its moratorium?
2. Can the city justify the use of either or both of the two options proposed?
3. You are the city planner. Suggest a third proposal for managing development resulting from the expansion of mineral exploration in the area.

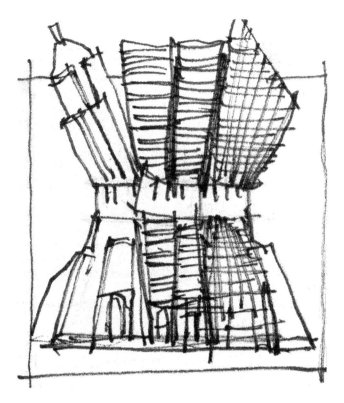

Figure 12 Credit: David D. Boeck

Cases

The following cases will be useful to you as you attempt to analyze this chapter's wicked problem:

Nollan v. California Coastal Commission, 482 U.S. 825 (1987)
Dolan v. City of Tigard, 512 U.S. 374 (1994)
Construction Industry Association of Sonoma County v. City of Petaluma, 522 F.2d 897 (9th Cir. 1975)
Golden v. Planning Board of the Town of Ramapo, 30 N.Y.2d 359 (1972)

Nollan v. California Coastal Commission

483 U.S. 825 (1987)

Facts
Nollan bought a beachfront property under the condition that the original structure could be demolished and replaced with a new residence. Public beaches were

---

within walking distance on either side of the property, but would be obstructed from public view upon construction of the new home. When Nollan applied for a permit from the California Coastal Commission, the permit was granted on the condition that Nollan provide a public access easement across the property. Nollan filed suit arguing the required easement constituted a taking. During the appeals process, Nollan demolished the lot's existing structure and built a three-bedroom home.

Issue

Does requiring an easement as a condition for the issuance of a land-use permit violate the Fifth and Fourteenth Amendments?

Held

Yes. It is undisputed that if the Commission had required Nollan to convey an easement outright, it would have constituted a taking. A land regulation will not trigger a Fifth Amendment taking if it substantially advances a permissible state interest, while not denying an owner economically viable property use. The Supreme Court held that conditioning the building permit on Nollan providing a public easement did not advance a legitimate state interest because the state's objectives of banning beachfront development and easement access do not serve the same purpose.

Discussion

The right to exclude others is a fundamental property right, one which would have been permanently and substantially diminished if Nollan were required to create an easement across his property.

Case Excerpt

Given, then, that requiring uncompensated conveyance of the easement out-right would violate the Fourteenth Amendment, the question becomes whether requiring it to be conveyed as a condition for issuing a land-use permit alters the outcome. We have long recognized that land-use regulation does not effect a taking if it "substantially advance[s] legitimate state interests" and does not "den[y] an owner economically viable use of his land," *Agins* v. *Tiburon*, 447 U. S. 255, 260 (1980). See also *Penn Central Transportation Co.* v. *New York City*, 438 U. S. 104, 127 (1978) ("[A] use restriction may constitute a 'taking' if not reasonably necessary to the effectuation of a substantial government purpose"). Our cases have not elaborated on the standards for determining what constitutes a "legitimate state interest" or what type of connection between the regulation and the state interest satisfies the requirement that the former "substantially advance" the latter. They have made clear, however, that a broad range of governmental purposes and regulations satisfies these requirements. See *Agins* v. *Tiburon, supra*, at 260–262 (scenic zoning); *Penn Central Transportation Co.* v. *New York City, supra* (landmark preservation); *Euclid* v. *Ambler Realty Co.*, 272 U. S. 365 (1926) (residential zoning); Laitos & Westfall, Government Interference with Private Interests in Public Resources, 11 Harv. Envtl. L. Rev. 1,

66 (1987). The Commission argues that among these permissible purposes are protecting the public's ability to see the beach, assisting the public in overcoming the "psychological barrier" to using the beach created by a developed shorefront, and preventing congestion on the public beaches. We assume, without deciding, that this is so – in which case the Commission unquestionably would be able to deny the Nollans their permit outright if their new house (alone, or by reason of the cumulative impact produced in conjunction with other construction) would substantially impede these purposes, unless the denial would interfere so drastically with the Nollans' use of their property as to constitute a taking. See *Penn Central Transportation Co.* v. *New York City, supra.*

The Commission argues that a permit condition that serves the same legitimate police-power purpose as a refusal to issue the permit should not be found to be a taking if the refusal to issue the permit would not constitute a taking. We agree. Thus, if the Commission attached to the permit some condition that would have protected the public's ability to see the beach notwithstanding construction of the new house – for example, a height limitation, a width restriction, or a ban on fences – so long as the Commission could have exercised its police power (as we have assumed it could) to forbid construction of the house altogether, imposition of the condition would also be constitutional. Moreover (and here we come closer to the facts of the present case), the condition would be constitutional even if it consisted of the requirement that the Nollans provide a viewing spot on their property for passersby with whose sighting of the ocean their new house would interfere. Although such a requirement, constituting a permanent grant of continuous access to the property, would have to be considered a taking if it were not attached to a development permit, the Commission's assumed power to forbid construction of the house in order to protect the public's view of the beach must surely include the power to condition construction upon some concession by the owner, even a concession of property rights, that serves the same end. If a prohibition designed to accomplish that purpose would be a legitimate exercise of the police power rather than a taking, it would be strange to conclude that providing the owner an alternative to that prohibition which accomplishes the same purpose is not.

The evident constitutional propriety disappears, however, if the condition substituted for the prohibition utterly fails to further the end advanced as the justification for the prohibition. When that essential nexus is eliminated, the situation becomes the same as if California law forbade shouting fire in a crowded theater, but granted dispensations to those willing to contribute $100 to the state treasury. While a ban on shouting fire can be a core exercise of the State's police power to protect the public safety, and can thus meet even our stringent standards for regulation of speech, adding the unrelated condition alters the purpose to one which, while it may be legitimate, is inadequate to sustain the ban. Therefore, even though, in a sense, requiring a $100 tax contribution in order to shout fire is a lesser restriction on speech than an outright ban, it would not pass constitutional muster. Similarly here, the lack of nexus between the condition and the original purpose of the building restriction converts that purpose to something other than what it was. The purpose then becomes, quite simply, the obtaining of an easement to serve some valid governmental purpose, but without payment of compensation. Whatever may be the outer limits of "legitimate state interests" in the takings and land-use context, this is not one of them. In short, unless the permit condition serves the same governmental purpose as the development ban, the building restriction is not a valid regulation of land use but "an out-and-out plan of extortion." *J. E. D. Associates, Inc. v. Atkinson*, 121 N. H. 581, 584, 432 A. 2d 12, 14–15 (1981); see Brief for United States as *Amicus Curiae* 22, and n. 20. See also *Loretto v. Teleprompter Manhattan CATV Corp.*, 458 U. S., at 439, n. 17.

The Commission claims that it concedes as much, and that we may sustain the condition at issue here by finding that it is reasonably related to the public need or burden that the Nollans' new house creates or to which it contributes. We can accept, for purposes of discussion, the Commission's proposed test as to how close a "fit" between the condition and the burden is required, because we find that this case does not meet even the most untailored standards. The Commission's principal contention to the contrary essentially turns on a play on the word "access." The Nollans' new house, the Commission found, will interfere with "visual access" to the beach. That in turn (along with other shorefront development) will interfere with the desire of people who drive past the Nollans' house to use the beach, thus creating a "psychological barrier" to "access." The Nollans' new house will also, by a process not altogether clear from the Commission's opinion but presumably potent enough to more than offset the effects of the psychological barrier, increase the use of the public beaches, thus creating the need for more "access." These burdens on "access" would be alleviated by a requirement that the Nollans provide "lateral access" to the beach.

Rewriting the argument to eliminate the play on words makes clear that there is nothing to it. It is quite impossible to understand how a requirement that people already on the public beaches be able to walk across the Nollans' property reduces any obstacles to viewing the beach created by the new house. It is also impossible to understand how it lowers any "psychological barrier" to using the public beaches, or how it helps to remedy any additional congestion on them caused by construction of the Nollans' new house. We therefore find that the Commission's imposition of the permit condition cannot be treated as an exercise of its land-use power for any of these purposes. Our conclusion on this point is consistent with the approach taken by every other court that has considered the question, with the exception of the California state courts. See *Parks v. Watson*, 716 F. 2d 646, 651–653 (CA9 1983); *Bethlehem Evangelical Lutheran Church v. Lakewood*, 626 P. 2d 668, 671–674 (Colo. 1981); *Aunt Hack Ridge Estates, Inc. v. Planning Comm'n*, 160 Conn. 109, 117–120, 273 A. 2d 880, 885 (1970); *Longboat Key v. Lands End, Ltd.*, 433 So. 2d 574 (Fla. App. 1983); *Pioneer Trust & Savings Bank v. Mount Prospect*, 22 Ill. 2d 375, 380, 176 N. E. 2d 799, 802 (1961); *Lampton v. Pinaire*, 610 S. W. 2d 915, 918–919 (Ky. App. 1980); *Schwing v. Baton Rouge*, 249 So. 2d 304 (La. App.), application denied, 259 La. 770, 252 So. 2d 667 (1971); *Howard County v. JJM, Inc.*, 301 Md. 256, 280–282, 482 A. 2d 908, 920–921 (1984); *Collis v. Bloomington*, 310 Minn. 5, 246 N. W. 2d 19 (1976); *State ex rel. Noland v. St. Louis County*, 478 S. W.

173

2d 363 (Mo. 1972); *Billings Properties, Inc. v. Yellowstone County,* 144 Mont. 25, 33–36, 394 P. 2d 182, 187–188 (1964); *Simpson v. North Platte,* 206 Neb. 240, 292 N. W. 2d 297 (1980); *Briar West, Inc. v. Lincoln,* 206 Neb. 172, 291 N. W. 2d 730 (1980); *J. E. D. Associates v. Atkinson,* 121 N. H. 581, 432 A. 2d 12 (1981); *Longridge Builders, Inc. v. Planning Bd. of Princeton,* 52 N. J. 348, 350–351, 245 A. 2d 336, 337–338 (1968); *Jenad, Inc. v. Scarsdale,* 18 N. Y. 2d 78, 218 N. E. 2d 673 (1966); *MacKall v. White,* 85 App. Div. 2d 696, 445 N. Y. S. 2d 486 (1981), appeal denied, 56 N. Y. 2d 503, 435 N. E. 2d 1100 (1982); *Frank Ansuini, Inc. v. Cranston,* 107 R. I. 63, 68–69, 71, 264 A. 2d 910, 913, 914 (1970); *College Station v. Turtle Rock Corp.,* 680 S. W. 2d 802, 807 (Tex. 1984); *Call v. West Jordan,* 614 P. 2d 1257, 1258–1259 (Utah 1980); *Board of Supervisors of James City County v. Rowe,* 216 Va. 128, 136–139, 216 S. E. 2d 199, 207–209 (1975); *Jordan v. Menomonee Falls,* 28 Wis. 2d 608, 617–618, 137 N. W. 2d 442, 447–449 (1965), appeal dism'd, 385 U. S. 4 (1966). See also *Littlefield v. Afton,* 785 F. 2d 596, 607 (CA8 1986); Brief for National Association of Home Builders et al. as *Amici Curiae* 9–16.

JUSTICE BRENNAN argues that imposition of the access requirement is not irrational. In his version of the Commission's argument, the reason for the requirement is that in its absence, a person looking toward the beach from the road will see a street of residential structures including the Nollans' new home and conclude that there is no public beach nearby. If, however, that person sees people passing and repassing along the dry sand behind the Nollans' home, he will realize that there is a public beach somewhere in the vicinity. *Post,* at 849–850. The Commission's action, however, was based on the opposite factual finding that the wall of houses completely blocked the view of the beach and that a person looking from the road would not be able to see it at all. App. 57–59.

Even if the Commission had made the finding that JUSTICE BRENNAN proposes, however, it is not certain that it would suffice. We do not share JUSTICE BRENNAN's confidence that the Commission "should have little difficulty in the future in utilizing its expertise to demonstrate a specific connection between provisions for access and burdens on access," *post,* at 862, that will avoid the effect of today's decision. We view the Fifth Amendment's Property Clause to be more than a pleading requirement, and compliance with it to be more than an exercise in cleverness and imagination. As indicated earlier, our cases describe the condition for abridgment of property rights through the police power as a "*substantial* advanc[ing]" of a legitimate state interest. We are inclined to be particularly careful about the adjective where the actual conveyance of property is made a condition to the lifting of a land-use restriction, since in that context there is heightened risk that the purpose is avoidance of the compensation requirement, rather than the stated police-power objective.

We are left, then, with the Commission's justification for the access requirement unrelated to land-use regulation:

"Finally, the Commission notes that there are several existing provisions of pass and repass lateral access benefits already given by past Faria Beach Tract applicants as a result of prior coastal permit decisions. The access required as a condition of this permit is part of a comprehensive program to provide continuous public access along Faria Beach as the lots undergo development or redevelopment." App. 68.

That is simply an expression of the Commission's belief that the public interest will be served by a continuous strip of publicly accessible beach along the coast. The Commission may well be right that it is a good idea, but that does not establish that the Nollans (and other coastal residents) alone can be compelled to contribute to its realization. Rather, California is free to advance its "comprehensive program," if it wishes, by using its power of eminent domain for this "public purpose," see U. S. Const., Amdt. 5; but if it wants an easement across the Nollans' property, it must pay for it.

Dolan v. City of Tigard

512 U.S. 374 (1994)

Facts
Dolan owned a commercial business in the Central Business District of the city of Tigard. Under Tigard's comprehensive land use plan and floodwater plan, the issuance of a permit for Dolan to expand her store was dependent on the dedication of land for both a pedestrian pathway and for a greenway to facilitate stormwater drainage. Dolan was denied a variance from the Planning Commission to be exempted from dedicating roughly 10 percent of her property to the city. The Land Use Board of Appeals and the Oregon Court of Appeals affirmed findings that there was reasonable relationship between the city's desire to dedicate a greenway and provide alternative transportation options and Dolan's proposed development.

Issue
Did the degree of exactions required of Dolan by the city bear the necessary relationship to the projected impact of her proposed development project?

Held
No. While it is evident that Dolan's expansion will increase the amount of impervious surface, thereby taxing the city's stormwater drainage system, the city's tentative findings about the impact did not conclusively show the substantial relationship between the required exaction and Dolan's proposed development. The Supreme Court found the same with regards to the exaction required for the pedestrian pathway.

Discussion
Until *Dolan*, the Court had not been in a position to decide the degree of connection between exactions and the projected impact of proposed development once an essential nexus had been found, now known as the "rough proportionality" test.

Case Excerpt

On review, petitioners first argue that city must meet a higher standard than a "reasonable relationship," that there must be an "essential nexus" or "substantial relationship" between the impacts of the development and the dedication requirements; otherwise, imposing exactions as a condition of land use approval is an unconstitutional taking. They rely on *Nollan v. California Coastal Comm'n, supra*. Petitioners argue that, because city has not demonstrated an essential nexus between its exactions and the demands that petitioners' proposed use will impose on public services and facilities, the requisite substantial relationship is missing and, therefore, that the exactions imposed on them by city constitute a taking under the Fifth Amendment. As a fallback position, petitioners argue that city cannot demonstrate even a "reasonable relationship" between their development's impacts and city's exactions.

City responds that the "reasonable relationship" test which was widely applied in regulatory takings cases before the Supreme Court's decision in *Nollan* was not abandoned in *Nollan*. Under that test, city asserts, the dedication conditions that it imposed on petitioners do not constitute a taking under the Fifth Amendment.

A land-use regulation does not effect a "taking" of property, within the meaning of the Fifth Amendment prohibition against taking private property for public use without just compensation, if it substantially advances a legitimate state interest and does not deny an owner economically viable use of the owner's land. *Nollan v. California Coastal Comm'n, supra*, 483 U.S. at 835–36, 107 S.Ct. at 3147–48; *Keystone Bituminous Coal Assn. v. DeBenedictis*, 480 U.S. 470, 495, 107 S.Ct. 1232, 1247, 94 L.Ed.2d 472 (1987): *Agins v. City of Tiburon*, 447 U.S. 255, 260, 100 S.Ct. 2138, 2141, 65 L.Ed.2d 106 (1980). Requiring an uncompensated conveyance of the easement outright would violate the Fourteenth Amendment. *Nollan, supra*, 483 U.S. at 834, 107 S.Ct. at 3147.

Before the Supreme Court's decision in *Nollan*, federal and state courts struggled to identify the precise connection that must exist between the conditions incorporated into a regulation and the governmental interest that the regulation purports to further if the regulation is to be deemed to "substantially advance" that interest. In the midst of a range of tests set forth by various courts, the Ninth Circuit Court of Appeals concluded in *Parks v. Watson*, 716 F.2d 646, 652 (9th Cir.1983), that, at the very least, a condition requiring an applicant for a governmental benefit to forego a constitutional right is unlawful if the condition is not rationally related to the benefit conferred. By way of example, the *Parks* court discussed "subdivision exaction" cases, where a city allows a developer to subdivide in exchange for a contribution. In such cases, the court noted, "there is agreement among the states 'that the dedication should have some reasonable relationship to the needs created by the subdivision.'" *Id.* at 653. Thus, under the *Parks* analysis, exactions and impacts must be "reasonably related." In *Parks*, the court held that the exactions had "no rational relationship to any public purpose related to the [impacts of the development]" and, therefore, that the exactions could not be required without just compensation. *Id.* at 653.

In *Nollan,* the Court did not purport to abandon the generally recognized "reasonably related" test and, in fact, noted that its approach was "consistent with the approach taken by every other court that has considered the question, with the exception of the California state courts." 483 U.S. at 839, 107 S.Ct. at 3150 (citing a long list of exaction cases, beginning with *Parks v. Watson, supra*). The *Nollan* court stated:

"We can accept, for purposes of discussion, the Commission's proposed test [the 'reasonably related test'] as to how close a 'fit' between the condition and the burden is required, because we find that this case does not meet even the most untailored standards." *Id.* at 838, 107 S.Ct. at 3149.

Thus, we are unable to agree with petitioners that the *Nollan* court abandoned the "reasonably related" test. We recognize, however, that the *Nollan* court's application of that test does provide some guidance as to how closely "related" exactions must be to impacts. For example, the *Nollan* court stated that the evident constitutional propriety of an exaction disappears

"if the condition substituted for the prohibition utterly fails to further the end advanced as the justification for the prohibition. When that essential nexus is eliminated, the situation becomes the same as if California law forbade shouting fire in a crowded theater, but granted dispensations to those willing to contribute $100 to the state treasury." *Id.* at 837, 107 S.Ct. at 3148.

Petitioners read that passage as indicating that in *Nollan* the Supreme Court abandoned the "reasonably related" test for a more stringent "essential nexus" test. We do not read *Nollan* that way.

The quoted passage indicates that, for an exaction to be considered "reasonably related" to an impact, it is essential to show a nexus between the two, in order for the regulation to substantially advance a legitimate state interest, as required by *Agins v. City of Tiburon, supra,* 447 U.S. at 260, 100 S.Ct. at 2141. In *Nollan,* the Court stated that, "unless the permit condition serves the same governmental purpose as the development ban, the building restriction is not a valid regulation of land use but 'an out-and-out plan of extortion.' " *Nollan v. California Coastal Comm'n, supra,* 483 U.S. at 837, 107 S.Ct. at 3149. (citations omitted). *Nollan,* then, tells us that an exaction is reasonably related to an impact if the exaction serves the same purpose that a denial of the permit would serve. *See Dept. of Trans. v. Lundberg,* 312 Or. 568, 578, 825 P.2d 641, *cert. den.,* ___ U.S. ___, 113 S.Ct. 467, 121 L.Ed.2d 374 (1992) (sidewalk dedication requirement serves the same legitimate governmental purposes that would justify denying permits to develop commercially zoned properties).

In this case, we conclude that city's unchallenged factual findings support the dedication conditions imposed by city. The pedestrian/bicycle pathway condition had an essential nexus to the anticipated development because, as the city found in part

"the proposed expanded use of this site is anticipated to generate additional vehicular traffic, thereby increasing congestion on nearby collector and arterial streets. Creation of a convenient, safe pedestrian/bicycle pathway system as an alternative means of transportation could offset some of the traffic demand on these nearby streets and lessen the increase in traffic congestion." *Dolan v. City of Tigard, supra,* 22 Or LUBA at 622 (quoting City of Tigard Planning Commission Final Order at 20).

We are persuaded that the transportation needs of petitioners' employees and customers and the increased traffic congestion that will result from the development of petitioners' land do have an essential nexus to the development of the site, and that this condition, therefore, is reasonably related to the impact of the expansion of their business.

Because the development would involve covering a much larger portion of petitioners' land with buildings and parking, thus increasing the site's impervious area, the condition requiring petitioners to dedicate a portion of their property for improvement of a storm drainage system also is reasonably related to the impact of the expansion of their business. The increased impervious surface would be expected to increase the amount of storm water runoff from the site to Fanno Creek. We hold that there is an essential nexus between the increased storm water runoff caused by petitioners' development and the improvement of a drainage system to accommodate that runoff.

We agree with LUBA's conclusion that the challenged condition requiring dedication of portions of petitioners' property is not an unconstitutional taking of petitioners' property in violation of the Fifth Amendment.

Construction Industry Association of Sonoma County v. City of Petaluma, California

522 F.2d 897 (1975)

Facts
In the 1970s, the city of Petaluma, California, experienced tremendous population growth as it transformed into a "bedroom community" for workers in the San Francisco Bay Area. The city enacted a construction moratorium in 1971 to allow the city time to study changes in the housing market and to adopt short- and long-term plans. In 1972, the city passed a series of resolutions collectively known as the "Petaluma Plan," intended to curb sprawl, promote infill development, and promote the construction of low to moderate income housing. Landowners and the Construction Association of Sonoma County brought suit, claiming that the plan was unconstitutional.

Issue
Does the Petaluma Plan violate the due process clause of the Fourteenth Amendment?

Held
No. While the plan would have the effect of excluding some people who may want to live in Petaluma, it falls within the city's broad police powers to promote public welfare; Petaluma's desire to maintain its small town character and

open spaces, and to grow at a sustainable pace are sufficient reasons to exercise its police powers.

Discussion

All zoning regulations have the purpose and effect of exclusion to some degree, so courts must determine whether such exclusions bear a rational relationship to a legitimate state interest. The due process rights of landowners and developers are not automatically violated when a municipality rightfully exercises its police powers in its own self-interest.

Case Excerpt

Appellees claim that the Plan is arbitrary and unreasonable and, thus, violative of the due process clause of the Fourteenth Amendment. According to appellees, the Plan is nothing more than an exclusionary zoning device, designed solely to insulate Petaluma from the urban complex in which it finds itself. The Association and the Landowners reject, as falling outside the scope of any legitimate governmental interest, the City's avowed purposes in implementing the Plan – the preservation of Petaluma's small town character and the avoidance of the social and environmental problems caused by an uncontrolled growth rate.

In attacking the validity of the Plan, appellees rely heavily on the district court's finding that the express purpose and the actual effect of the Plan is to exclude substantial numbers of people who would otherwise elect to move to the City. 375 F.Supp. at 581. The existence of an exclusionary purpose and effect reflects, however, only *one* side of the zoning regulation. Practically all zoning restrictions have as a purpose and effect the *exclusion* of some activity or type of structure or a certain density of inhabitants. And in reviewing the reasonableness of a zoning ordinance, our inquiry does not terminate with a finding that it is for an exclusionary purpose. We must determine further whether the *exclusion* bears any rational relationship to a *legitimate state interest*. If it does not, then the zoning regulation is invalid. If, on the other hand, a legitimate state interest is furthered by the zoning regulation, we must defer to the legislative act. Being neither a super legislature nor a zoning board of appeal, a federal court is without authority to weigh and reappraise the factors considered or ignored by the legislative body in passing the challenged zoning regulation. The reasonableness, not the wisdom, of the Petaluma Plan is at issue in this suit.

It is well settled that zoning regulations "must find their justification in some aspect of the police power, asserted for the public welfare." *Village of Euclid v. Ambler Realty Co.*, 272 U.S. 365, 387, 47 S.Ct. 114, 118, 71 L.Ed. 303 (1926). The concept of the public welfare, however, is not limited to the regulation of noxious activities or dangerous structures. As the Court stated in *Berman v. Parker*, 348 U.S. 26, 33, 75 S.Ct. 98, 102, 99 L.Ed. 27 (1954):

The concept of the public welfare is broad and inclusive. The values it represents are spiritual as well as physical, aesthetic as well as monetary. It is within the power of the legislature to determine that the community should be beautiful as well as healthy, spacious as well as clean, well-balanced as well as carefully patrolled.

(citations omitted). *Accord, Village of Belle Terre v. Boraas,* 416 U.S. 1, 6, 9, 94 S.Ct. 1536, 39 L.Ed.2d 797 (1974).

In determining whether the City's interest in preserving its small town character and in avoiding uncontrolled and rapid growth falls within the broad concept of "public welfare," we are considerably assisted by two recent cases. *Belle Terre, supra,* and *Ybarra v. City of Town of Los Altos Hills,* 503 F.2d 250 (9th Cir. 1974), each of which upheld as not unreasonable a zoning regulation much more restrictive than the Petaluma Plan, are dispositive of the due process issue in this case.

In *Belle Terre* the Supreme Court rejected numerous challenges to a village's restricting land use to one-family dwellings excluding lodging houses, boarding houses, fraternity houses or multiple-dwelling houses. By absolutely prohibiting the construction of or conversion of a building to other than single-family dwelling, the village ensured that it would never grow, if at all, much larger than its population of 700 living in 220 residences. Nonetheless, the Court found that the prohibition of boarding houses and other multi-family dwellings was reasonable and within the public welfare because such dwellings present urban problems, such as the occupation of a given space by more people, the increase in traffic and parked cars and the noise that comes with increased crowds. According to the Court,

A quiet place where yards are wide, people few, and motor vehicles restricted are legitimate guidelines in a land-use project addressed to family needs. This goal is a permissible one within *Berman v. Parker, supra.* The police power is not confined to elimination of filth, stench, and unhealthy places. It is ample to lay out zones where family values, youth values, and the blessings of quiet seclusion, and clean air make the area a sanctuary for people.

416 U.S. at 9, 94 S.Ct. at 1541. While dissenting from the majority opinion in *Belle Terre* on the ground that the regulation unreasonably burdened the exercise of First Amendment associational rights, Mr. Justice Marshall concurred in the Court's express holding that a local entity's zoning power is extremely broad:

[L]ocal zoning authorities may properly act in furtherance of the objectives asserted to be served by the ordinance at issue here: *restricting uncontrolled growth,* solving traffic problems, keeping rental costs at a reasonable level, and making the community attractive to families. The police power which provides the justification for zoning is not narrowly confined. And, it is appropriate that we afford zoning authorities *considerable latitude in choosing the means by which to implement such purposes.*

416 U.S. at 13–14, 94 S.Ct. at 1543 (Marshall, J., dissenting) (emphasis added) (citations omitted).

Following the *Belle Terre* decision, this court in *Los Altos Hills* had an opportunity to review a zoning ordinance providing that a housing lot shall be contain not less than one acre and that no lot shall be occupied by more than one primary dwelling unit. The ordinance as a practical matter prevented poor people from living in Los Altos Hills and restricted the density, and thus the population, of the town. This court, nonetheless, found that the ordinance was rationally related to a legitimate governmental interest – *the preservation of the town's rural environment* – and, thus, did not violate the equal protection clause of the Fourteenth Amendment. 503 F.2d at 254.

Both the Belle Terre ordinance and the Los Altos Hills regulation had the purpose and effect of permanently restricting growth; nonetheless, the court in each case upheld the particular law before it on the ground that the regulation served a legitimate governmental interest falling within the concept of the public welfare: the preservation of quiet family neighborhoods (Belle Terre) and the preservation of a rural environment (Los Altos Hills). Even less restrictive or exclusionary than the above zoning ordinances is the Petaluma Plan which, unlike those ordinances, does not freeze the population at present or near-present levels. Further, unlike the Los Altos Hills ordinance and the various zoning regulations struck down by state courts in recent years, the Petaluma Plan does not have the undesirable effect of walling out any particular income class nor any racial minority group.

Although we assume that some persons desirous of living in Petaluma will be excluded under the housing permit limitation and that, thus, the Plan may frustrate some legitimate regional housing needs, the Plan is not arbitrary or unreasonable. We agree with appellees that unlike the situation in the past most municipalities today are neither isolated nor wholly independent from neighboring municipalities and that, consequently, unilateral land use decisions by one local entity affect the needs and resources of an entire region. *See, e. g., Golden v. Planning Board of Town of Ramapo,* 30 N.Y.2d 359, 334 N.Y.S.2d 138, 285 N.E.2d 291, *appeal dismissed,* 409 U.S. 1003, 93 S.Ct. 436, 34 L.Ed.2d 294 (1972); *National Land & Investment Co. v. Kohn,* 419 Pa. 504, 215 A.2d 597 (1965); Note, *Phased Zoning: Regulation of the Tempo and Sequence of Land Development,* 26 Stan.L.Rev. 585, 605 (1974). It does not necessarily follow, however, that the *due process* rights of builders and landowners are violated merely because a local entity exercises in its own self-interest the police power lawfully delegated to it by the state. *See Belle Terre, supra; Los Altos Hills, supra.* If the present system of delegated zoning power does not effectively serve the state interest in furthering the general welfare of the region or entire state, it is the state legislature's and not the federal courts' role to intervene and adjust the system. As stated *supra,* the federal court is not a super zoning board and should not be called on to mark the point at which legitimate local interests in promoting the welfare of the community are outweighed by legitimate regional interests. *See* Note, *supra,* at 608–11.

We conclude therefore that under *Belle Terre* and *Los Altos Hills* the concept of the public welfare is sufficiently broad to uphold Petaluma's desire to preserve its small town character, its open spaces and low density of population, and to grow at an orderly and deliberate pace.

Golden v. Planning Board of Town of Ramapo

30 N.Y.2d 359 (1972)

Facts

In the 1960s, faced with a population boom, the town of Ramapo began the process of developing a master land use plan and adopted a comprehensive zoning ordinance. In 1969, the town amended its ordinance to provide that residential subdivision development hinged on the issuance of a special permit, which would be granted pending the shown availability of essential services including public sanitation facilities; drainage facilities, public recreation facilities, including public schools; roads; and fire department services. Golden's application for preliminary approval of a residential subdivision plat was denied for failure to secure a special use permit.

Issue

Did Ramapo exceed its authority by conditioning development on the provision of specific infrastructure services and facilities?

Held

No. Phased growth is within the scope of current New York enabling legislation. Ramapo's zoning amendments were not exclusionary, but rather, sought to guarantee that all residential development would have access to a minimum threshold of public services and facilities, ensuring orderly, efficient growth consistent with the town's comprehensive land use plan.

Discussion

The power to zone is a police power vested in local municipalities by the state enabling legislation. However, statewide or regional planning systems have been suggested as a means of ensuring that land use policies are dictated by broader concerns than those of individual municipalities.

Case Excerpt

The Town of Ramapo, following an intensive study by highly-competent experts, amended its zoning ordinance by adding to it section 46-13.1, a section with extensive scope and detailed provisions. It broadly defines a developer as any landowner who proposes to erect and sell a dwelling or dwellings for residential use. Regardless of the district zone, any proposed development, as so broadly defined, is forbidden unless a special permit is obtained. Permits will be granted only if the land qualifies for enough assigned points under some five categories of available municipal facilities, namely, sewerage, drainage, park-recreation-public school facilities, roads, and firehouses. The purpose is to prohibit development until an acceptable level of supporting facilities exists. The town has committed itself, it is said, by its capital budget and capital improvement plans to insure eventual availability of supporting facilities. But in some areas this eventuality will not be realized for 18 years.

To prevent undue delay, the town allows for a crediting of points based on the scheduled improvements even if the town program should not be realized as planned, because of fiscal, economic, or political impediments. Because the effect of the ordinance is to freeze an owner's use for varying periods of time, up to 18 years, the town also allows the owner to apply for a reduction in tax assessments.

It is important to note how radically the Ramapo scheme differs from those used and adopted under existing enabling acts. The zoning acts, starting from 50 years ago, based on national models, provided simply for district zoning to control population density and some planning to protect preferred uses of land, such as single-family dwellings, from other uses considered less desirable or even harmful to residential living or environmental balance. Since the beginning, in this State and elsewhere, by amendment to the enabling acts by the Legislature, provision has been made for subdivision planning and, in some instances, planned unit development, to prevent large-scale developers from dumping homes wholesale in raw land areas without private and, to some extent, public facilities essential to the use of the homes. In more recent years, since World War II, the need for a much enlarged kind of land planning has become critical. The evils of uncontrolled urban sprawl on the one hand, and the suburban and exurban pressure to exclude urban population on the other hand, have created a massive conflict, with social and economic implications of the gravest character. Throughout the nation the conflict has risen or threatened and solutions are being sought in careful, intensive examination of the problem affecting those within and those without the localities to be regulated.

The President's National Commission on Urban Problems has made relevant recommendations, the American Law Institute is engaged in drafting a model land development code, and, in this State, the Office of Planning Coordination is working on a planning code. The conflict has surfaced in other States in efforts by municipalities to cut their own swaths in solving their difficulties, and, in every instance uncovered, the courts have struck down the efforts as unconstitutional or as invalid under enabling acts much like those in this State (*National Land & Inv. Co. v. Easttown Twp. Bd. of Adj.*, 419 Pa. 504, 524–533; *Concord Twp. Appeal*, 439 Pa. 466, 469–478; *Oakwood at Madison v. Township of Madison*, 117 N. J. Super. 11, 14–22; *Girsh Appeal*, 437 Pa. 237, 240–246; *Bristow v. City of Woodhaven*, 35 Mich. App. 205; *Lakeland Bluff v. County of Will*, 114 Ill. App. 2d 267, 275–280). Generally, there is the view that the conflict requires solution at a regional or State level, usually with local administration, and not by compounding the conflict with idiosyncratic municipal action (see ALI, Model Land Development Code [Tent. Draft No. 2, April 24, 1970], pp. xvii–xx; Model Land Development Code [Tent. Draft No. 1, April 24, 1968], pp. 189–195; New York State, Office of Planning Coordination, Planning Law Revision Study, Study Document No. 1, April 1969, at pp. 1–3; Report of National Commission on Urban Problems, pp. 208–217, 222–224, 235–240). The Ramapo ordinance flies in the face of and would frustrate these well-directed efforts.

Decisive of the present appeals, however, is the absence in the town of legislative authorization to postpone growth, let alone to establish unilaterally phased population levels, through the expedient of barring residential development for scheduled periods of up to 18 years. It has always been the rule that a municipality has only those land use powers delegated or necessarily implied (1 Anderson, American Law of Zoning, § 3.10). Existing enabling legislation does not grant the power upon which the Ramapo ordinance rests. And for policy reasons, one should not strain the reading of the enabling acts, even if straining would avail, to distort them, beyond any meaning ever attributed to them, except by the ingenious draftsmen of the Ramapo ordinance.

The enabling acts for the several classes of municipalities in the State are substantially alike. They followed the model acts drafted by the U. S. Department of Commerce in the 1920's, after an earlier zoning effort by New York City in 1916 (Report of National Commission on Urban Problems, p. 200; see L. 1916, ch. 497). Since then they have been amended, usually in identical fashion, as the need for broader powers was envisaged and accepted. Article 16 of the Town Law is the enabling act for towns. Section 261 in pertinent part provides: "For the purpose of promoting the health, safety, morals, or the general welfare of the community, the town board is hereby empowered by ordinance to regulate and restrict the height, number of stories and size of buildings and other structures, the percentage of lot that may be occupied, the size of yards, courts, and other open spaces, the density of population, and the location and use of buildings, structures and land for trade, industry, residence or other purposes;". This is a typical district zoning provision. It grants power to define permissible physical characteristics of land and structure; and says nothing about exercising control in time. The town would stretch the reference to "density of population" to give the town the powers it purports to exercise by the ordinance. Section 263, defining the purposes of district zoning, by any standard of statutory construction provides no help. The section reads: "Such regulations shall be made in accordance with a comprehensive plan and designed to lessen congestion in the streets, to secure safety from fire, flood, panic and other dangers; to promote health and general welfare; to provide adequate light and air; to prevent the overcrowding of land; to avoid undue concentration of population; to facilitate the adequate provision of transportation, water, sewerage, schools, parks and other public requirements. Such regulations shall be made with reasonable consideration, among other things, as to the character of the district and its peculiar suitability for particular uses, and with a view to conserving the value of buildings and encouraging the most appropriate use of land throughout such municipality." It does not broaden powers granted. Instead it is intended to be restrictive in two ways: first, by making certain that zoning regulations conform to a master plan; and second, by relating them directly to specified public purposes. In short, district zoning is permitted if, and only if, it is pursuant to a comprehensive plan and it serves the purposes listed (cf. *Udell v. Haas*, 21 N Y 2d 463, 469).

Going beyond district zoning, the statute provides for subdivision platting (§ 276 *et seq.*). It does not provide support for the procedures essayed in the Ramapo ordinance. But what is important is that even intensive subdivision regulation was required to be authorized by statute before towns could control subdivision developers. Statutory authorization was all the more important because the then drastic regulation required the developers to provide private and public facilities for the wholesale distribution of homes and to provide moneys and bonds to make sure that they performed as promised. Notably, no developer is forbidden to develop for a period of years.

The urgent need to control the tempo and sequence of land development has been recognized by courts, government commissions, and commentators (see Cutler, Legal and Illegal Methods of Controlling Community Growth, 1961 Wis. L. Rev. 370; Fagin, Regulating the Timing of Urban Development, 20 Law & Contemp. Prob. 298; Report of National Commission on Urban Problems, pp. 245, 251; New York State, Office of Planning Coordination, Planning Law Revision Study, Draft Outline, pp. 13, 17). Techniques to control the rate, nature and sequence of community development are plentiful although not all are presently authorized or comport with constitutional limitations. Thus, in *Albrecht Realty Co. v. Town of New Castle* (8 Misc 2d 255) the Town of New Castle in Westchester County sought to control growth by placing a moratorium on the issuance of building permits for unspecified periods and with no apparent object other than controlling growth. The measure was voided because the enabling act did not authorize "a direct regulation of the rate of growth" (at p. 256). For another technique, in California the purchase of "development rights" or a time-limited easement by the local government reportedly has been employed. The community is saved the expense of purchasing the fee simple of the owner. It obtains flexibility by the power to release land for development while landowners are compensated. The method is also said to justify assessing or taxing the owner at a lower rate (see Cutler, *op. cit.*, *supra*, at p. 394). A similar approach is followed in England and has been recently recommended by the President's National Commission on Urban Problems (Report, at p. 251; Mandelker, Notes from the English: Compensation in Town and County Planning, 49 Cal. L. Rev. 699; see, also, Ann. Zoning – With Compensation, 41 ALR 3d 636).

A common technique is minimum area zoning. If it does not amount to prohibitory zoning, minimum lot requirements may be used to regulate the tempo and sequence of land development (see *Matter of Josephs v. Town Bd. Of Town of Clarkstown*, 24 Misc 2d 366). Unfortunately, however, the method is often used as an exclusionary or prohibitory device.

Finally, there is the technique sought to be exercised by Ramapo – a technique partaking somewhat of the motivation for and methods used in holding zones.

Holding zones, that is, areas reserved for future development, if legislatively authorized and carefully circumscribed, can validly and effectively implement land planning. Both the interests of localities and the broader interests of the State and its large metropolitan areas can be reconciled. Indeed, it has been suggested by the National Commission on Urban Problems that enabling legislation grant communities such power. The devising and authorization of new powers, one of which is to create holding or delayed development zones, is a chief concern of the State Office of Planning Coordination. Indeed, it plays a prominent role in its proposed legislation. Notably, in delayed development schemes limitations are invariably suggested, limitations absent in the Ramapo ordinance (e.g., 3- to 5-year limits, regional and State agency review, provision for compensation). Such limitations may be essential if the delegation is to be valid constitutionally. Aside from considerations of unlimited delegation, without the standards which universally circumscribe the conduct of administrative agencies, the limitations reflect basic doctrine that even the State's zoning power is not unlimited. As observed by the Pennsylvania Supreme Court, "Zoning is a means by which a governmental body can plan for the future – it may not be used as a means to deny the future" (*National Land & Inv. Co. v. Easttown Twp. Bd. of Adj.*, 419 Pa. 504, *supra*, at p. 528). Again, in *Concord Twp. Appeal* (439 Pa. 466, *supra*), it observed, "Communities must deal with the problems of population growth. They may not refuse to confront the future by adopting zoning regulations that effectively restrict population to near present levels" (at p. 474).

Either by legislation limited by decisional rule, or by decisional rule alone a limited amount of restraint in time has been held valid in controlling development, even without compensation. Thus, in the State of Washington it was suggested that the legislatively authorized right to impress "holding zones" on private property beyond the immediate reaches of present development, must be reasonably limited in its duration (*State ex rel. Randall v. Snohomish County*, 79 Wn. 2d 619; see, also, *Westwood Forest Estates v. Village of South Nyack*, 23 N Y 2d 424, 428–429). Significantly, the time limitations should be brief, or reasonably fixed, and justified by emergency or statutory authorization.

It is not necessary now, as observed later, to confront the serious constitutional issues raised by mandatory delayed development. The crux of the matter in these cases is that before wrestling with the constitutional issues the Ramapo ordinance is destroyed at the threshold. It lacks statutory authorization, and this despite the fact that its reach is more ambitious than any before essayed even with enabling legislation.

By the unsupportable extrapolation from existing enabling acts, one may not usurp the unique responsibility of the Legislature, even where it has failed to act. What is worse, to do this, as a State Legislature would not, without considering the social and economic ramifications for the locality, region, and State, and without limitations essential to an intelligent delegation, is unsound as well as invalid. Moreover, to allow Ramapo's idiosyncratic solution, which would then be available to any other community like Ramapo, may end indefinitely the possibility of commanding better legislation for land planning, just because such legislation requires some diminution in the local control now exercised under the zoning acts.

There are, to be sure, the constitutional issues in the case. Some relate to the power of government to deprive the landowner of any reasonable use of his land for a period of years, up to 18 years, without compensation. These are knotty problems confronting the draftsmen of a land development code. The problems are not insuperable. The initial, principal land zoning case, *Euclid v. Ambler Co.* (272 U. S. 365), held rather flatly, as far back as 1926, that an owner may be made to suffer a substantial loss in the economic potential of his land without compensation. But it has always been made clear that an owner could not be deprived of all reasonable use nor could his use be postponed for more than a short time, even if only to prevent an overloading of municipal facilities (*Westwood Forest Estates v. Village of South Nyack*, 23 N Y 2d 424, 428–429, *supra*; see, also, *Arverne Bay Constr. Co. v. Thatcher*, 278 N.Y. 222, 232; *People ex rel. St. Albans-Springfield Corp. v. Connell*, 257 N.Y. 73, 83). Be that as it may, for many reasons these constitutional issues are better reserved for future consideration. There is little doubt that the compulsion of current interests and conflicts will require a re-examination of much legal and judicial thinking in this area. The problem, however, is not only legal. As some students of the subject have pointed out, it is not enough to regulate land development. There must be incentive to develop, or else there will be little new housing except that which government could afford to build (Mandelker, The Zoning Dilemma, pp. 47–51). These are just some of the problems that the Ramapo ordinance glosses over as it attacks the problem for one town alone, a device that maybe a few more towns like Ramapo could adopt, but not all, without destroying the economy and channelling the demographic course of the State to suit their own insular interests.

At least one of the concurring opinions at the Appellate Division raised another constitutional question, namely, the power of the town to adjust tax assessments as provided in the ordinance (see concurring opn. of Mr. Justice HOPKINS, 37 A D 2d 236, 244–246). The point would be a salient one, if reached. It and the other constitutional questions need not and should not be reached because it is enough that the enabling acts do not permit the arrogation of power that the Ramapo ordinance projects.

Consequently, although the town had no power under the enabling act to adopt the ordinance in question, this does not mean that the town is not faced with a grave problem. It is. So are the many towns and villages in the State, and elsewhere in the country. But there is no doubt that the Ramapos, in isolation, cannot solve their problems alone, legally, under existing laws, or socially, politically, or economically. For the time being, the Ramapos must do what they can with district zoning and subdivision platting control. They may not declare moratoria on growth and development for as much as a generation. They may not separately or in concert impair the freedom of movement or residence of those outside their borders, even by ingenious schemes. Nor is it important whether their intention is to exclude, if that is the effect of their arrogated powers.

The exclusionary effect of local efforts to preserve the country's Edens has been largely noted. Professor Roberts, in an important essay, explores the conditions bedevilling places like Ramapo but also assesses the calamitous effects of ill-advised parochial devices (E. F. Roberts, The Demise of Property Law, 57 Cornell L. Rev. 1). The problems of development of the larger community run so deep, he suggests that: "'Snob zoning,' of course, may best be 'solved' by the legislature. This really is the lesson contained in *Girsh* which seems, moderately enough, to suggest that a regional planning mechanism should be devised to create a pluralist suburbia in which each class could find its proper place. More interest, however, is being generated by the notion of statewide land-use planning which presumably would allow each class its niche outside center city.

187

Whether this interest in formulating state planning derives from a concern for the lower orders or reflects instead an irritation at the lack of order when a multitude of tiny hamlets makes any planning impossible, is difficult to tell." (at p. 37). To leave vital decisions controlling the mix and timing of development to the unfettered discretion of the local community invites disaster.

A glance at other legislation in this State reveals that regional or co-ordinated planning is not new to the Legislature, albeit the steps thus far taken may one day be regarded as quite primitive compared with what, necessarily, is to be. Article 12-B of the General Municipal Law contains a congeries of provisions authorizing optional metropolitan, regional, and county planning boards. Their powers are still rather limited. Perhaps most interesting is section 239-l of that article which authorizes a scheme for mandatory co-ordination in counties or regions of various kinds of zoning action by the included municipalities. The legislation is significant evidence of the activity and understanding of the Legislature in land use planning, into which Ramapo would thrust itself beyond the limits now authorized by law.

A glance at history suggests that Ramapo's plan to have public services installed in advance of development is unrealistic. Richard Babcock, the distinguished practitioner in land development law, some years ago addressed himself to the natural desire of communities to stay development while they caught up with the inexorable thrust of population growth and movement. He observed eloquently that this country was built and is still being built by people who moved about, innovated, pioneered, and created industry and employment, and thereby provided both the need and the means for the public services and facilities that followed (Babcock, The Zoning Game, at pp. 149–150). Thus, the movement has not been in the other direction, first the provision of public and utility services and then the building of homes, farms, and businesses. This court has said as much, in effect, in *Westwood Forest Estates v. Village of South Nyack* (23 N Y 2d 424, *supra*) unanimously and in reliance on commonplace authority and precedent.

As said earlier, when the problem arose outside the State the judicial response has been the same, frustrating communities, intent on walling themselves from the mainstream of development, namely, that the effort was invalid under existing enabling acts or unconstitutional (*National Land & Inv. Co. v. Easttown Twp. Bd. of Adj.*, 419 Pa. 504, *supra*; *Girsh Appeal*, 437 Pa. 237, *supra*; *Bristow v. City of Woodhaven*, 35 Mich. App. 205, *supra*; *Lakeland Bluff v. County of Will*, 114 Ill. App. 2d 267, *supra*; *Concord Twp. Appeal*, 439 Pa. 466, *supra*; *Oakwood at Madison v. Township of Madison*, 117 N. J. Super 11, *supra*). The response may not be charged to judicial conservatism or self-restraint. In short, it has not been illiberal. It has indeed reflected the larger understanding that American society is at a critical crossroads in the accommodation of urbanization and suburban living, with effects that are no longer confined, bad as they are, to ethnic exclusion or "snob" zoning (see Roberts, *op. cit.*, *supra*, at pp. 36–49). Ramapo would preserve its nature, delightful as that may be, but the supervening question is whether it alone may decide this or whether it must be decided by the larger community represented by the Legislature. Legally, politically, economically, and sociologically, the base for determination must be larger than that provided by the town fathers.

Primer on Growth Management as an Issue for Planners

Response to Urban Sprawl

Sprawl is dispersed, auto-dependent development outside compact urban and village centers, along highways, and in rural countryside. This land development pattern is problematic for a number of reasons, including the cost of extending infrastructure. Development that is spread out requires the creation of a significant amount of new infrastructure, including: roads, water and sewer systems, and schools and libraries. These costs are typically paid for by the tax payer. However, in cities where growth is so rapid, the costs are often shifted by the city to the developers of new properties and their buyers.

The Relationship between Residential Subdivisions and Suburban Sprawl

When we think about sprawl, our minds are quickly drawn to post World War II development patterns. Prior to World War II, there were two standard development patterns: Urban and rural. Urban areas were characterized by density and connectivity. These areas were segregated by income and race but still required diverse interactions given the need for movement across the urban expanse. Rural areas, by contrast, were served by a small strip of commercial and institutional buildings, including a city hall, general store, and school, among other necessities. Those living in rural areas typically expected to travel some distance to visit these establishments. This division lasted until the period following World War II.

Urban neighborhoods deteriorated significantly during the war years. The rationing of building materials, as well as the labor needed to maintain and construct homes, weighed heavily on living quarters in the urban core. To further the prosperity associated with the war effort, the federal government made it possible for the first time for young GI families to build new homes outside the city center. There was an instantaneous demand for this type of single-family housing. The suburbs were born out of this demand, as tract after tract of farmland was subdivided and converted into single-family housing. As anticipated, family sizes grew exponentially as a result of this transition. Male heads of household continued to drive their new cars to the city to work, returning home at day's end for a home-cooked meal.

It was not long until businesses followed families to the suburbs. Strip malls lined auto-oriented streets, giving suburban families access to all of the commodities their new lives in the suburbs demanded. Soon after, the companies who employed these heads of household also found their way out to the suburbs. As a result, these suburban areas expanded and changed character from exclusively residential areas to mini cities. As the suburbs expanded, families found themselves moving further and further from the urban cores. New suburbs emerged and home and lot sizes expanded.

This venture was costly on a number of fronts. First, and most significantly, the suburban migration took a heavy toll on those low-income, minority families, who did not have access to the amount of capital needed to flee the cities. Even those who had the means to flee often found themselves unwelcome in suburban areas governed by restrictive covenants that disallowed minorities from living in these communities. This process, sometimes referred to as the "white flight," had a significant effect on urban vitality in general and the ability of minority families to gain access to better infrastructure. In this regard, the history of suburbanization and outmigration continues to haunt central cities that seek to draw families with means back into them. The long-term disinvestment in social and economic infrastructure is a difficult barrier for city planners to overcome.

Suburbanization was also fiscally irresponsible. Historic development practices in the United States placed the burden of paying for new infrastructure on cities. After all, property owners pay taxes that go into the general fund out of which these expenditures are paid. Theoretically, each new unit of development brings revenue to this fund that will pay for the cost of infrastructure. This theory, however, has proven to be flawed. Property tax rates are a political issue. Most property owners do not wish to have to pay taxes for anything beyond meeting their own needs. As such, mileage rates are kept low and rarely cover the cost of installing new infrastructure. In addition, the money from the property taxes follows development, rather than leading it. Local governments find themselves playing perpetual games of catch up as a result of this mismatch. Also, while property tax revenue paid into the general fund is supposed to cover the cost of both installing new and maintaining and replacing existing infrastructure, most of these funds are spent on new infrastructure. The result has been a further decay in the urban fabric in areas where infrastructure needs are not met.

The Advent of Growth Management

Beginning in the 1970s, a small number of cities and states across the nation began to experiment with growth management policies. These policies did not replace comprehensive planning and zoning schemes. Rather, they supplemented these regulations by helping prioritize the time, location, and character of new development. Many of these policies incentivized or prioritized new development occurring in areas already served by adequate infrastructure. In the alternative, cities embracing growth management strategies sought at the very least to ensure that developers paid to install the infrastructure that served the communities they developed through exactions, dedications, or fees in lieu. Upon implementation of these strategies, cities found themselves justifying these strategies in courts of law. These cases, as described below, are also a quintessential part of the regulatory takings jurisprudence which has evolved since the 1970s.

Nollan v. California Coastal Commission

In *Nollan v. California Coastal Commission*, the property owner applied to the California Coastal Commission (CCC) for a permit to replace an existing beach bungalow with a larger home, a request that was very much in character with development in the area. The CCC agreed to grant the permit on the condition that the Nollans provide an easement for public passage across their property. The Nollans challenged the exaction sought by CCC on the grounds that it was a regulatory taking. The Nollans successfully claimed that the condition upon which the permit was based was a taking because there was no rational nexus between the permit requirement and the purpose

190

of the building restriction. While the High Court agreed that the easement was a good idea given the lack of connectivity of two public beaches at high tide, they said the CCC would have to pay for the use of the Nollans' private property.

This case was an important first challenge of the types of exaction that would be later be used widely by cities to require developers to pay for the costs associated with their developments. In general, courts have found that such requirements are appropriate if there is a direct relationship between a cost or issue arising as a part of the proposed development and the regulation itself. It was not until the subsequent ruling in the *Dolan v. City of Tigard* case that the court offered guidance regarding the acceptable degree of the exaction.

Dolan v. City of Tigard

Dolan sought to expand her hardware store and the city conditionally agreed to issue the permit in exchange for a dedication of a portion of the property in question. This dedication, amounting to roughly 10 percent of the land, was requested for the purpose of expanding the city's storm drainage infrastructure and bike pathway. Dolan prevailed in her regulatory takings suit when she demonstrated that even if there was a relationship between the building permit and the exaction sought by the city, the magnitude of the connection was out of proportion. In *Dolan*, the U.S. Supreme Court adopted a rough proportionality test that shifts the burden to the city to show that there is a reasonable relationship between the exaction and the proposed development.

In both of these instances, the municipality saw the opportunity to pay for needed infrastructure by conditioning development upon dedications of land. The court did not object to this approach in principle, but did establish a specific threshold for determining when a municipality exceeds its authority. In the absence of such clarity, state and local governments that utilize growth management tools must exercise caution to ensure that they are not invalidated on takings grounds. The tools described below typically have been utilized to help manage growth.

Growth Management Tools

MORATORIA

A moratorium is a legislative act wherein a city council, for example, will pass an ordinance limiting growth for a certain period. Moratoria are permitted in such cases where study is necessary to solve an impending problem. In *Construction Industry Association of Sonoma County v. City of Petaluma*, the courts upheld a one-year moratorium on new residential development so that the city could develop the "Petaluma Plan" to ensure that future residential development efforts were balanced and met the needs of all residents. In Chapter 10 on regulatory takings, you read the Supreme Court case involving the moratorium on development around Lake Tahoe. As you may recall, the High Court held that the temporary suspension of development rights is legally acceptable if a city is not exercising any unnecessary delay in the study of the problem at hand. In that case, the time was necessary for the regional planning council to hire experts to study the relationship between land development practices and the dimunition of water quality.

URBAN GROWTH BOUNDARIES

Cities may use Urban Growth Boundaries (UBGs) to contain growth. A city, by legislative action, may draw an imaginary boundary within the city's geographical limits in which it seeks to contain development. This strategy allows jurisdictions to encourage property owners to develop properties closer to the urban core before leapfrogging out into the fringe areas of the urban boundaries. As areas within UBGs develop, cities must revisit and revise UBGs. UBG policies sometimes permit development in these fringe areas prior to the expansion of the urban growth boundary on the condition that property owners install the infrastructure that is necessary to connect them to existing services. In some instances, these added costs disincentivize leapfrog development. This tool, while effective at encouraging infill and more dense development, can result in the exaggeration of property values and, if unchecked, result in affordable housing issues.

POINTS SYSTEMS

Some local governments have employed strategies to prioritize new development based on time, location, and amenities. Local ordinances employing a points system identify a particular threshold when development can take place. Developers are given points for developing in areas that are already adequately served by infrastructure. Additional points are given to development that incorporates features important to the city such as green space, low impact design, dedications of land for public purposes, among other amenities. Points systems were first evaluated by New York's High Court in *Golden v. Town Planning Board of Ramapo*. There the court found that these systems were legally defensible so long as they were related to the priorities imbedded in a city's comprehensive planning document.

ADEQUATE PUBLIC FACILITIES REQUIREMENTS

Adequate Public Facilities Requirements (APFs) seek to ensure that new development is only permitted in those areas where infrastructure is either in place or planned for. In this way, cities are able to control the location and timing of development by connecting it with the availability of roads, schools, and water and sewerage systems, among other necessary infrastructure. Rather than following development, cities using APF requirements can direct the location of development. Like UBG policies, most APFs allow for developers in other locations to install infrastructure in places not prioritized for development by the city. While this may raise the cost of development in these areas, these policies do help avert regulatory takings challenges.

There are a multitude of other tools being utilized to support growth management activities. These tools will survive legal scrutiny if they are established as a part of a city's comprehensive planning efforts. Given the rights of private property owners to develop, growth management schemes must make development possible in the foreseeable future. This approach must be driven, in part, on market demand with special attention paid to issues of social equity. Like zoning, property owners are not entitled to the highest and best use of their lands. Courts use a reasonableness standard, coupled with the traditional regulatory takings analysis, to determine if growth management tools are justified.

Response to Wicked Problem

The city of Nostalgia is legitimately concerned about the possible impacts of oil and gas exploration activities on the city, particularly on its housing market. Such activities customarily result in raised rents, impacting affordable housing supplies. Exploration activities do not typically create a market for the construction of new housing until mineral deposits are located and long-term plans for extraction are made. A moratorium on the construction of all new residential development might be appropriate to estimate the current and future supply and demand for housing in the city, particularly affordable housing. If a moratorium is passed, experts must be immediately retained to study this issue. There is no limit on the amount of time the moratorium can be in place so long as the city is not exercising unnecessary delay in studying the issue and developing a regulatory solution to the same. As a general rule, six months to one year is a common time frame for a moratorium of this type.

The two regulatory responses proposed by the city in this case have been upheld in other contexts. The rate of development ordinance is similar to the one at the heart of the conflict in the *Petaluma* case. The city's proposed limit of 50 units per year with a further requirement that only 5 of those units be developed as multi-family use would be suspect if that limit did not correspond with the findings of the market demand study. The adequate public facilities proposal, modeled after the one in Ramapo, is more like a Nollan-Dolan exaction. These are permissible as long as there is a reasonable relationship that is roughly proportional to the burden imposed. In either case, the selected strategy should be tied to the city's comprehensive plan to ensure that private property owners and, ultimately, the courts understand the basis for these activities.

The city planner must stay abreast of current and future local housing needs. It is his or her responsibility to ensure that growth.

Discussion Prompts

- Growth management typically seeks to control the amount, time, location, and character of new development on the basis of the availability of adequate infrastructure to support development. What type of infrastructure is typically considered by cities, counties, and states who implement growth management? How do they typically judge the availability/adequacy of existing infrastructure?
- Opponents of growth management often suggest that the real intention of such programs is to prevent growth. Is this true? Present an argument to the contrary.
- When Florida's Governor Rick Scott ran for election, he took aim at the state's growth management program as have other tea party politicians. What are their primary concerns about growth management schemes? Are these concerns justified?

Bibliography

Anthony, J. (2003). The Effects of Florida's Growth Management Act on Housing Affordability. *Journal of the American Planning Association*, 69:3, 282–295.

Chapin, Timothy S., Connerly, Charles E., and Higgins, Harrison T. (2007).*Growth Management in Florida: Planning for Paradise*. Chippenham, Wiltshire: Antony Rowe Ltd.

Ingram, Gregory K. and Hong, Yu-Hung (2009). *Evaluating Smart Growth: State and Local Policy Outcomes*. Cambridge, MA: Lincoln Institute of Land Policy.

RuBino, Richard G. and Starnes, Earl M. (2008). *Lessons Learned? The History of Planning in Florida*. Tallahassee, FL: Sentry Press, Inc.

Stroud, N. (1988). Legal Considerations of Development Impact Fees. *Journal of the American Planning Association*, 54:1, 29–37.

14

HISTORIC PRESERVATION AND URBAN DESIGN

Governmental entities at the federal, state, and local levels are often called upon to incentivize the preservation of historic structures, even though these are often privately owned. Historically significant structures have been recognized as a vital part of local infrastructure. Similarly, these entities are often asked to promote a particular aesthetic in a community through the enactment of urban design regulations. Historic preservation and urban design regulations are often controversial because of their subjective natures as well as the burden that they impose on private property owners for the benefit of the community at large.

Historic Preservation and Urban Design Wicked Problem

The city of X has recently replaced its zoning regulations with a form-based code. Please assess the legality of the following provisions of the code.

This code, among other elements, seeks to encourage development that is mixed use and well designed. Per the language of the code, transect two is a historic district. The regulations for the district require that all new construction be designed so that it is in harmony with the historic structures that surround it. Transect two contains structures from the 1920s to the present. Most of the structures, however, date back to the 1930s and 1940s. Jane owns a vacant lot within transect two. She seeks to open a franchise of a White Castle, a business that is known for being housed in a white building that looks somewhat like a castle. The City Council, based on the recommendations of planning staff and the planning commission, has denied Jane's application to build the White Castle in the form proposed but has said that it will approve her plans if she removes the turrets and flags from the design and paints the structure grey. What is Jane's best legal argument?

Cases

The following cases will be useful to you as you attempt to analyze this chapter's wicked problem:

Penn Central Transportation Co. v. City of New York, 438 U.S. 104 (1978)
Figarsky v. Historic District Commission, 171 Conn. 198 (1976)
State ex. rel Stoyanoff v. Berkeley, 458 S.W.2d 305 (1970)

Figure 13 Credit: David D. Boeck

Penn Central Transportation Co. v. City of New York

438 U.S. 104 (1978)

Facts

In the interest of historic preservation, New York City enacted a law that created a system for owners of designated buildings of historical importance to alter their properties. In 1968, Penn Central Transportation Company, owners of Grand Central Terminal, entered into a contract to build a multi-story office building above the Terminal, which was a designated landmark. After the Landmark Preservation Commission denied two successive applications submitted by Penn Central for construction, Penn Central filed suit, claiming that the denial constituted a taking.

Issue

Does the application of restrictions on development under the City's Landmark Preservation Law to Grand Central Terminal constitute a taking under the Fifth and Fourteenth Amendments?

Held

No. Determining whether a government action has constituted a taking depends on an assessment of the economic impact of the regulation on the property owner, the owner's distinct investment-backed expectations, and the character of the governmental action. The city's law did not transfer control of the property away from Penn Central, affect the present use of the terminal as it had been used for 65 years, prohibit Penn from submitting future applications for development, or prevent Penn transferring its air rights.

Discussion

The Supreme Court has repeatedly used its three-prong test established in *Penn Central* in assessing whether a government actor has created a regulatory taking requiring compensation under the Fifth and Fourteenth Amendments.

Case Excerpt

Before considering appellants' specific contentions, it will be useful to review the factors that have shaped the jurisprudence of the Fifth Amendment injunction "nor shall private property be taken for public use, without just compensation." The question of what constitutes a "taking" for purposes of the Fifth Amendment has proved to be a problem of considerable difficulty. While this Court has recognized that the "Fifth Amendment's guarantee … [is] designed to bar Government from forcing some people alone to bear public burdens which, in all fairness and justice, should be borne by the public as a whole," *Armstrong* v. *United States*, 364 U. S. 40, 49 (1960), this Court, quite simply, has been unable to develop any "set formula" for determining when "justice and fairness" require that economic injuries caused by public action be compensated by the government, rather than remain disproportionately concentrated on a few persons. See *Goldblatt* v. *Hempstead*, 369 U. S. 590, 594 (1962). Indeed, we have frequently observed that whether a particular restriction will be rendered invalid by the government's failure to pay for any losses proximately caused by it depends largely "upon the particular circumstances [in that] case." *United States* v. Central *Eureka Mining Co.*, 357 U. S. 155, 168 (1958); see *United States* v. *Caltex, Inc.*, 344 U. S. 149, 156 (1952).

In engaging in these essentially ad hoc, factual inquiries, the Court's decisions have identified several factors that have particular significance. The economic impact of the regulation on the claimant and, particularly, the extent to which the regulation has interfered with distinct investment-backed expectations are, of course, relevant considerations. See *Goldblatt* v. *Hempstead*, *supra*, at 594. So, too, is the character of the governmental action. A "taking" may more readily be found when the interference with property can be characterized as a physical invasion by government, see, *e. g.*, *United States* v. *Causby*, 328 U. S. 256 (1946), than when interference arises from some public program adjusting the benefits and burdens of economic life to promote the common good.

"Government hardly could go on if to some extent values incident to property could not be diminished without paying for every such change in the general law," *Pennsylvania Coal Co.* v. *Mahon*, 260 U. S. 393, 413 (1922), and this Court has accordingly recognized, in a wide variety of contexts, that government may execute laws or programs that adversely affect recognized economic values. Exercises of the taxing power are one obvious example. A second are the decisions in which this Court has dismissed "taking" challenges on the ground that, while the challenged government action caused economic harm, it did not interfere with interests that were sufficiently bound up with the reasonable expectations of the claimant to constitute "property" for Fifth Amendment purposes. See, *e. g., United States* v. *Willow River Power Co.*, 324 U. S. 499 (1945) (interest in high-water level of river for runoff for tailwaters to maintain power head is not property); *United States* v. *Chandler-Dunbar Water Power Co.*, 229 U. S. 53 (1913) (no property interest can exist in navigable waters); see also *Demorest* v. *City Bank Co.*, 321 U. S. 36 (1944); *Muhlker* v. *Harlem R. Co.*, 197 U. S. 544 (1905); Sax, Takings and the Police Power, 74 Yale L. J. 36, 61–62 (1964).

More importantly for the present case, in instances in which a state tribunal reasonably concluded that "the health, safety, morals, or general welfare" would be promoted by prohibiting particular contemplated uses of land, this Court has upheld land-use regulations that destroyed or adversely affected recognized real property interests. See *Nectow* v. *Cambridge*, 277 U. S. 183, 188 (1928). Zoning laws are, of course, the classic example, see *Euclid* v. *Ambler Realty Co.*, 272 U. S. 365 (1926) (prohibition of industrial use); *Gorieb* v. *Fox*, 274 U. S. 603, 608 (1927) (requirement that portions of parcels be left unbuilt); *Welch* v. *Swasey*, 214 U. S. 91 (1909) (height restriction), which have been viewed as permissible governmental action even when prohibiting the most beneficial use of the property. See *Goldblatt* v. *Hempstead, supra*, at 592–593, and cases cited; see also *Eastlake* v. *Forest City Enterprises, Inc.*, 426 U. S. 668, 674 n. 8 (1976).

Zoning laws generally do not affect existing uses of real property, but "taking" challenges have also been held to be without merit in a wide variety of situations when the challenged governmental actions prohibited a beneficial use to which individual parcels had previously been devoted and thus caused substantial individualized harm. *Miller* v. *Schoene*, 276 U. S. 272 (1928), is illustrative. In that case, a state entomologist, acting pursuant to a state statute, ordered the claimants to cut down a large number of ornamental red cedar trees because they produced cedar rust fatal to apple trees cultivated nearby. Although the statute provided for recovery of any expense incurred in removing the cedars, and permitted claimants to use the felled trees, it did not provide compensation for the value of the standing trees or for the resulting decrease in market value of the properties as a whole. A unanimous Court held that this latter omission did not render the statute invalid. The Court held that the State might properly make "a choice between the preservation of one class of property and that of the other" and since the apple industry was important in the State involved, concluded that the State had not exceeded "its constitutional powers by deciding upon the destruction of one class of property [without compensation] in order to save another which, in the judgment of the legislature, is of greater value to the public." *Id.*, at 279.

Again, *Hadacheck* v. *Sebastian,* 239 U. S. 394 (1915), upheld a law prohibiting the claimant from continuing his otherwise lawful business of operating a brickyard in a particular physical community on the ground that the legislature had reasonably concluded that the presence of the brickyard was inconsistent with neighboring uses. See also *United States* v. Central *Eureka Mining Co., supra* (Government order closing gold mines so that skilled miners would be available for other mining work held not a taking): *Atchison, T. & S. F. R. Co.* v. *Public Utilities Comm'n,* 346 U. S. 346 (1953) (railroad may be required to share cost of constructing railroad grade improvement); *Walls* v. *Midland Carbon Co.,* 254 U. S. 300 (1920) (law prohibiting manufacture of carbon black upheld); *Reinman* v. *Little Rock,* 237 U. S. 171 (1915) (law prohibiting livery stable upheld); *Mugler* v. *Kansas,* 123 U. S. 623 (1887) (law prohibiting liquor business upheld).

Goldblatt v. *Hempstead, supra,* is a recent example. There, a 1958 city safety ordinance banned any excavations below the water table and effectively prohibited the claimant from continuing a sand and gravel mining business that had been operated on the particular parcel since 1927. The Court upheld the ordinance against a "taking" challenge, although the ordinance prohibited the present and presumably most beneficial use of the property and had, like the regulations in *Miller* and *Hadacheck,* severely affected a particular owner. The Court assumed that the ordinance did not prevent the owner's reasonable use of the property since the owner made no showing of an adverse effect on the value of the land. Because the restriction served a substantial public purpose, the Court thus held no taking had occurred. It is, of course, implicit in *Goldblatt* that a use restriction on real property may constitute a "taking" if not reasonably necessary to the effectuation of a substantial public purpose, see *Nectow* v. *Cambridge, supra;* cf. *Moore* v. *East Cleveland,* 431 U. S. 494, 513–514 (1977) (STEVENS, J., concurring), or perhaps if it has an unduly harsh impact upon the owner's use of the property.

Pennsylvania Coal Co. v. *Mahon,* 260 U. S. 393 (1922), is the leading case for the proposition that a state statute that substantially furthers important public policies may so frustrate distinct investment-backed expectations as to amount to a "taking." There the claimant had sold the surface rights to particular parcels of property, but expressly reserved the right to remove the coal thereunder. A Pennsylvania statute, enacted after the transactions, forbade any mining of coal that caused the subsidence of any house, unless the house was the property of the owner of the underlying coal and was more than 150 feet from the improved property of another. Because the statute made it commercially impracticable to mine the coal, *id.,* at 414, and thus had nearly the same effect as the complete destruction of rights claimant had reserved from the owners of the surface land, see *id.,* at 414–415, the Court held that the statute was invalid as effecting a "taking" without just compensation. See also *Armstrong* v. *United States,* 364 U. S. 40 (1960) (Government's complete destruction of a materialman's lien in certain property held a "taking"); *Hudson Water Co.* v. *McCarter,* 209 U. S. 349, 355 (1908) (if height restriction makes property wholly useless "the rights of property … prevail over the other public interest" and compensation is required). See generally Michelman, Property, Utility, and Fairness: Comments on the Ethical Foundations of "Just Compensation" Law, 80 Harv. L. Rev. 1165, 1229–1234 (1967).

Finally, government actions that may be characterized as acquisitions of resources to permit or facilitate uniquely public functions have often been held to constitute "takings." *United States* v. *Causby*, 328 U. S. 256 (1946), is illustrative. In holding that direct overflights above the claimant's land, that destroyed the present use of the land as a chicken farm, constituted a "taking" *Causby* emphasized that Government had not "merely destroyed property [but was] using a part of it for the flight of its planes." *Id.*, at 262–263, n. 7. See also *Griggs* v. *Allegheny County*, 369 U. S. 84 (1962) (overflights held a taking); *Portsmouth Co.* v. *United States*, 260 U. S. 327 (1922) (United States military installations' repeated firing of guns over claimant's land is a taking); *United States* v. *Cress*, 243 U. S. 316 (1917) (repeated floodings of land caused by water project is a taking); but see *YMCA* v. *United States*, 395 U. S. 85 (1969) (damage caused to building when federal officers who were seeking to protect building were attacked by rioters held not a taking). See generally Michelman, *supra*, at 1226–1229; Sax, Takings and the Police Power, 74 Yale L. J. 36 (1964).

In contending that the New York City law has "taken" their property in violation of the Fifth and Fourteenth Amendments, appellants make a series of arguments, which, while tailored to the facts of this case, essentially urge that any substantial restriction imposed pursuant to a landmark law must be accompanied by just compensation if it is to be constitutional. Before considering these, we emphasize what is not in dispute. Because this Court has recognized, in a number of settings, that States and cities may enact land-use restrictions or controls to enhance the quality of life by preserving the character and desirable aesthetic features of a city, see *New Orleans* v. *Dukes,* 427 U. S. 297 (1976); *Young* v. *American Mini Theatres, Inc.,* 427 U. S. 50 (1976); *Village of Belle Terre* v. *Boraas,* 416 U. S. 1, 9–10 (1974); *Berman* v. *Parker,* 348 U. S. 26, 33 (1954); *Welch* v. *Swasey,* 214 U. S., at 108, appellants do not contest that New York City's objective of preserving structures and areas with special historic, architectural, or cultural significance is an entirely permissible governmental goal. They also do not dispute that the restrictions imposed on its parcel are appropriate means of securing the purposes of the New York City law. Finally, appellants do not challenge any of the specific factual premises of the decision below. They accept for present purposes both that the parcel of land occupied by Grand Central Terminal must, in its present state, be regarded as capable of earning a reasonable return, and that the transferable development rights afforded appellants by virtue of the Terminal's designation as a landmark are valuable, even if not as valuable as the rights to construct above the Terminal. In appellants' view none of these factors derogate from their claim that New York City's law has effected a "taking."

They first observe that the airspace above the Terminal is a valuable property interest, citing *United States* v. *Causby, supra*. They urge that the Landmarks Law has deprived them of any gainful use of their "air rights" above the Terminal and that, irrespective of the value of the remainder of their parcel, the city has "taken" their right to this superjacent airspace, thus entitling them to "just compensation" measured by the fair market value of these air rights.

Apart from our own disagreement with appellants' characterization of the effect of the New York City law, see *infra,* at 134–135, the submission that appellants may establish a "taking" simply by showing that they have been denied the ability to exploit a property interest that they heretofore had believed was available for development is quite simply untenable. Were this the rule, this Court would have erred not only in upholding laws restricting the development of air rights, see *Welch* v. *Swasey, supra,* but also in approving those prohibiting both the subjacent, see *Goldblatt* v. *Hempstead,* 369 U. S. 590 (1962), and the lateral, see *Gorieb* v. *Fox,* 274 U. S. 603 (1927), development of particular parcels. "Taking" jurisprudence does not divide a single parcel into discrete segments and attempt to determine whether rights in a particular segment have been entirely abrogated. In deciding whether a particular governmental action has effected a taking, this Court focuses rather both on the character of the action and on the nature and extent of the interference with rights in the parcel as a whole – here, the city tax block designated as the "landmark site."

Secondly, appellants, focusing on the character and impact of the New York City law, argue that it effects a "taking" because its operation has significantly diminished the value of the Terminal site. Appellants concede that the decisions sustaining other land-use regulations, which, like the New York City law, are reasonably related to the promotion of the general welfare, uniformly reject the proposition that diminution in property value, standing alone, can establish a "taking," see *Euclid* v. *Ambler Realty Co.,* 272 U. S. 365 (1926) (75% diminution in value caused by zoning law); *Hadacheck* v. *Sebastian,* 239 U. S. 394 (1915) (87 1/2% diminution in value); cf. *Eastlake* v. *Forest City Enterprises, Inc.,* 426 U. S., at 674 n. 8, and that the "taking" issue in these contexts is resolved by focusing on the uses the regulations permit. See also *Goldblatt* v. *Hempstead, supra.* Appellants, moreover, also do not dispute that a showing of diminution in property value would not establish a "taking" if the restriction had been imposed as a result of historic-district legislation, see generally *Maher* v. *New Orleans,* 516 F. 2d 1051 (CA5 1975), but appellants argue that New York City's regulation of individual landmarks is fundamentally different from zoning or from historic-district legislation because the controls imposed by New York City's law apply only to individuals who own selected properties.

Stated baldly, appellants' position appears to be that the only means of ensuring that selected owners are not singled out to endure financial hardship for no reason is to hold that any restriction imposed on individual landmarks pursuant to the New York City scheme is a "taking" requiring the payment of "just compensation." Agreement with this argument would, of course, invalidate not just New York City's law, but all comparable landmark legislation in the Nation. We find no merit in it.

It is true, as appellants emphasize, that both historic-district legislation and zoning laws regulate all properties within given physical communities whereas landmark laws apply only to selected parcels. But, contrary to appellants' suggestions, landmark laws are not like discriminatory, or "reverse spot," zoning: that is, a land-use decision which arbitrarily singles out a particular parcel for different, less favorable treatment than the neighboring ones. See 2 A. Rathkopf, The Law of Zoning and Planning 26-4, and n. 6 (4th ed. 1978). In contrast to discriminatory zoning, which is the antithesis of land-use control as part of some comprehensive plan, the New York City law embodies a comprehensive plan to preserve structures of historic or aesthetic interest wherever they might be found in the city, and as noted, over 400 landmarks and 31 historic districts have been designated pursuant to this plan.

Equally without merit is the related argument that the decision to designate a structure as a landmark "is inevitably arbitrary or at least subjective, because it is basically a matter of taste," Reply Brief for Appellants 22, thus unavoidably singling out individual landowners for disparate and unfair treatment. The argument has a particularly hollow ring in this case. For appellants not only did not seek judicial review of either the designation or of the denials of the certificates of appropriateness and of no exterior effect, but do not even now suggest that the Commission's decisions concerning the Terminal were in any sense arbitrary or unprincipled. But, in any event, a landmark owner has a right to judicial review of any Commission decision, and, quite simply, there is no basis whatsoever for a conclusion that courts will have any greater difficulty identifying arbitrary or discriminatory action in the context of landmark regulation than in the context of classic zoning or indeed in any other context.

Next, appellants observe that New York City's law differs from zoning laws and historic-district ordinances in that the Landmarks Law does not impose identical or similar restrictions on all structures located in particular physical communities. It follows, they argue, that New York City's law is inherently incapable of producing the fair and equitable distribution of benefits and burdens of governmental action which is characteristic of zoning laws and historic-district legislation and which they maintain is a constitutional requirement if "just compensation" is not to be afforded. It is, of course, true that the Landmarks Law has a more severe impact on some landowners than on others, but that in itself does not mean that the law effects a "taking." Legislation designed to promote the general welfare commonly burdens some more than others. The owners of the brickyard in *Hadacheck,* of the cedar trees in *Miller* v. *Schoene,* and of the gravel and sand mine in *Goldblatt* v. *Hempstead,* were uniquely burdened by the legislation sustained in those cases. Similarly, zoning laws often affect some property owners more severely than others but have not been held to be invalid on that account. For example, the property owner in *Euclid* who wished to use its property for industrial purposes was affected far more severely by the ordinance than its neighbors who wished to use their land for residences.

In any event, appellants' repeated suggestions that they are solely burdened and unbenefited is factually inaccurate. This contention overlooks the fact that the New York City law applies to vast numbers of structures in the city in addition to the Terminal – all the structures contained in the 31 historic districts and over 400 individual landmarks, many of which are close to the Terminal. Unless we are to reject the judgment of the New York City Council that the preservation of landmarks benefits all New York citizens and all structures, both economically and by improving the quality of life in the city as a whole – which we are unwilling to do – we cannot conclude that the owners of the Terminal have in no sense been benefited by the Landmarks Law. Doubtless appellants believe they are more burdened than benefited by the law, but that must have been true, too, of the property owners in *Miller, Hadacheck, Euclid,* and *Goldblatt.*

Appellants' final broad-based attack would have us treat the law as an instance, like that in *United States* v. *Causby,* in which government, acting in an enterprise capacity, has appropriated part of their property for some strictly governmental purpose. Apart from the fact that *Causby* was a case of invasion of airspace that destroyed the use of the farm beneath and this New York City law has in nowise impaired the present use of the Terminal, the Landmarks Law neither exploits appellants' parcel for city purposes nor facilitates nor arises from any entrepreneurial operations of the city. The situation is not remotely like that in *Causby* where the airspace above the property was in the flight pattern for military aircraft. The Landmarks Law's effect is simply to prohibit appellants or anyone else from occupying portions of the airspace above the Terminal, while permitting appellants to use the remainder of the parcel in a gainful fashion. This is no more an appropriation of property by government for its own uses than is a zoning law prohibiting, for "aesthetic" reasons, two or more adult theaters within a specified area, see *Young* v. *American Mini Theatres, Inc.,* 427 U. S. 50 (1976), or a safety regulation prohibiting excavations below a certain level. See *Goldblatt* v. *Hempstead.*

Rejection of appellants' broad arguments is not, however, the end of our inquiry, for all we thus far have established is that the New York City law is not rendered invalid by its failure to provide "just compensation" whenever a landmark owner is restricted in the exploitation of property interests, such as air rights, to a greater extent than provided for under applicable zoning laws. We now must consider whether the interference with appellants' property is of such a magnitude that "there must be an exercise of eminent domain and compensation to sustain [it]." *Pennsylvania Coal Co.* v. *Mahon,* 260 U. S., at 413. That inquiry may be narrowed to the question of the severity of the impact of the law on appellants' parcel, and its resolution in turn requires a careful assessment of the impact of the regulation on the Terminal site.

Unlike the governmental acts in *Goldblatt, Miller, Causby, Griggs,* and *Hadacheck,* the New York City law does not interfere in any way with the present uses of the Terminal. Its designation as a landmark not only permits but contemplates that appellants may continue to use the property precisely as it has been used for the past 65 years: as a railroad terminal containing office space and concessions. So the law does not interfere with what must be regarded as Penn Central's primary expectation concerning the use of the parcel. More importantly, on this record, we must regard the New York City law as permitting Penn Central not only to profit from the Terminal but also to obtain a "reasonable return" on its investment.

Appellants, moreover, exaggerate the effect of the law on their ability to make use of the air rights above the Terminal in two respects. First, it simply cannot be maintained, on this record, that appellants have been prohibited from occupying *any* portion of the airspace above the Terminal. While the Commission's actions in denying applications to construct an office building in excess of 50 stories above the Terminal may indicate that it will refuse to issue a certificate of appropriateness for any comparably sized structure, nothing the Commission has said or done suggests an intention to prohibit *any* construction above the Terminal. The Commission's report emphasized that whether any construction would be allowed depended upon whether the proposed addition "would harmonize in scale, material, and character with [the Terminal]." Record 2251. Since appellants have not sought approval for the construction of a smaller structure, we do not know that appellants will be denied any use of any portion of the airspace above the Terminal.

Second, to the extent appellants have been denied the right to build above the Terminal, it is not literally accurate to say that they have been denied *all* use of even those pre-existing air rights. Their ability to use these rights has not been abrogated; they are made transferable to at least eight parcels in the vicinity of the Terminal, one or two of which have been found suitable for the construction of new office buildings. Although appellants and others have argued that New York City's transferable development-rights program is far from ideal, the New York courts here supportably found that, at least in the case of the Terminal, the rights afforded are valuable. While these rights may well not have constituted "just compensation" if a "taking" had occurred, the rights nevertheless undoubtedly mitigate whatever financial burdens the law has imposed on appellants and, for that reason, are to be taken into account in considering the impact of regulation. Cf. *Goldblatt* v. *Hempstead,* 369 U. S., at 594 n. 3.

On this record, we conclude that the application of New York City's Landmarks Law has not effected a "taking" of appellants' property. The restrictions imposed are substantially related to the promotion of the general welfare and not only permit reasonable beneficial use of the landmark site but also afford appellants opportunities further to enhance not only the Terminal site proper but also other properties.

Figarsky v. Historic District Commission of the City of Norwich

171 Conn. 198 (1976)

Facts

In 1963, Figarsky purchased a building that would eventually become located within the city of Norwich's historic district. Rather than rehabilitating the structure, Figarsky applied for a permit to demolish the building, but was told that issuance of the permit was dependent on a certificate of appropriateness from the Historic District Commission. After a public hearing, the Commission denied Figarsky's application for a certificate of appropriateness.

Issue

Did the Historic District Commission act illegally, arbitrarily, and abuse its authority when it denied Figarsky's application to demolish a building in the City's historic district?

Held

No. In order to be constitutional, the exercise of police powers must have a reasonable relationship to promoting public welfare. Connecticut's enabling legislation recognized the intangible benefits of historical preservation, allowing the city of Norwich the authority to exercise its police powers to preserve areas or landmarks of historic importance. Admittedly, Figarsky's building was itself of little historic value, but it served as a crucial barrier to encroaching development, helping the district maintain its unique character.

Discussion

If a regulation leaves a property owner unable to make a reasonable use of the property, rendering it of little or no value to the owner, then a valid regulation may be deemed confiscatory. Relief is only appropriate in extreme instances of such deprivation, not merely for limiting the owner's greatest potential economic use of the property.

Case Excerpt

The plaintiffs' principal claim is that the Norwich historic district ordinance, implementing the state enabling act, is unconstitutional as applied to them, and that the denial of their application for a certificate of appropriateness to demolish their building amounts to a taking of their property for public use without compensation. More specifically, they contend that the ordinance is "vague aesthetic legislation," incapable of application in accordance with mandates of due process, and that because of the denial of their application they will be forced to expend large sums in the maintenance of their property without being able to put it to any practical use.

Neither the constitution of the United States, amendments five and fourteen, nor the constitution of Connecticut, article first, § 11, deny the state the power to regulate the uses to which an owner may devote his property.

"All property is held subject to the right of government to regulate its use in the exercise of the police power, so that it shall not be injurious to the rights of the community, or so that it may promote its health, morals, safety and welfare. The power of regulation by government is not unlimited; it cannot, as we have stated, be imposed unless it bears a rational relation to the subjects which fall fairly within the police power and unless the means used are not within constitutional inhibitions. The means used will fall within these inhibitions whenever they are destructive, confiscatory, or so unreasonable as to be arbitrary. *Euclid v. Ambler Realty Co.,* 272 U.S. 365, 47 Sup. Ct. 114 [71 L. Ed. 303]. Regulations may result to some extent, practically in the taking of property, or the restricting its uses, and yet not be deemed confiscatory or unreasonable. Courts will not substitute their judgment for the legislative judgment when these considerations are fairly debatable. They will regard their validity… from the standpoint of existing conditions and present times." *State* v. *Hillman,* 110 Conn. 92, 105, 147 A. 294. When, as here, a legislative enactment is challenged in its application as beyond the scope or as an abuse of the state's police power, two issues are raised: first, whether the object of the legislation falls within the police power; and second, whether the means by which the legislation attempts to reach that object are reasonable. *Windsor* v. *Whitney,* 95 Conn. 357, 369, 111 A. 354.

"To be constitutionally valid, a regulation made under the police power must have a reasonable relation to the public health, safety, morality and welfare." *State* v. *Gordon,* 143 Conn. 698, 703, 125 A.2d 477; *DeMello* v. *Plainville,* 170 Conn. 675, 679, 368 A.2d 71. No contention is made that the historic district ordinance contributes to the health or safety of the public; our inquiry is limited to whether the preservation of historic areas in a static form serves the amorphous concept of "the public welfare." See *Opinion of the Justices,* 333 Mass. 773, 778, 128 N.E.2d 557. "The concept of the public welfare is broad and inclusive… The values it represents are spiritual as well as physical, aesthetic as well as monetary. It is within the power of the legislature to determine that the community should be beautiful as well as healthy, spacious as well as clean, well-balanced as well as carefully patrolled." *Berman* v. *Parker,* 348 U.S. 26, 33, 75 S. Ct. 98, 99 L. Ed. 27. It is apparent from the language of the enabling statute that the General Assembly, in enacting those statutes, was cognizant not only of the intangible benefits to be derived from historic districts, such as an increase in the public's awareness of its New England heritage, but of the economic benefits to be reaped as well, by augmenting the value of properties located within the old sections of the state's cities and towns, and encouraging tourism within the state. In a number of recent cases, it has been held that the preservation of a historical area or landmark as it was in the past falls within the meaning of general welfare and, consequently, the police power. See, e.g., *Maher* v. *New Orleans,* 516 F.2d 1051, 1060 (5th Cir.); *Annapolis* v. *Anne Arundel County,* 271 Md. 265, 316 A.2d 807; *Lutheran Church in America* v. *City of New York,* 35 N.Y.2d 121, 316 N.E.2d 305; *Rebman* v. *Springfield,* 111 Ill. App.2d 430, 250 N.E.2d 282; *Opinion of the Justices,* supra, 773; see 1 Rathkopf, Zoning and Planning (4th Ed.), c. 15; 82 Am. Jur.2d, Zoning and Planning, § 40. We cannot deny that the preservation of an area or cluster of buildings with exceptional historical and architectural significance may serve the public welfare.

The plaintiffs argue that the Norwich ordinance constitutes "vague aesthetic legislation," and point to our statement in *DeMaria* v. *Planning & Zoning Commission,* 159 Conn. 534, 541, 271 A.2d 105, that "vague and undefined aesthetic considerations alone are insufficient to support the invocation of the police power," and our dictum to the same effect. *Gionfriddo* v. *Windsor,* 137 Conn. 701, 704, 81 A.2d 266. The "aesthetic considerations" involved in the Norwich ordinance are not, however, "vague and undefined"; § 7–147f of the General Statutes, incorporated by reference into the ordinance, sets out with some specificity the factors to be considered by the commission in passing upon an application for a certificate of appropriateness. Nor, as we pointed out in the preceding discussion, do "aesthetic considerations alone" provide the basis for the ordinance. Furthermore, as long ago as *Windsor v. Whitney*, 95 Conn. 357, 368, 111 A. 354, we commented that the question of the relationship between aesthetics and the police power was not a settled question. In *State v. Kievman*, 116 Conn. 458, 465, 165 A. 601, we stated that a land use regulation was not invalid simply because it was based in part on aesthetic considerations. And in *Murphy, Inc. v. Westport*, 131 Conn. 292, 302, 40 A.2d 177, we indicated that aesthetic considerations may have a definite relation to the public welfare. Although we need not directly decide the issue in the present case, we note that other jurisdictions have recognized that "aesthetic considerations alone may warrant an exercise of the police power." *People v. Stover*, 12 N.Y.2d 462, 467, 191 N.E.2d 272, appeal dismissed, 375 U.S. 42, 84 S. Ct. 147, 11 L. Ed.2d 107; see 1 Rathkopf, op. cit., c. 14.

Having determined that the ordinance creating the Norwich historic district constitutes a valid exercise of the state's police power, we are left with the question of whether the application of that ordinance to the plaintiffs' property amounts to an unconstitutional deprivation of their property without compensation. In this context, it has often been noted that the police power, which regulates for the public good the uses to which private property may be put and requires no compensation, must be distinguished from the power of eminent domain, which takes private property for a public use and requires compensation to the owner. See, e.g., *DeMello v. Plainville*, 170 Conn. 675, 679–80, 368 A.2d 71, and cases cited therein. The difference is primarily one of degree, and the amount of the owner's loss is the basic criterion for determining whether a purported exercise of the police power is valid, or whether it amounts to a taking necessitating the use of the power of eminent domain. See Sax, "Takings and the Police Power," 74 Yale L.J. 36. "A regulation which otherwise constitutes a valid exercise of the police power may, as applied to a particular parcel of property, be confiscatory in that no reasonable use may be made of the property and it becomes of little or no value to the owner... See, e.g., *Pennsylvania Coal Co. v. Mahon*, 260 U.S. 393, 43 S. Ct. 158, 67 L. Ed. 322; *Brecciaroli v. Commissioner of Environmental Protection*, 168 Conn. 349, 354, 362 A.2d 948; *Horwitz v. Waterford*, 151 Conn. 320, 323, 197 A.2d 636; *Dooley v. Town Plan & Zoning Commission*, 151 Conn. 304, 311–12, 197 A.2d 770; *Vartelas v. Water Resources Commission*, 146 Conn. 650, 657, 153 A.2d 822." *DeMello v. Plainville*, supra, 680; see *Penn Central Transportation Co. v. City of New York*, 50 App. Div.2d 265, 377 N.Y.S.2d 20.

Whether the denial of the plaintiffs' application for a certificate of appropriateness to demolish their building has rendered the Norwich ordinance, as applied to them, confiscatory, must be determined in the light of their particular circumstances as they have been shown to exist. *Bartlett v. Zoning Commission*, 161 Conn. 24, 31, 282 A.2d 907; *Dooley v. Town Plan & Zoning Commission*, 151 Conn. 304, 311, 197 A.2d 770. In regulating the use of land under the police power, the maximum possible enrichment of a particular landowner is not a controlling purpose. *Goldblatt v. Hempstead*, 369 U.S. 590, 82 S. Ct. 987, 8 L. Ed.2d 130; *Hyatt v. Zoning Board of Appeals*, 163 Conn. 379, 383, 311 A.2d 77; *Damick v. Planning & Zoning Commission*, 158 Conn. 78, 83, 256

A.2d 428. It is only when the regulation practically destroys or greatly decreases the value of a specific piece of property that relief may be granted, provided it promotes substantial justice. *Culinary Institute of America, Inc.* v. *Board of Zoning Appeals,* 143 Conn. 257, 261, 121 A.2d 637. "The extent of that deprivation must be considered in light of the evils which the regulation is designed to prevent." *Chevron Oil Co.* v. *Zoning Board of Appeals,* 170 Conn. 146, 152, 365 A.2d 387; see General Statutes § 7–147f.

The plaintiffs had the burden of proving that the historic district commission acted illegally, arbitrarily, in a confiscatory manner or in abuse of discretion. *Byington* v. *Zoning Commission,* 162 Conn. 611, 613, 295 A.2d 553. This the plaintiffs failed to do. See *Maher* v. *New Orleans,* 516 F.2d 1051, 1067 (5th Cir.); *Penn Central Transportation Co.* v. *City of New York,* supra, 274. The plaintiffs went no further than to present evidence that their house was unoccupied and in need of extensive repairs. There was no evidence offered that the house, if repaired, would not be of some value, or that the proximity of the McDonald's hamburger stand rendered the property of practically no value as a part of the historic district.

The Norwich historic district commission, after a full hearing, lawfully, reasonably and honestly exercised its judgment. The trial court was correct in not substituting its own judgment for that of the commission. *Bora* v. *Zoning Board of Appeals,* 161 Conn. 297, 300, 288 A.2d 89.

State ex rel. Stoyanoff v. Berkeley

458 S.W.2d 305 (1970)

Facts

Stoyanoff applied for a building permit to construct a single-family residence in the city of Ladue, one of the most desirable residential suburbs in the St. Louis area. Although the proposed residence complied with all of the requirements of the city's zoning ordinance, the city's Architectural Board, created by ordinance, rejected the application on the basis that Stoyanoff's ultramodern design would clash with the neighborhood's dominant architectural style of traditional homes and would have a substantial adverse effect on the market values in the neighborhood. Stoyanoff brought suit, alleging that the Architectural Board was not authorized by the state's enabling legislation and that the exercise of police powers based on aesthetics was unreasonable.

Issue

Did the city exceed its authority by creating an Architectural Board to review building permit applications?

Held

No. Ordinances 131 and 281, which established Ladue's Architectural Board, conform to Missouri's enabling legislation that explicitly mentions that municipal zoning regulations can consider the suitability of particular uses given the character of an area and the impact of such uses on property values. Although the board's architectural standards for conformity were vague, the ordinance's focus on sustaining property values and owners' welfare was considered paramount.

Discussion

By assuring potential and current owners that property purchased in a residential area is likely to retain its value, zoning helps to stabilize property values. The idea that zoning serves to promote the general welfare extends to the preservation of property values.

Case Excerpt

Section 89.020 provides: "For the purpose of promoting health, safety, morals or the general welfare of the community, the legislative body of all cities, towns, and villages is hereby empowered to regulate and restrict the height, number of stories, and size of buildings and other structures, the percentage of lot that may be occupied, the size of yards, courts, and other open spaces, the density of population, the preservation of features of historical significance, and the location and use of buildings, structures and land for trade, industry, residence or other purposes." Section 89.040 provides: "Such regulations shall be made in accordance with a comprehensive plan and designed to lessen congestion in the streets; to secure safety from fire, panic and other dangers; to promote health *and the general welfare*; to provide adequate light and air; to prevent the overcrowding of land; to avoid undue concentration of population; to preserve features of historical significance; to facilitate the adequate provision of transportation, water, sewerage, schools, parks, and other public requirements. *Such regulations shall be made with reasonable consideration, among other things, to the character of the district and its peculiar suitability for particular uses, and with a view to conserving the values of buildings and encouraging the most appropriate use of land throughout such municipality.*" (Italics added.)

Relators say that "Neither Sections 89.020 or 89.040 nor any other provision of Chapter 89 mentions or gives a city the authority to regulate architectural design and appearance. There exists no provision providing for an architectural board and no entity even remotely resembling such a board is mentioned under the enabling legislation." Relators conclude that the City of Ladue lacked any power to adopt Ordinance 131 as amended by Ordinance 281 "and its intrusion into this area is wholly unwarranted and without sanction in the law." As to this aspect of the appeal relators rely upon the 1961 decision of State ex rel. Magidson v. Henze, Mo.App., 342 S.W.2d 261. That case had the identical question presented. An Architectural Control Commission was set up by an ordinance of the City of University City. In its report to the Building Commissioner, the Architectural Control Commission disapproved the Magidson application for permits to build four houses. It was commented that the proposed houses did not provide for the minimum number of square feet, and "In considering the existing character of this neighborhood, the Commission is of the opinion that houses of the character proposed in these plans are not in harmony with and will not contribute to nor protect the general welfare of this neighborhood" (loc. cit. 264). The court held that § 89.020, RSMo 1949, V.A.M.S., does not grant to the city the right to impose upon the landowner aesthetic standards for the buildings he chooses to erect.

As is clear from the affidavits and attached exhibits, the City of Ladue is an area composed principally of residences of the general types of Colonial, French Provincial and English Tudor. The city has a comprehensive plan of zoning to maintain the general character of buildings therein. The Magidson case, supra, did not consider the effect of § 89.040, supra, and the italicized portion relating to the character of the district, its suitability for particular uses, and the conservation of the values of buildings therein. These considerations, sanctioned by statute, are directly related to the general welfare of the community. That proposition has support in a number of cases cited by appellant. State ex rel. Carter v. Harper, Building Commissioner, 182 Wis. 148, 196 N.W. 451, 454, quotes Chicago B. & Q. Ry. Co. v. People of State of Illinois ex rel. Drainage Commissioners, 200 U.S. 561, 26 S.Ct. 341, 50 L.Ed. 596, 609, "'We hold that the police power of a state embraces regulations designed to promote the public convenience or the general prosperity, as well as regulations designed to promote the public health, the public morals or the public safety.'" In Marrs v. City of Oxford (D.C.D.Kan.) 24 F.2d 541, 548, it was said, "The stabilizing of property values, and giving some assurance to the public that, if property is purchased in a residential district, its value as such will be preserved, is probably the most cogent reason back of zoning ordinances." See also People v. Calvar Corporation et al., Sup., 69 N.Y.S.2d 272, 279 (aff'd 286 N. Y. 419, 36 N.E.2d 644); Kovacs v. Cooper, Judge, 336 U.S. 77, 69 S.Ct. 448, 93 L.Ed. 513, 526; Wulfsohn v. Burden, 241 N.Y. 288, 150 N.E. 120, 122 [3], 43 A.L.R. 651; and Price et al. v. Schwafel (Cal.), 92 Cal. App.2d 77, 206 P.2d 683, 685. The preamble to Ordinance 131, quoted above in part, demonstrates that its purpose is to conform to the dictates of § 89.040, with reference to preserving values of property by zoning procedure and restrictions on the use of property. This is an illustration of what was referred to in Deimeke v. State Highway Commission, Mo., 444 S.W.2d 480, 484, as a growing number of cases recognizing a change in the scope of the term "general welfare." In the Deimeke case on the same page it is said, "Property use which offends sensibilities and debases property values affects not only the adjoining property owners in that vicinity but the general public as well because when such property values are destroyed or seriously impaired, the tax base of the community is affected and the public suffers economically as a result."

Relators say further that Ordinances 131 and 281 are invalid and unconstitutional as being an unreasonable and arbitrary exercise of the police power. It is argued that a mere reading of these ordinances shows that they are based entirely on aesthetic factors in that the stated purpose of the Architectural Board is to maintain "conformity with surrounding structures" and to assure that structures "conform to certain minimum architectural standards of appearance." The argument ignores the further provisos in the ordinance: "* * * and that unsightly, grotesque and unsuitable structures, *detrimental to the stability of value and the welfare of surrounding property, structures, and residents,* and *to the general welfare and happiness of the community,* be avoided, and that appropriate standards of beauty and conformity be fostered and encouraged." (Italics added.) Relators' proposed residence does not descend to the "'patently offensive character of vehicle graveyards in close proximity to such highways'" referred to in the Deimeke case, supra (444 S.W.2d 484). Nevertheless, the aesthetic factor to be taken into account by the Architectural Board is not to be considered alone. Along with that inherent factor is the effect that the proposed residence would have upon the property values in the area. In this time of burgeoning urban areas, congested with people and structures, it is certainly in keeping with the ultimate ideal of general welfare that the Architectural Board, in its function, preserve and protect existing areas in which structures of a general conformity of architecture have been erected. The area under consideration is clearly, from the record, a fashionable one. In State ex rel. Civello v. City of New Orleans, 154 La. 271, 97 So. 440, 444, the court said, "If by the term 'aesthetic considerations' is meant a regard merely for outward appearances, for good taste in the matter of the beauty of the neighborhood itself, we do not observe any substantial reason for saying that such a consideration is not a matter of general welfare. The beauty of a fashionable residence neighborhood in a city is for the comfort and happiness of the residents, and it sustains in a general way the value of property in the neighborhood." See also People v. Stover, 12 N.Y.2d 462, 240 N.Y.S. 2d 734, 191 N.E.2d 272, 274 [3]; State ex rel. Saveland Park Holding Corp. v. Wieland, 269 Wis. 262, 69 N.W.2d 217, 222; Reid v. Architectural Board of Review of the City of Cleveland Heights, 119 Ohio App. 67, 192 N.E.2d 74, 77; and Oregon City v. Hartke, 240 Or. 35, 400 P.2d 255, 261, for pronouncements of the principle that aesthetics is a factor to be considered in zoning matters.

In the matter of enacting zoning ordinances and the procedures for determining whether any certain proposed structure or use is in compliance with or offends the basic ordinance, it is well settled that courts will not substitute their judgments for the city's legislative body, if the result is not oppressive, arbitrary or unreasonable and does not infringe upon a valid preexisting nonconforming use. Landau et al. v. Levin, 358 Mo. 77, 213 S.W.2d 483, 485 [2–4]; Flora Realty & Investment Co. v. City of Ladue, 362 Mo. 1025, 246 S.W.2d 771, 777 [1]; Wrigley Properties, Inc. et al. v. City of Ladue, Mo., 369 S.W.2d 397, 400 [2–4]. The denial by appellant of a building permit for relators' highly modernistic residence in this area where traditional Colonial, French Provincial and English Tudor styles of architecture are erected does not appear to be arbitrary and unreasonable when the basic purpose to be served is that of the general welfare of persons in the entire community.

In addition to the above-stated purpose in the preamble to Ordinance 131, it establishes an Architectural Board of three members, all of whom must be architects. Meetings of the Board are to be open to the public, and every application for a building permit, except those not affecting the outward appearance of a building, shall be submitted to the Board along with plans, elevations, detail drawings and specifications, before being approved by the Building Commissioner. The Chairman of the Board shall examine the application to determine if it conforms to proper architectural standards in appearance and design and will be in general conformity with the style and design of surrounding structures and conducive to the proper architectural development of the city. If he so finds, he approves and returns the application to the Building Commissioner. If he does not find conformity, or has doubt, a full meeting of the Board is called, with notice of the time and place thereof given to the applicant. The Board shall disapprove the application if it determines the proposed structure will constitute an unsightly, grotesque or unsuitable structure in appearance, detrimental to the welfare of surrounding property or residents. If it cannot make that decision, the application shall be returned to the Building Commissioner either with or without suggestions or recommendations, and if that is done without disapproval, the Building Commissioner may issue the permit. If the Board's disapproval is given and the applicant refuses to comply with recommendations, the Building Commissioner shall refuse the permit. Thereafter provisions are made for an appeal to the Council of the city for review of the decision of the Architectural Board. Ordinance 281 amends Ordinance 131 only with respect to the application initially being submitted to and considered by all members of the Architectural Board.

Relators claim that the above provisions of the ordinance amount to an unconstitutional delegation of power by the city to the Architectural Board. It is argued that the Board cannot be given the power to determine what is unsightly and grotesque and that the standards, "whether the proposed structure will conform to proper architectural standards in appearance and design, and will be in general conformity with the style and design of surrounding structures and conducive to the proper architectural development of the City * * *" and "the Board shall disapprove the application if it determines that the proposed structure will constitute an unsightly, grotesque or unsuitable structure in appearance, detrimental to the welfare of surrounding property or residents * *," are inadequate. First cited is State ex rel. Continental Oil Company v. Waddill, Mo., 318 S.W.2d 281, which held an ordinance provision unconstitutional which clothed the City Planning Committee with arbitrary discretion without a definite standard or rule for its guidance, following the general rule in Lux v. Milwaukee Mechanics' Ins. Co., 322 Mo. 342, 15 S.W.2d 343, 345. In the Lux case, as well as in State ex rel. Ludlow v. Guffey, Mo., 306 S.W.2d 552, exceptions to the general rule were stated to be "in situations and circumstances where necessity would require the vesting of discretion in the officer charged with the enforcement of an ordinance, as where it would be either impracticable or impossible to fix a definite rule or standard, or where the discretion vested in the officer relates to the enforcement of a police regulation requiring prompt exercise of judgment" (306 S.W.2d 557). The ordinance here is similar to the ordinance in the Guffey case wherein it was held that general standards of the ordinance were sufficient. Although it was said that neither of

the above-stated exceptions applied in the Guffey case, the impracticality of setting forth a completely comprehensive standard insuring uniform discretionary
action by the city council was discussed. It was held that the general standards
were sufficient and that the procedure for determining whether the proposed
filling station would or would not promote the "health, safety, morals or general
welfare of the community" or would or would not adversely affect "the character of the neighborhood, traffic conditions, public utility facilities and other
matters pertaining to the general welfare" (306 S.W.2d 558) was sufficient to
provide against the exercise of arbitrary and uncontrolled discretion by the city
council. Here, as in the Guffey case, the procedures are for public hearings with
notice to the applicant, not only by the Architectural Board but also by the City
Council on appeal on the factual issues to be determined under the ordinance.
An applicant's rights are safeguarded in this respect, and thus distinguished is
the ordinance which was condemned in State ex rel. Magidson v. Henze, supra.
Otherwise, in the respect that the Magidson case did not consider the purpose
of § 89.040, supra, it should no longer be followed. Ordinances 131 and 281
are sufficient in their general standards calling for a factual determination of
the suitability of any proposed structure with reference to the character of the
surrounding neighborhood and to the determination of any adverse effect on
the general welfare and preservation of property values of the community. Like
holdings were made involving Architectural Board ordinances in State ex rel.
Saveland Park Holding Corp. v. Wieland, 269 Wis. 262, 69 N.W.2d 217, and
Reid v. Architectural Board of Review of the City of Cleveland Heights, 119
Ohio App. 67, 192 N.E.2d 74, supra.

Historic Preservation and Urban Design as an Issue for Planners

Federal Preservation Law and the National Register of Historic Places

Congress enacted the National Historic Preservation Act (NHPA) in 1966 due, at least
in part, to concerns that "historic properties significant to the Nation's heritage are
being lost or substantially altered, often inadvertently, with increasing frequency" (16
U.S.C. 470(b)(3)). The act created the National Register of Historic Places, authorizing the Secretary of Interior to list "districts, sites, buildings, structures, and objects
significant in American history, architecture, archaeology, engineering, and culture"
(16 U.S.C. 470a(a)(1)(A)). As the statutory language clearly denotes, the meaning of
the term significance is vital to the discussion of what should be preserved as historic.
Mason (2004, p. 64) contends:

> A "statement of significance" gathers together all the reasons why a build-
> ing or a place should be preserved, why it is meaningful or useful, and what
> aspects require most urgent protection. Once defined, significance is used as
> a basis for policy, planning and design decisions.

In spite of the importance of the term, the statute is devoid of clear guidance regarding its meaning. The Department of Interior, through the rulemaking authority of the National Parks Service, crafted guidelines that attempt to insert objectivity into the process of determining whether a particular landmark is historically significant. The evaluation criteria suggest that a property may be deemed historic if:

- The quality of significance in American history, architecture, archeology, engineering, and culture is present in districts, sites, buildings, structures, and objects that possess integrity of location, design, setting, materials, workmanship, feeling, and association, <u>and</u>:

A. That are associated with events that have made a significant contribution to the broad patterns of our history; or
B. That are associated with the lives of significant persons in or past; or
C. That embody the distinctive characteristics of a type, period, or method of construction, or that represent the work of a master, or that possess high artistic values, or that represent a significant and distinguishable entity whose components may lack individual distinction; or
D. That have yielded or may be likely to yield, information important in history or prehistory.

Applicants bear the burden of establishing that the potential landmark meets some of the established criteria.

A National Register listing may not be enough to protect designated public housing communities from demolition. Should demolition be considered, listing merely requires that a heightened review process be initiated. While the listing does not guarantee total protection from demolition for a listed structure, it does provide a mechanism for additional scrutiny when listed landmarks or the properties surrounding them are slated for change. One such protection is laid out in Section 106 of the NHPA (16 U.S.C. 470(f)). Federal agencies that undertake projects scheduled to affect either listed properties or those eligible for listing must take into account the effect of the proposed project on the historic property. This consideration typically occurs as part of either the environmental assessment (EA) or the environmental impact statement (EIS), which is prepared as a part of the federal agency's review as required by the National Environmental Policy Act (NEPA) (16 U.S.C. 470f, 36 CFR Part 800)). Both NHPA and NEPA are procedural in nature. Collectively, the acts do not mandate that a reviewing agency take a particular course of action with respect to the preservation of a listed or eligible structure. Instead, the laws require agencies to "seek ways to avoid, minimize, or mitigate any adverse effects on historic properties" through consultation and the evaluation of alternatives (36 C.F.R. 800.1(a) and 800.6(a)).

State Preservation Efforts and the Role of State Historic Preservation Officers

States also have their own preservation statutes and funds. State Historic Preservation Officers implement these laws. States may have their own registers of historic preservation. Their priorities for preservation are directly tied to the history and values of the particular state. For example, New Mexico's State Preservation Law focuses heavily on the preservation of pre-history and Native American artifacts. These state laws also establish the parameters for preservation at the local level.

Local Regulation of Historic Places

Local governments may enact their own historic preservation ordinances. It is typical for a local government to create an advisory board. These advisory boards are typically responsible for crafting the local inventory of historic resources and the ordinance that regulates them. A local government may create its own historic register to protect or incentivize the protection of historic structures. It may do this on an individual basis or through the creation of historic districts. These regulations typically require that new development or remodeling activities occurring within a historic district or structure are reviewed by the local historic preservation board for architectural compatibility. This board recommends to a higher level governing body, either the planning commission or the city council, whether the proposed development should be approved. This recommendation is one of many factors that are considered in review processes involving historic structures or areas. Local preservation ordinances have been long upheld by the courts, as demonstrated in the holdings of *Penn Central* and *Figarsky*. Generally, preservation requirements will not be deemed regulatory takings if they do not completely alleviate the use of the properties in question or, in the alternative, if there is some scheme that allows the property owner another means to capture lost value such as an arrangement to transfer development rights.

Urban Design

Cities have long attempted to create regulatory tools to protect and/or develop a particular aesthetic. Historic preservation ordinances, particularly those that create historic districts, are a good example of this type of regulation. The regulations attempt to bring cohesiveness between new and existing development in areas that have an existing aesthetic. Similar tools are used to mandate the theme of new developments. This approach to planning became increasingly popular with the emergence of traditional neighborhood design and new urbanism.

As the *Stoyanoff* case demonstrates, conditioning development on a particular design paradigm is permissible under police powers. These codes are typically administered by city staff or local architectural review boards. Courts will review such regulations for vagueness and the application of the same for clarity and fairness in application. For these reasons, many cities have begun to offer photographs or pattern books as part of these regulations.

Response to Wicked Problem

The city of X's form-based code and the rules governing transect two fall within the police powers that permit both urban design and historic preservation. The strongest argument Jane may have against the code generally may be the requirement that "all new construction be designed so that it is in harmony with the historic structures that surround it." The term harmony is vague at best given the different periods of architecture represented in the transect. It would be difficult for anyone to discern how to build a new structure that was in harmony with all surrounding buildings. While not covered in this book, Jane might also be able to attack this regulation as an affront to a registered trademark. White Castle restaurants are known for their castle design. Their white color, turrets, and flags are defining features. The city should consider amending this planning restriction to add clarity. In addition, the city must balance its desire for a design aesthetic with economic vitality. Both are important to the overall well-being of a community.

Discussion Prompts

- The importance of community aesthetics is becoming a more universal discussion in planning practice as part of a movement toward placemaking. What is the role of aesthetics in placemaking?
- Does zoning alone lead to the creation of attractive space? What other tools accompany zoning ordinance in the name of beautification?

Bibliography

Baer, W. C. (1995). When Old Buildings Ripen for Historic Preservation: A Predictive Approach to Planning. *Journal of the American Planning Association*, 61:1, 82–94.

Duany, Andres and Talen, Emily (2002). Making the Good Easy: The Smart Code Alternative. *Fordham Urban Law Journal*, 29:April, 1444.

Mason, Randall (2004). Fixing Historic Preservation: A Constructive Critique of "Significance". *Places*, 16:1, available at: https://escholarship.org/uc/item/74q0j4j2 (last accessed July 27, 2015).

Sitkowski, Robert and Ohm, Brian (2006). Form-Based Land Development Regulations. *The Urban Lawyer*, 28:Winter, 163.

Sternberg, E. (2000). Integrative Theory of Urban Design. *Journal of the American Planning Association*, 66:3, 265–278.

Talen, Emily and Ellis, Cliff (2002). Beyond Relativism: Reclaiming the Search for Good City Form. *JPER*, 22:1, 36–49.

Tappendorf, J. (2002). Architectural Design Regulations: What Can a Municipality Do to Protect Against Unattractive, Inappropriate, and Just Plain Ugly Structures? *The Urban Lawyer*, 34:4, 961–969.

INDEX

Page numbers in **bold** illustrate tables.

historic preservation 203–4; *Hawaii Housing Authority* v. *Midkiff* 124; *Kelo v. City of New London* 98–103; within larger redevelopment plans 105–6; *Penn Central Transportation Co. v. City of New York* 203–4; and police power 207; and public land use requirements 104, 207
enabling acts 3, 183–4
English common law system 6
environmental assessment (EA) 218
environmental impact statement (EIS) 214
equal protection *see* due process and equal protection
exclusionary zoning: affordable housing 163–6; growth management 187–8; holding-zone creation 165; and legitimate state interests 179–81; limitations on manufactured homes 165; limited construction of multi-family housing 165; Mount Laurel Doctrine 163–4; NIMBYism (Not In My Backyard) 164; as unconstitutional exercise of police power 156–60; unrelated persons ordinances 165–6
expedited permitting, affordable housing 167

farming *see* agricultural pursuits/uses
Fifth Amendment: compensation and regulatory takings 111–16; compensation and temporary takings 120–4; denial of economically viable use of land 117–19; due process under 104; Just Compensation Clause 120–4; landmark laws as takings 196–204; moratoria and regulatory takings 125–9; and private property protection 89; takings under 103–4
First Amendment: adult entertainment 148–9; *Bigelow v. Virginia* 147; *Central Hudson Gas & Electric Company v. Public Services Commission* 147; *City of Ladue v. Gilleo* 137–40, 146–7; *City of Renton v. Playtime Theatres, Inc.* 142–6; commercial speech 147–8; freedom of speech 137–40; governmental interest 147–8; identity of the speaker 139; *Metromedia, Inc. v. City of San Diego* 140–2; and other societal interests 141; religious uses 149–50; sign ordinance 146–7; wicked problem 135–6, 150
First English Evangelical Lutheran Church of Glendale v. County of Los Angeles: moratoria 132–3; regulatory takings 120–4
flexible zoning: area variances 56; Board of Zoning Adjustment 5, 59, 84–5; *Cheney v. Village 2 New Hope, Inc.* 68; *Collard v. Incorporated Village of Flower Hill* 67,

72; conditional zoning 71–2; *Crooked Creek Conservation and Gun Club, Inc. v. Hamilton County North Board of Zoning Appeals* 65–6, 72; *Dallen v. City of Kansas City* 64, 74; density zoning 68; *Ecogen, LLC v. Town of Italy* 65, 74; flexible zoning tools 69; floating zones 67, 69, 70; form-based codes 5, 69; form-based codes and traditional neighborhood development 74–5; master-variance developments 70–1; moratoria and interim zoning 65, 69, 73–4; overlay zoning 69, 74; overview of 5, 68–9; performance zoning 69, 73; planned-unit developments (PUD) 68, 69, 70–1; reasonableness of, challenges to 64; as of right zoning 71; *Rodgers v. Village of Tarrytown* 66–7; special exception permits (variances) 66; spot zoning 55, 67; standard-based approaches (PUDs) 71; use variances 56–7, 59, 84–5; voluntary-design conditional zoning 72; voluntary-restriction zoning 72; wicked problem 62–3, 75; *see also* incentive zoning (bonus zoning)
floating zones 67, 69, 70
floor area ratio (FAR) 72
form-based codes 5, 69, 74–5
Fourteenth Amendment: *City of Cleburne v. Cleburne Living Center* 80–3; communicative and noncommunicative aspects 141–2; covenants under 33–4; due process and growth management 178–81; Equal Protection Clause 80–1, 160–1; equal protection rights 85–6; and heightened standards of review 81–2; higher levels of protection, special groups 85; irrational prejudice 80; landmark laws as takings 196–204; racial discrimination and rezoning for affordable housing 160–2; right of due process 83–6
freedom of speech: *City of Ladue v. Gilleo* 137–40, 146–7; commercial speech 147–8; content-based speech regulations 143–5, 147; degrees of protection 146–7; identity of the speaker 139

gender, equal protection 81, 85–6
general welfare: and affordable housing 154–5; and Architectural Boards 210–11, 213; and multi-family housing 153–5; police power and 154–5
Gilbert v. Showerman (nuisance law) 22
Goldblatt v. Hempstead: and individual burden 114, 202–3; regulatory takings 112, 113, 197, 199, 201
Golden v. Planning Board of Town of Ramapo 192